The Panama Canal

The Panama Canal

The Crisis in Historical Perspective

UPDATED EDITION

Walter LaFeber

New York   Oxford   OXFORD UNIVERSITY PRESS   1989

Oxford University Press

Oxford   New York
Toronto   Melbourne   Auckland
Nairobi   Dar es Salaam   Cape Town
Petaling Jaya   Singapore   Hong Kong   Tokyo
Delhi   Bombay   Calcutta   Madras   Karachi

and associated companies in
Berlin   Ibadan

First published by Oxford University Press, New York, 1978

First issued as an Oxford University Press paperback, in an expanded edition, 1979

Library of Congress Cataloging-in-Publication Data
LaFeber, Walter.
The Panama Canal : the crisis in historical perspective / Walter LaFeber.—Updated ed.
p.   cm.   Includes bibliographical references.
ISBN 0-19-505930-1
1. United States—Foreign relations—Panama.   2. Panama—Foreign relations—United States.
3. Panama Canal (Panama)—History. I. Title.
E183.8.P2L33   1989   327.7307287—dc20   89-36284   CIP

9 8 7 6 5 4 3 2 1

Printed in the United States of America
on acid-free paper

For Scott and Suzanne

Preface to Updated Edition

This new edition is published on the seventy-fifth anniversary of the opening of the Panama Canal. The passageway remains an efficient miracle. The story of United States–Panama relations, however, is less happy. The last half of the 1980s has marked the most tumultuous and dangerous era in the relationship. Why those years turned tragic had less to do with the Canal (indeed, the 1978 treaties have worked successfully) than with the larger foreign policies of the Reagan administration and the Noriega regime. A new Chapter VII tells the story of the 1978 treaties. A new Chapter VIII attempts to explain the increasingly disastrous relationship of the 1980s. The Bibliographical Essay has been updated. Other chapters remain as they were in the first edition except for a few minor changes.

I owe a large debt to those who gave me helpful advice for this edition: Andrew Zimbalist of Smith College: Bill Walker of Ohio Wesleyan University; Eduardo Vallarino of Cambridge, Massachusetts; and Rebecca Earle of Oxford, England. Dawn Drost typed the manuscript and the revisions, as well as taking care of many other details, with her usual efficiency and good humor. I am indebted to Agnes Sagan for her work as a research assistant. To others I owe special thanks for long personal friendships that I exploited for help with this edition: Tom Holloway of Cornell University; Lloyd Gardner of Rutgers University; Max Miller, now Press Secretary to Congressman Ron Dellums; David Wechsler of West Chester, Pennsylvania; Gerry McCauley, who helped place this manuscript originally and revive it now; and Sheldon Meyer, who once again shepherded it through Oxford Press.

Ithaca, New York   *W. L.*
January 1989

Preface to First Edition

In January 1964, four United States soldiers died, 85 others were wounded, and 24 Panamanians were killed with nearly 200 wounded during four days of warfare between the troops and Panamanian mobs. Most North Americans soon forgot about the killings. Vietnam, inflation, and Watergate pre-empted headlines for the next ten years. But Panamanians did not forget. The riots had been triggered by their determination to exercise some control over the great waterway that divides their country and dominates the economy. During the following decade they worked incessantly to gain that control. North Americans were consequently surprised in 1974 when Secretary of State Henry Kissinger, acquiescing to Panamanian pressure, suddenly agreed in principle to return the Canal Zone.

Intense debate broke out in the United States. Thirty-eight Senators, four more than needed to defeat a new treaty, publicly announced their opposition to surrendering any control over the Canal. They were joined by conservative organizations which began concerted letter-writing campaigns to newspapers and politicians, and by the Zonians—some 10,000 North Americans living in the Zone—who feared loss of jobs, or at least security, if Panama operated the waterway.

On the other side, the State Department began systematic lobbying and education efforts designed to convince Congress and the public that it was in their best interest to share control with Panama. The Panamanian government bought the services of a high-powered public relations firm to take its case directly to the North Americans. By mid-1977, the United States and Panama agreed on the treaty's essential points, but the debate within the United States continued.

Observers estimated that despite the Department of State's efforts, Senate opposition to a new pact grew in early 1977. Secretary of State Cyrus Vance admitted in June that while treaty negotiations progressed, the Carter administration lacked the votes to pass the agreement through the Senate. Knowledgeable Panamanians and North Americans agreed that if the treaty did not pass, large-scale, anti-United States rioting could erupt in Panama, causing more deaths, leading to a sabotaging and closing of the Canal, and poisoning relations between Washington and Latin America.

Strangely, the historic debate had to be conducted amidst vast ignorance about how and why the post-1964 crisis developed. Discussion was shaped more by gut feelings than by historical knowledge. As a Canal Zone official told me in the summer of 1976, "We believe that 80 percent of Americans agree with us that we must keep the Canal under our control. Unfortunately, half of those Americans are not sure where the Panama Canal is located."

The crisis can only be understood by comprehending its historical development. The history does not begin in 1974 or 1964, nor can it be understood by learning simply about Theodore Roosevelt's boast of 1911 that "I took the Canal." The problem developed over three-quarters of a century, and this history, especially the growing dependence of Panama upon the waterway, is inseparable from the crisis itself.

Yet there is no full-length survey of relations between the United States and Panama, and no adequate study exists in either English or Spanish of Panamanian political and economic history since 1903. A host of well-written and beautifully illustrated books has appeared on the glamorous era of canal building, but little on the development of the current crisis.

This book attempts to fill that void and contribute to the debate by emphasizing the forces of the past which shaped the 1974–77 treaty negotiations. About one-quarter of the work analyzes the post-1968 years, but that period is undecipherable without the larger historical context provided in the first five chapters. The book is only a survey. It is to be hoped that scholars will amplify and correct parts of it in longer analyses; in this way one gap in United States diplomatic history will be filled.

Out of the survey four themes emerge. First, contrary to a prevalent belief, Panama did not magically materialize at Theodore Roosevelt's command. The drive for Panamanian independence, the development of a demanding, often chauvinistic nationalism, long preceded Roosevelt. Panama is not an artificial nation created solely by North American beneficence.

Second, the United States did not buy the Canal area in 1903 and does not own it. This is not well understood, particularly after Republican presidential candidate Ronald Reagan emphasized, with notable success, that North American claims to the Canal and Texas were equally valid. Reagan, incidentally, received important advice on the question from Arnulfo Arias, exiled to Miami by the Panamanian military regime which overthrew his government in 1968. Arias is one of the more important and colorful characters in this account. Contrary to Reagan's statements, from the beginning Washington officials claimed control but not full ownership of the Zone. Negotiations between the 1930s and 1970s were marked by a notable North American reluctance to discuss the point. Washington found the status quo satisfactory.

Unfortunately for the United States, a long-term status quo in international relations is a contradiction in terms. A third thesis attempts to place Panamanian-United States relations within the ever changing international and particularly Latin American context. Those relations cannot be understood without realizing that since 1945 the United States has waged not one, but three types of Cold Wars. The first (1945–56) involved the United States and Russia. The second (1945-early 1970s) was waged by many nations; it is discussed in Chapter IV. The third (the post-1973 years) has been marked by a relative decline in United States power to deal with a fragmented world, and particularly with the peoples of the southern hemisphere. This Third Cold War is discussed in detail in Chapter VI. The second and third of these wars, the book argues, helped shape both Panama's aspirations and its power to deal effectively with the United States.

Finally, the problems of the 1970s must be analyzed within the context of long-term developments within Panama itself. Those developments have been strongly influenced by an informal United States colonial policy exerted over the entire Isthmus, not merely the Canal Zone. The difference between North American domination of the country and Washington's control of the Zone, the book argues, is that in the former the colonialism is informal and indirect, while in the latter it is formal and direct. Panamanian history has also been molded by a racism that afflicts natives as well as foreigners living on the Isthmus, and by the country's almost total dependence on the Canal for its economic salvation. Politically, the emergence of the National Guard (the Panamanian army and police) has been most important. The Guard replaced an elite, wealthy, familial-based, and highly irresponsible oligarchy which long mismanaged the nation. The relative decline of the oligarchy and the corresponding rise of the militaristic, United States-trained Guard are, along with a vigorous and sometimes radical student movement, the most notable political characteristics of contemporary Panama.

This book resulted from a National Endowment of the Humanities grant to the Cornell History Department for experimental undergraduate seminars. Michael Kammen developed the plan, and I am indebted to him for many things, including his suggestion that I teach one of the seminars. In preparing for that course no full-length treatment of United States-Panamanian relations could be found that brought the story into the mid-1970s, hence the idea for this book. That idea led to a trip in 1976 to Panama with Professor Thomas Holloway of Cornell. Holloway was a U.S. Army translator in Panama during the 1964 riots. His help in introducing me to Panama and its people, as well as his criticism of this manuscript, have been especially important. As always, Professors Lloyd Gardner of Rutgers, and Joel Silbey and Richard Polenberg of Cornell, have been candid critics, a necessary part of being the best of friends. The book owes much to conversations with Professor Thomas McCormick of the University of Wisconsin regarding his work on United States-Latin American relations. Chris Muenzen performed bibliographical work and some research as an undergraduate research assistant at Cornell. For two years his work has been invaluable. Between 1976 and 1978 the Cornell freshmen and sophomores enrolled in the NEH-sponsored seminar not only uncovered fresh materials and sources, but were a pleasure to work with. It was a class the professor, at least, looked forward to meeting.

Zbigniew Brzezinski, National Security Advisor on the White House Staff, and the staffs at the Lyndon Johnson Presidential Library in Austin, Texas, and the Dwight D. Eisenhower Presidential Library in Abilene, Kansas, helped declassify documents from the 1950s and 1960s, as has the Freedom of Information Office in the Department of State. William Rogers, Chaplain at Cornell and expert on Latin American affairs; Jeff Bialos, a Cornell Honors student; Eric Edelman, now at Yale Graduate School; and the superb Cornell University Library staff (paticularly Caroline Spicer and Barbara P. Berthelsen) were generous with information and their discoveries of materials on United States–

Panamanian affairs. Pat Guilford typed much of the final manuscript with a good humor which neither it nor I deserved. I am indebted to persons in Panama and to Panamanian and United States officials in this country who provided information. For various reasons they are sometimes not cited by name in this account. Finally, without the confidence and help of Sheldon Meyer, Editor at Oxford University Press, Gerry McCauley, Marie Noll, and, above all, Sandra, the past year would have been considerably more leisurely, but less interesting, and I am grateful to them.

Ithaca, New York   *W.L.*
August 1977

Contents

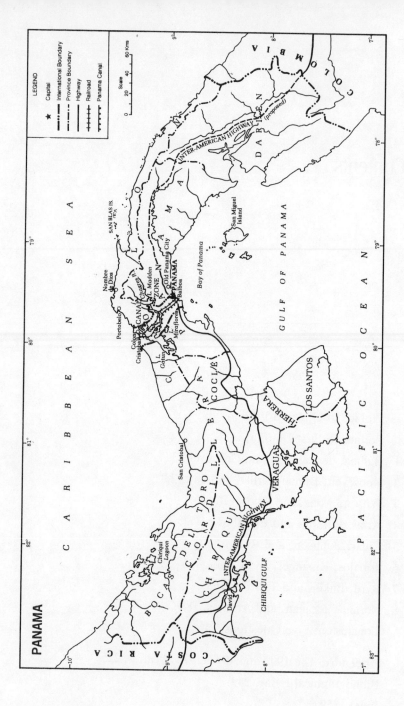

PANAMA

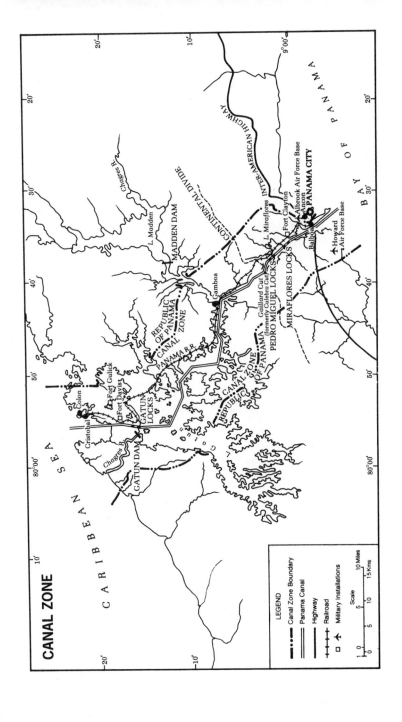

CANAL ZONE

CARIBBEAN SEA

BAY OF PANAMA

Chagres R.

L. Madden

MADDEN DAM

CONTINENTAL DIVIDE

REPUBLIC OF PANAMA

CANAL ZONE

PANAMA R.R.

Gamboa

Gaillard Cut
(formerly Culebra Cut)

PEDRO MIGUEL LOCKS

MIRAFLORES LOCKS

L. Miraflores

Fort Clayton

Albrook Air Force Base

PANAMA CITY

Ancon

Balboa

Howard
Air Force Base

INTER-AMERICAN HIGHWAY

REPUBLIC OF PANAMA

CANAL ZONE

Gatun L.

Fort Gulick

Colon

Fort Davis

Cristobal

GATUN LOCKS

GATUN DAM

Chagres R.

9° 00'

30'

20'

10'

80° 00'

LEGEND
.–..–.. Canal Zone Boundary
════ Panama Canal
───── Highway
┼┼┼┼ Railroad
□ ✈ Military Installations

Scale
0 1   5   10 Miles
0   5   10   15 Kms

The Panama Canal

1

Balboa,
de Lesseps,
and Cromwell

Panama was a crossroads of global trade, the keystone of the great Spanish Empire, a century before the first white settlers struggled ashore at Massachusetts Bay. From its beginnings, the Isthmus was destined to be "the center of the universe," to use the later phrase of the Latin American liberator, Simón Bolívar. The prize has been neither easily seized nor cheaply held. Spanish explorer Rodrigo de Bastidas first landed in the area during the spring of 1501, wandered through a hundred-mile zone desperately searching for treasure, and returned empty-handed to his ship. Bastidas became the first of many who sought fame and fortune in Panama and departed with neither.

A member of his crew, however, found fame if not fortune. Vasco Nuñez de Balboa decided to settle in Hispaniola (Santo Domingo), but in 1510 hurriedly traveled to Panama as a stowaway to escape creditors. He became one of the nearly 800 Spaniards who settled on the Isthmus. Then one by one they began to die, of what they did not know. The Spaniards greatly feared the many poisonous snakes which infest the country's jungles, but their killer was doubtless the tiny mosquito that carried yellow fever and malaria. Soon only sixty Spaniards remained. The stowaway seized command of the group despite protests from the

3

King's appointed agents. Balboa promptly restored discipline and hope. The Spaniards replenished their supplies through brutal raids on Indian settlements, but Balboa, who was considerably more enlightened and humane than most European conquerors, took the radical step of befriending Indians.

His rewards were immediate, among them the beautiful daughter of a chief for a mistress, and information about a great "South Sea" washing shores stocked with gold. After an epic march of nearly a month, Balboa stood atop a peak in eastern Panama on September 25, 1513, and was the first European to see the Pacific. The Indians designated the "South Sea" correctly. The Pacific lies to the south of part of the country. (From certain points, it is even possible to watch the sun rise over the Pacific.) The natives, however, were less than accurate about the gold to be found.

As a good Spaniard, Balboa nevertheless took no chances. He claimed the water and all the shores it touched for the King of Castile. Perhaps he hoped that in return for the Pacific Ocean the King might forgive his seizure of power in the settlement. But Balboa delayed sending the good news to Spain, and he soon lost his power to the jealous governor of Darien, Pedro Arias Dávila. History records Dávila as "Pedrarias the Cruel," and with good reason. He probably killed or enslaved—or both— as many as two million Indians. (The figure leads to speculation that when Balboa landed, Panama's population was larger than it is in the 1980s— one measure of the area's importance before 1500 and the impact of slaughters thereafter.) After convicting him on trumped-up charges of treason, Pedrarias the Cruel had Balboa publicly strangled by the official executioner. The explorer's grave has never been found.

The name "Panama" apparently derived from an Indian term meaning "many fish." But it could also have come from the word "panaba," or "far away," the reply Indians usually gave explorers who demanded the location of the nearest gold mine.[1] Balboa doubtless would have thought the second term more appropriate.

Pedrarias the Cruel expanded his domains by founding the City of Panama on the Pacific shore in 1519. That success triggered the first survey in 1534 for building a canal between the new city and Nombre de Dios, the major Spanish port on the Caribbean coast (renamed Portobelo in the 1590s). For thirty years Spanish officials pondered the idea of

1. Jules B. Billard, "Panama, Link Between Oceans and Continents," *National Geographic*, CXXXVII (March 1970), 430–431; excellent background is in David Howarth, *Panama, Four Hundred Years of Dreams and Cruelty* (New York, 1966), esp. pp. 30–40.

a waterway until finally deciding against it, in part because the King concluded, after much consultation with his religious advisers, that if God wanted the oceans to meet he would have built the canal Himself. The Spanish instead linked the two port cities with a "Royal Road," a narrow, stone trail wide enough only for two loaded mules to pass. A few yards of smooth, partly buried stones can still be seen. Longer parts of the trail were regularly explored four centuries later by Boy Scout troops from the Canal Zone.

The Destruction of the Spanish Empire

Along this rough highway mule trains carried gold and silver from the port at Panama City across to Nombre de Dios, where the riches were packed aboard galleons for the Atlantic crossing. The Spanish extracted as much as 200,000 tons of silver from their holdings, and uncountable amounts of gold. Panama City was one of the three richest centers in the new world (Lima and Mexico City were the other two). Nombre de Dios became a key port for the Spanish Empire and the site of annual trade fairs whose riches strained even Spanish imaginations. By 1572, however, Spain's holdings were both too opulent and relatively unarmed, an easy target for the British pirate Francis Drake. His privateers seized Spanish galleons, raided the rich trading areas, and finally established a base off the Panamanian coast so they could more systematically loot the defenseless Spanish colonies.

For commiting such theft, Queen Elizabeth bestowed a knighthood on Drake. But in the larger sense, Drake's appearance suddenly transformed Panama into an arena for a struggle to the death between an established empire and an aspiring empire. Appropriately, Drake died of the fever in 1596 while in Portobelo preparing to loot Spanish treasure ships. Others quickly took his place, and their robberies helped build the foundations of the British Empire. In 1671 Henry Morgan hit the Spanish jugular, Panama City. After Spanish officials and most of the inhabitants fled, powder stores exploded. A month later Morgan left the incinerated city with hundreds of prisoners and 175 mule-loads of treasure.

The Spanish never attempted to rebuild the ruins. They moved to a better fortified area several miles west, where the present Panama City was founded in 1673. Today in the old city the roofless, crumbling walls of a once-majestic cathedral face toward the ocean. On one side stand barracks of the Panamanian army, the National Guard; on another, attendants clean the stables for the Guard's horses; and on the third side are hovels holding refugees from Panama City slums who use the 300-year-old ruins of the cathedral as one side of their own tarpaper or aluminum-sheet shacks.

The Appearance of a New North American Empire

Panama's fortunes were roped to the fast sinking Spanish Empire. In 1739 Portobelo was finally destroyed by a British fleet commanded by Edward Vernon (after whom a young North American, Lawrence Washington, named his estate in Virginia colony). Spain terminated Portobelo's port monopoly and destroyed Panama's autonomy by attaching it to the Viceroyalty of New Granada (now known as Colombia). Panamanians began a century-and-a-half long struggle to regain their independence, but the main colonial conflict was occurring in the north, where the British eliminated the French as a rival in 1763. Twenty years later, Great Britain in turn was defeated by a large, newly born empire. In 1800 the United States moved its seat of government to the new Washington City, which, like old Panama City of 300 years before, was built amidst swamps and fever. During the next twenty years officials of Washington City paid close attention to the Caribbean region.

They watched the Latin Americans taking advantage of Spain's struggle for survival in Europe's Napoleonic Wars to crumble the remaining shell of the Spanish Empire and declare independence. Fighting for political autonomy, plagued by centuries of corrupt Spanish administrators, lacking an economic base, the Central American area seemed to lie open before aggressive North American and British empire-builders. Great Britain, conqueror of both Napoleon and the secrets of the steam engine, held the greatest economic and military power in history. Quite often where the Manchester businessman gained a foothold, London governmental officials followed to extend the mixed blessings of an imperial bureaucracy. The new Latin America had escaped Spanish rule only to face the danger of being victimized by expansionists from the north and empire-builders from the east.

In 1823 United States President James Monroe warned that the British should not again try their luck at empire-building in the Western Hemisphere. The Monroe Doctrine admonished Europeans to plant no more colonies and refrain from interfering with American interests in the new world. In return, the President carefully promised "not to interfere in the internal concerns" of Europeans. The United States consequently committed itself to containing the expansion of the world's greatest power. It seemed a mismatch, for the North Americans had few manufactured products with which to compete in the new markets, no navy to protect their interests (the British fleet had more ships than the United States Navy had cannon), and shared less common heritage with Latin America than geography seemed to indicate. As Monroe's Secretary of State, John Quincy Adams, explained in 1821, there was "no prospect that [Latin Americans] would establish free or liberal institutions of government. . . . They have not the first elements of good or free government. Arbitrary power, military and ecclesiastical, was stamped upon their habits, and upon all their institutions."[2] Nor did Adams believe that commerce would link North and South America in the foreseeable future.

Adams changed his mind about Latin America's importance, although not about its talents for "free government." No one more feared British expansionism, or was more sensitive to the political implications of England's commercial conquests, than Adams. In 1819 he forced Spain to surrender Florida. Suddenly North American territory was washed by the Caribbean. Merchants from Baltimore and New York had a new foothold from which to exploit Latin American markets. In the same 1819 treaty, Adams obtained Spanish claims to the Pacific coast of North America. The United States now possessed a strength not even England enjoyed: rapidly growing trading posts spreading along the shore of the eastern Pacific which served as bases for merchants and whalers who plied South and North American coasts. But these settlements were so far separated from the cities of the East Coast that a passage through the Isthmus and up along the Pacific shores became a necessity for the United States.

The interest of North Americans in Panama consequently grew naturally out of their quest for continental and commercial empire. Their initial involvement in the Isthmus occurred in 1825–26, at the midpoint of the most expansionist half-century in United States history. A group of wealthy and politically influential New York businessmen, claiming Central American support, announced the creation of a canal comapny to build an isthmian passageway. The announcement was premature and the investment capital moved into less riskier ventures closer to home, but it was the private businessmen and promoters, mostly northeastern Whigs involved in commercial expansion abroad, who kept alive the

2. Charles Francis Adams, ed., *Memoirs of John Quincy Adams*, 12 vols. (Philadelphia, 1874–77), V, 323–326.

spark of interest in a canal for the next twenty years. Washington officials were preoccupied with more immediate foreign policy problems.[3]

The United States government did make one announcement of consequence for a future canal. In 1825 the Latin American nations planned to meet in Panama City to develop common commercial and political policies. An invitation was sent to Washington, much against the wishes of Simón Bolívar who believed—correctly—that the United States did not desire to cooperate politically. After long debates, Adams (now the President) and Congress accepted the invitation, but Adams instructed the two North American delegates not to enter into any type of alliance with the other nations. The two emissaries failed to reach the conference in time, but a policy had been set: Washington officials were determined to maintain complete freedom of action in handling Latin America. The call for a separate hemispheric system sounded grand in the Monroe Doctrine, but in reality Monroe and his successors never allowed their hands to be tied by Latin Americans when dealing with either problems or opportunities in the Caribbean.

Interest in a canal intensified during the next twenty years. When the President of New Granada offered contracts on a possible rail or ship crossing through the Isthmus, President Andrew Jackson, at the request of the Senate, sent Charles A. Biddle to investigate the possibilities in both Panama and Nicaragua, the only other route which seemed to have the potential of Panama's. Biddle succumbed to a disease common in such situations: he began to bargain with the New Granada government for his own private concession to build the passageway. Jackson admired aggressive, self-made men (like himself), but he had to call Biddle home in disgrace. Other groups tried unsuccessfully to pick up Biddle's plan. Then in 1846 a breakthrough occurred.

By that time the British had established settlements along the Nicaraguan coast where a possible eastern terminus of a canal might be built. In 1846 rumor spread through the Caribbean that London businessmen next planned to conquer Panama. The United States diplomatic representative in Colombia, Benjamin Bidlack, was under instructions to thwart any attempt by another power to gain special rights in Panama. As Colombian fear of Britain intensified, Bidlack seized the opportunity to negotiate a treaty in which the United States guaranteed both the rights of transit across the Isthmus and Colombian control over the area.

---

3. This draws from Harvey E. Wilkinson, "Early American Interest in an Isthmian Canal," Unpublished Honors Thesis, Cornell University, 1977.

In return, the North Americans received a guarantee of free access to any future canal. With fast footwork and ambiguous language, President James K. Polk sent the treaty to the Senate with the assurance that no entangling alliance was involved. He warned that if the United States failed to seize the opportunity, the British surely would move to control the Isthmus. In the 1840s such a warning usually proved as catalytic as an anti-Soviet appeal would be a century later. In this case, however, the Senate intermittently debated the treaty for one-and-a-half years before accepting its historic responsibility on the Isthmus.

As the Senators understood, the United States was venturing into dangerous territory. The British were not only consolidating their hold on the eastern Nicaraguan coast, but selecting sites on the Pacific side for a possible canal. The United States and England seemed on a collision course in Central America. John M. Clayton, Secretary of State in Zachary Taylor's Whig administration during 1850, searched for alternatives. The slave controversy so divided the North Americans that a united front against Great Britain was difficult to form. As a Whig and a native of Delaware, moreover, Clayton had long been interested in extending his nation's commerce while avoiding conflict with the British navy, whose cannons could destroy that commerce in short order. Yet a clash seemed possible, particularly after United States interest in the Isthmus area increased with the discovery of gold in California during the late 1840s. By 1850 thousands of overly hopeful North Americans moved through Panama and Nicaragua to find their fortune in California.

Clayton asked the British if a deal could be made. The London Foreign Office was cool. It preferred simply to strengthen its hold in Central America. The Secretary of State then played his high card. United States diplomats had negotiated treaties with Nicaragua and Honduras giving Washington exclusive rights to build canals in those two nations. Clayton not only threatened to send these pacts to the Senate for ratification, but told the British (and stretched the truth to good effect), that some Central American states "have offered and asked to be annexed to the United States already." The British quickly became interested in defusing the issue. As finally written, the Clayton-Bulwer treaty of 1850 provided that the two nations would cooperate in building any isthmian canal, and neither would try to fortify or control it exclusively. Militant Democrats predictably condemned Clayton for not shoving the British out of Nicaragua entirely, but in retrospect the treaty was clearly a triumph of North American diplomacy. It prevented possible war with the world's most formidable power, made the United States an equal partner in any canal enterprise, and—more importantly—it gave Washington time to solve internal problems of slavery, time to develop its own military power, time to become so strong in the Caribbean that it could someday push the British aside and build the canal alone.

The discovery of California gold telescoped that time. A railroad across the 3000-mile-wide United States would not be completed until 1869, but between 1851 and 1855 New York City financiers built a transcontinental railway by laying 48 miles of rails between Panama City and the Atlantic side of the Isthmus. No one could doubt that the United States was the dominant foreign power in the Colombian province. But it was nevertheless "foreign," and when the Pacific Mail Company named the Atlantic terminal "Aspinwall" after its president, the Colombians insisted on "Colon" and made their point stick by returning any mail addressed to Aspinwall with the stamp "Destination unknown." Thus the North Americans lost the first of several battles over nomenclature to Latin American nationalism.

The railroad was not built cheaply. Nine thousand laborers died in the swamps during the five years of construction, "a life for every railroad tie," as the saying went. For the owners, of course, the price was not unbearable; they did not die of yellow fever. They indeed became very rich. During the fourteen years after the line opened in 1855, 600,000 travelers used it and as much as $750 million in gold bullion moved from California to the eastern United States along the Panama Railroad. Through 1905 it paid nearly $38 million in dividends to the owners, returned prosperity to Panama after more than a century of decline, and made the Isthmus once again crossroads of the Western world.

In retrospect, however, two other results were of greatest significance. First, United States interests held a hammerlock on the Isthmus. No one could doubt this after the completion of the railroad and the simultaneous landing of American troops to restore order after the failure of a traveler to pay for a piece of watermelon led to a riot and then the so-called "Watermelon War." This marked the first landing of United States forces under the 1846 treaty. Second, nationalism flourished with the railroad's fortunes. The first daily newspaper appeared (*The Panama Star and Herald,* still in existence), and Panamanians began to wonder why their new wealth had to be shared with the faraway Colombians. Not coincidentally, one of the bloodiest of Panamanian uprisings against Colombian control occurred in the mid-1850s. But of equal significance historically, the "Watermelon War" turned into the first of many anti-Yankee riots in Panama.

De Lesseps

During the last half of the nineteenth century, Panamanian nationalism continued to ripen, but North American control was suddenly challenged in 1878. Ferdinand de Lesseps, famed builder of the Suez Canal, announced he would build a sea-level canal across Panama. President Rutherford B. Hayes solemnly warned the United States would never accept a canal under non-American control. To make his point, Hayes dispatched warships to the Panamanian coast as a warning that the 1846 treaty prohibited de Lesseps' venture. The Colombians paid little attention and de Lesseps began digging. The Frenchman, however, made fatal mistakes. Attempting to emulate his Suez success, he determined to build a sea-level passageway across Panama instead of a multi-tiered lock system. After a decade he had completed less than half of what he planned to accomplish in six years. French engineers could not stop mud and rock slides from filling the newly dug cuts.

But worse, de Lesseps failed in waging all-out warfare against malaria and yellow fever, the "black vomit" that claimed victims in twenty-four hours. Workers wrote their wills before leaving for Panama, a few had the foresight to bring their coffins with them from France. As one reporter described Colon, it was

> a foul hole, by comparison, the ghettoes of White Russia, the slums of Toulon, Naples, and old Stamboul . . . deserve prizes for cleanliness. There are neither sewers nor street cleaners . . . toilets are quite unknown, all the rubbish is thrown into the swamps or onto rubbish heaps. Toads splash in the liquid muck . . . , rats infest the solid filth . . . , snakes hunt both toads and rats; clouds of mosquitoes swarm into the homes.[4]

As many as 20,000 died before de Lesseps gave up in 1889. Panama had ruined his and his son's fortunes and reputations. French courts found them and several associates guilty of fraud and bribery in raising funds for the canal. The son went to jail, and was allowed out only to visit his father, a broken man who spent days staring at the fire, gazing at a three-year-old newspaper, and trying vainly to recognize his son. Left behind was a partially dug canal and a small French cemetery outside Panama City where, as a later visitor said, "little crosses corrode in the

---

4. Quoted in Sheldon B. Liss, *The Canal: Aspects of United States-Panamanian Relations* (Notre Dame, Ind., 1967), p. 16.

tropic air."[5] De Lesseps joined the growing ranks of those who, like Balboa and Drake, had tried and failed to tame the Isthmus.

The North Americans meanwhile never let up in their pressure against France or the Clayton-Bulwer treaty. They followed the lead of Secretary of State William Seward who had fit Panama into his spectacular vision of global commercial empire by telling a group of New York capitalists in 1869 that they must lead in building a canal. Since "we are Americans," Seward proclaimed, "we are charged with responsibilities of establishing on the American continent a higher condition of civilization and freedom" than has existed elsewhere. But "that destiny can only be attained" by cutting a canal which could carry the earth's goods cheaply by navigation. Seward had sounded the theme: since North Americans enjoyed the freest of all governmental systems, and since that system rested on booming production and commercial exchanges, the world would be served by a canal that made the exporting of both the system's freedoms and goods easier and cheaper.[6] The future of civilization hinged on an American-built canal. Given that assumption, de Lesseps' challenge was immoral as well as a strategic threat, and the Clayton-Bulwer treaty an impediment rather than an obligation.

One modest State Department message to London in 1881 stated that North Americans must single-handedly control a canal in order to claim "our rightful and long-established claim to priority on the American continent."[7] As United States power developed, so did the passion for freedom to expand as Washington saw fit. When the British rejected such an argument, the North Americans nevertheless went ahead and signed a treaty in 1884 which gave them rights to build a canal in Nicaragua—without British participation. Due in part to political party jealousies, the United States Senate refused to ratify the pact.

The 1890s Watershed

But the pressure did not abate. Indeed, interest in a canal leaped ahead during the 1890s, as an economic panic marked the nadir of a two-decade downturn in prices. Businessmen and governmental officials

5. Billard, "Panama," p. 414.
6. George E. Baker, ed., *The Works of William H. Seward,* 5 vols. (Boston, Mass., 1853–83), V, 590.
7. U.S. Department of State, *Papers Relating to the Foreign Relations of the United States, 1881* (Washington, D.C., 1882), p. 555. (Hereafter cited: *FRUS,* followed by year and volume.)

feared class warfare in the slum-ridden urban areas, and in 1894 Secretary of State Walter Quintin Gresham worried deeply over "symptoms of revolution" which were appearing, symptoms which he believed could be eradicated only if jobs were created by shipping the glut of United States iron, steel, and agricultural products to foreign markets. As the business periodical *Bradstreet's* observed in 1895, a canal would give the country "a decided advantage over other nations" in the "future development of the South American and Oriental countries."[8]

Similar words were sounded by the powerful Democratic Senator from Alabama, John T. Morgan, and Chambers of Commerce representatives. The National Nicaraguan Canal Convention called for an isthmian passage so, in Morgan's words, the United States could have "access to the eastern Asiatic countries for our cotton." When the British landed troops in Nicaragua in 1894 to collect an indemnity for the arrest of a diplomatic official, the State Department and the North American press were in an uproar. London officials backed down, so much so that they finally released their grip on Mosquitia and the potential canal entrances. When a revolt erupted in Nicaragua during 1896, U.S. Marines, not British sailors, landed to protect foreign citizens and property. The old order was passing, and Monroe's doctrine was realized as the North Americans accelerated their drive for a canal.

In 1893–94 a giant step was taken when a government dominated by white planters seized control of Hawaii and asked Washington to annex the islands. In 1898 the William McKinley administration did so. The new territory served both as a naval base to protect Pacific entrances to a canal, and as a port for ships that sailed through a canal en route to Asian markets.

During the 1890s the first giant battleships of the modern U.S. Navy were built. According to the theories of Alfred Thayer Mahan, the best-known military strategist of the time, a canal was essential if the ships were to move quickly from one ocean to the other in order to protect both coasts and American markets worldwide. A canal, Mahan argued, would "enable the Atlantic coast to compete with Europe, on equal terms as to distance, for the markets of Asia," and reduce the distance to the western coast of Latin America by half.[9] The need for a passageway became dramatically apparent during the war against Spain in 1898. The battleship *Oregon* spent 68 days sailing from the West Coast of the

8. *Bradstreet's,* December 28, 1895, p. 820; the Gresham quote in analyzed in Walter LaFeber, *The New Empire* (Ithaca, N.Y., 1963), pp. 197–201.
9. Alfred Thayer Mahan, "The Isthmus and Sea Power," *Atlantic Monthly,* LXXII (October 1893), 470–472.

United States to battle stations in Cuba *via* the tip of South America, a trip that would have taken one-third the time if a canal had existed.

The 1898 war introduced the United States as a great world power. Specifically, the conflict made the nation supreme in the Caribbean region. The country emerged from "the splendid little war," as Secretary of State John Hay aptly called it, with Cuba, Puerto Rico, a great (if little tested) fleet, and British recognition that the days of the Clayton-Bulwer treaty were numbered. The cry for a canal intensified. Brooks Adams, John Quincy Adams's brilliant if eccentric grandson, and close friend of arch-expansionists Theodore Roosevelt and Senator Henry Cabot Lodge, had prophesied North American "economic supremacy" in world markets. The apparent fulfillment of that prophecy after 1898, Adams bragged, "knocked the stuffing out of me." "America has been irresistibly impelled to produce a large industrial surplus," he argued. "The expansion of any country must depend on the markets for its surplus product." Since "China is the only region which now provides almost boundless possibilities of absorption," an isthmian canal "to the Pacific must be built."[10]

President William McKinley was equally direct in his Annual Message of December 1898. A canal, McKinley observed, was "demanded by the annexation of the Hawaiian Islands and the prospective expansion of our influence and commerce in the Pacific." He emphasized the waterway must be controlled by the United States.[11] Brooks Adams and other acute observers believed Great Britain actually had little choice but to become the junior partner in an Anglo-Saxon empire. Not only did United States power appear awesome, but the London government was increasingly preoccupied with a rising Germany and a rebellion in South Africa where the Boer farmers were unexpectedly humiliating British troops.

With Great Britain busy elsewhere, in 1900 the United States Senate considered a bill that would build a Nicaraguan canal without regard for the Clayton-Bulwer treaty. That threat prodded British officials to negotiate with Secretary of State Hay (a noted Anglophile), to work out an alternative. Hay finally agreed with British Ambassador Lord Pauncefote that under a new treaty the United States could build and control a canal, but would not fortify it. The Senate rebelled against the non-fortification pledge, as did a hero of the 1898 war, a self-proclaimed expansionist, and Republican candidate for Vice-President of the United States in 1900,

10. Quoted in Charles S. Campbell, *The Transformation of American Foreign Relations, 1865–1900* (New York, 1976), p. 154.
11. *Ibid.*, p. 314.

Theodore Roosevelt. Though a close friend of Hay, Roosevelt warned that a fresh treaty was necessary. The Secretary of State threatened to resign, muttering privately that "There will always be 34 percent of the Senate on the blackguard side of every question," then thought better of it and negotiated a second treaty with Pauncefote. Hay warned friends that in dealing with the Senate one should not underrate "the power of ignorance and spite, acting upon cowardice," but this time he had nothing to fear. The agreement directly abrogated the 1850 pact and implicitly gave the United States the sole right to fortify a canal. The treaty was negotiated during the weeks that President William McKinley, who had been shot, lingered near death, and then passed away. The White House was now in the hands of that "wild man," as one of McKinley's advisers called Theodore Roosevelt.

The only remaining question concerned the location of the passageway. Since the 1870s most knowledgeable observers had assumed the site would be Nicaragua. In 1901 the Walker Commission, a group of engineers named by McKinley to examine the prospects for a canal, also reported favorably on the Nicaraguan route. That conclusion received strong endorsement from Senator Morgan. But the Walker Commission made the recommendation reluctantly, believing the Nicaragua river system too shallow for a large canal. The Commission agreed with most engineers (and Theodore Roosevelt) that the Panama route was preferable, especially since de Lesseps had completed part of the work on the Isthmus. The Commission nevertheless concluded that building the canal in Panama would be considerably more expensive than the Nicaraguan route, for the New Panama Canal Company—a group of Frenchmen who had bought out the ruined de Lesseps company—was asking $109 million for its assets and concessionary rights to build in Panama.

The Titans: Cromwell and Bunau-Varilla

At this juncture two remarkable men reversed the movement toward the Nicaraguan route. William Nelson Cromwell headed a New York City law firm prestigious in 1900 (and even more prestigious a half-century later when two of Sullivan and Cromwell's senior partners, John Foster Dulles and Arthur Dean, became important United States diplomats in the Cold War). In 1896 Cromwell emerged as the New Panama Canal Company's agent in the United States and served as legal counsel for the Panama Railroad Company. Four years later the forty-eight-year-old lawyer miraculously prevented the inclusion in the Republican Party

platform of a plank favoring the Nicaraguan canal. His means for working the miracle were direct: he contributed $60,000 to the party through
the party chairman, and confidant of McKinley, Senator Mark Hanna of
Ohio.[12] Cromwell later charged this and other expenses to the Canal
Company and apparently collected nearly a million dollars in fees.

The exact amount of money involved in the canal transactions will
never be known. Cromwell burned many of his papers and most of the
remainder, particularly those relating to Panama, were destroyed by
several of his surviving law partners, including Dulles.[13] Cromwell nevertheless deserved whatever he was paid, for between 1896 and 1902 he
single-handedly fended off the commitment to the Nicaraguan route. In
1913 the head of a congressional investigation into the canal transactions
called Cromwell "the most dangerous man the country has produced
since the days of Aaron Burr." His abilities were apparent in a description written by a New York reporter in 1908:

> Mr. Cromwell is about 5 feet 8 inches high, and medium in build. . . . He
> can smile as sweetly as a society belle and at the same time deal a blow at a
> business foe that ties him in a hopeless tangle of financial knots. . . . He is
> a wizard with figures and a shorthand writer of wonderful skill. . . . He is
> one of the readiest talkers in town. . . . He talks fast, and when he wishes
> to, never to the point. . . . [He] has an intellect that works like a flash of
> lightning, and it swings about with the agility of an acrobat.[14]

In November 1901 Cromwell's wizardry with figures and politics convinced the anxious New Panama Canal Company in Paris to drop its
price from $109 million to $40 million, thereby making the Panama route
less expensive that the Nicaraguan. The Walker Commission now recommended Panama to the Senate as a better buy.

The New Panama Canal Company's decision to lower the price occurred after bitter debate. Arguments became so heated that Parisian
police were called in to calm one meeting. In the end, however, a faction
led by Phillipe Bunau-Varilla triumphed. "A somewhat picturesque per-
sonage," as a contemporary described him, the vain and trimly mus-
tached Bunau-Varilla viewed "the earth . . . like a school globe which
he, the teacher, made to revolve at his pleasure."[15] At twenty-six,
Bunau-Varilla was chief engineer on the de Lesseps project in Panama

12. William Roscoe Thayer, *The Life and Letters of John Hay,* 2 vols. (Boston, Mass.,
1915), II, 307.
13. Erhard to Dulles, June 16, 1954, Papers of John Foster Dulles, Princeton University.
14. Quoted in Dwight C. Miner, *The Fight for the Panama Route* (New York, 1940), pp.
76–77.
15. Thayer, *Hay,* II, 315.

before falling victim to the fever. After returning to Paris he embarked upon a career of building railroads in the Belgian Congo, constructing flood controls in Rumania, serving as an editor of *Le Matin* in Paris, and, in 1893, playing a central role in the formation of the New Panama Canal Company.

Realizing that the company's rights would expire in 1904, Bunau-Varilla raced against time. In the mid-1890s he tried to convince Russians to buy the claims and build the canal. After all, he told them, if the Anglo-Saxons controlled Panama as well as Suez, they would rule the world's commerce. When the Czar's government did not respond, he used the same argument in discussions with the British, only transforming the reference to Anglo-Saxons into North Americans. Busy elsewhere, London officials were preparing to leave the Caribbean in Washington's hands. The second Hay-Pauncefote treaty made this clear to Bunau-Varilla, and in 1902 he left Paris to join Cromwell in the United States. Just before the Frenchman arrived, however, the House passed, by an overwhelming vote of 308–2, a bill sponsored by William P. Hepburn of Iowa which ordered the canal to be built in Nicaragua. The pro-Nicaragua lobby, led by Senator Morgan, had scored an impressive victory.

Reaching Washington in late January 1902, Bunau-Varilla joined Cromwell and Senator Hanna in pushing for an amendment sponsored by Republican Senator John C. Spooner of Wisconsin. When attached to the Hepburn bill, the Spooner amendment instructed President Roosevelt to buy the Canal Company's claims for $40 million and build the passageway in Panama if he could obtain a treaty from Colombia. If he failed, Roosevelt was to deal with Nicaragua. Within six months Bunau-Varilla, Cromwell, and Hanna collected the votes to pass the Spooner amendment. The trio was even blessed by an act of God. In May a volcano erupted on the Caribbean island of Martinique, covering a city of 30,000 inhabitants with hot lava. Bunau-Varilla immediately notified all Senators that Nicaragua could suffer the same disaster.

Nicaraguan authorities made the mistake of claiming publicly that no active volcanoes had shaken their country since 1835. Bunau-Varilla, however, knew that Momotombo had erupted just several months before, and that in 1901 the Nicaraguan government even issued a postage stamp showing Momotombo magnificently belching lava. The Frenchman bought out the Washington dealers' supply of these stamps, then placed one on each Senator's desk with the simple notation, "Official testimony regarding volcanic activity in Nicaragua." The Senate and House passed the Spooner amendment (the House so totally reversing itself that it passed the Panama bill 260–8), and Roosevelt signed the new measure into law on June 28.[16]

Happily following instructions, Roosevelt and Hay opened negotiations with Colombia. In January 1903, after a good deal of arm-twisting, Hay convinced the Colombian ambassador in Washington to sign a treaty that gave the United States a 99-year lease on a six-mile-wide canal zone. In return, the United States would pay Colombia $10 million plus an annual payment of $250,000. The United States Senate ratified the pact, but in August 1903 the Colombian Senate not only rejected it, but did so unanimously. The Bogotá government wanted more money. A leading Colombian historian later wrote that his nation feared the loss of sovereignty in Panama to the powerful North Americans, and believed itself entitled to a larger sum, particularly since the United States-owned isthmian railroad had earned millions in profits of which Colombia received nothing.[17] Left unsaid was that the Colombians hoped to stall until October 1904 when the Canal Company's rights would expire. Colombia could then collect all of the $40 million ticketed for Bunau-Varilla's and Cromwell's organization.

Roosevelt was livid. During the next several months he exhausted his rich vocabulary, calling the Colombians everything from "inefficient bandits" to "a corrupt pithecoid community." The sardonic Hay hid an equal anger behind his condescending smile and sarcastic words. At one time in 1902 he considered outright purchase of Panama from Colombia, then dropped the scheme, agreeing with a visitor's comment that Colombians viewed Panama "as a financial cow to be milked for the benefit of the country at large."[18] In August 1903 the Secretary of State wondered whether he should turn to deal with Nicaragua or instead begin "the far more difficult and multifurcate scheme of building the Panama Canal *malgré* Bogotá."[19]

Roosevelt's mind began to move in the same direction. He would be "delighted" if Panama became independent, TR wrote a friend in October, but "I cast aside the proposition made at this time to foment the secession of Panama. Whatever other governments can do, the United States cannot go into the securing by such underhand means, the seces-

16. The best account of the lobbying effort is Charles D. Ameringer, "The Panama Canal Lobby of Philippe Bunau-Varilla and William Nelson Cromwell," *American Historical Review,* LXVII (January 1963), 345–363.
17. Germán Arciniegas, *Caribbean: Sea of the New World* (New York, 1946, 1954), p. 437.
18. Thayer, *Hay,* II, 303–304.
19. Dana G. Munro, *Intervention and Dollar Diplomacy in the Caribbean, 1900–1921* (Princeton, 1964), p. 49.

sion."[20] As usual, he worked more directly. Roosevelt began drafting a message to Congress suggesting that the simpler method would be to send the navy to seize the Isthmus.

The New Four-Hundred-Year-Old Panama

Roosevelt never sent that particular message, for Panamanian national-ists had long been awaiting such an opportunity. These nationalists, contrary to North American myths too long propagated in textbooks, did not suddenly spring up full-grown at Roosevelt's command. The belief that Panama should exist as a separate, independent country was neither artificially created suddenly in 1903 nor propagated in Washing-ton before it took hold in Panama City. The Panamanian nationalism of 1902–03 formed only one part of an ancient story, although, as it turned out, the most important chapter.

The point demands emphasis. Nothing is more important in under-standing the 1960s–80s crisis in United States-Panamanian relations than to realize the Panamanians are acutely conscious of their four centuries' long history, and that their ardent nationalism arising from this con-sciousness developed at the same time United States expansionism con-quered a continent and, while building a worldwide empire, laid claims on Panama itself. Throughout the nineteenth century, the two national-isms were on a collision course.

After Colombia declared its independence from Spain in 1821, it was never able to control Panama completely. In part this failure was due to the type of person the Isthmus attracted—the rootless, lawless, transient who obeyed no authority. This element remained in Panama, as a later observer noted, becoming "a community of gamblers, jockeys, boxers, and cockfighters."[21] At the other end of the social spectrum a small propertied elite—an "oligarchy"—developed that resembled the North American elite of 1776: both developed valuable economic and political interests apart from the mother country, and neither saw any reason to share their wealth with colonizers. Colombia, moreover, was separated from the Isthmus as the United States was from England. The mountains and jungles in eastern Panama that bordered Colombia were so dense that in 1903 North Americans could reach Panama more easily and

20. Elting E. Morison, ed., *The Letters of Theodore Roosevelt*, 6 vols. (Cambridge, Mass., 1951), III, 628.
21. Jan Morris, "A Terminal Case of American Perpetuity," *Rolling Stone*, Jan. 1, 1976, p. 47.

quickly by steamer than Colombians could by horse. In the 1970s, despite new technology, the Inter-American Highway had not breached those jungles after thirty years of intermittent effort.

Separated from the supposed mother country, holding a mobile, rebellious, independent population, Panama never developed the quasifeudal, mercantilist characteristics of neighboring Latin American nations. Movement and trade were freer, liberalism seemed more natural. The land-owning oligarchs notably profited from such laissez-faire sentiment, but it also shaped the thought of most politically active Panamanians.[22] They were individualistic, nationalistic, and ripe for revolt.

They first rebelled against Colombia (then New Granada), in 1830, again in 1831, and as many as fifty times between 1840 and 1903. In 1840 one of Panama's great historical figures, Colonel Tomás Herrera, led the movement to create an independent state. A Panamanian Congress ruled the area until 1842 when Colombia regained the Isthmus by making extensive promises to grant Panama more autonomy. Four years later, Colombia signed the Bidlack treaty, an act, a later Panamanian historian argued, which sharply reduced Colombian sovereignty since the pact allowed the United States to guarantee transit rights across the Isthmus.[23]

These first rebellions were accompanied—indeed partially caused—by the development of an ideology that nurtured Panamanian nationalism thereafter. Comprised of certain European philosophies (particularly Benthamism), anti-Colombian feeling, and historical memories of the once-magnificent Panamanian past, its critical ingredient was "the geographical myth"—the belief that Panamanians were predestined to control the crossroads of the world. In the hands of Justo and Pablo Arosemena, the ideology also assumed strong anti-imperialist feelings, focused initially against Colombia, then as early as the 1850s against the United States. Panamanians were not immune to the strong currents of nationalism that swept through the Western world in the midnineteenth century, and it is striking that their new ideology, with its anti-imperialist component, was shaped at the same time North Americans constructed their own "Manifest Destiny"—a conviction that they

22. Ricaurte Soler, *Formas Ideológicas de la Nación Panameña* (San José, Costa Rica, 1972), pp. 16, 83–84.
23. Ramon M. Valdes, "La Independencia del Istmo de Panama; Sus Antecedentes, Sus Cause y su Justification," November 1903, in Buchanan to Hay, Dec. 28, 1903, Dispatches, Panama, National Archives, Record Group 59 (hereafter NA, RG 59), Microfilm. State Department translation. Frank Otto Gatell, "Canal in Retrospect—Some Panamanian and Colombian Views," *Americas*, XV (July 1958), 26–27.

were predestined to conquer a continent and exploit such vital hemispheric areas as Panama.[24]

A major collision seemed imminent as early as 1855–56 when, during a rebellion against Colombia, Panamanian mobs threatened United States citizens and property. Washington was watching over its Caribbean interests closely, especially in the isthmian area that was carrying the riches of California eastward on a North-American-owned railroad. The Navy Department instructed its commander in the area that Colombia must maintain order; if it did not, he could use force whenever necessary.[25] The uprising won new rights from Colombia, and Panama ran its internal affairs until the Bogotá regime cracked down again in 1863. The Panamanians, however, had tasted independence and wanted more.

Revolts occurred sporadically until 1884–85 when rebels seized control of the Isthmus. They made the mistake of attacking the Panama Railroad and United States shipping. President Grover Cleveland's administration was known for its anti-imperialist, "little America" policies, but Cleveland vividly demonstrated that on canal issues he ranked with Seward and other noted expansionists: the President sent eight warships and landed 400 men in Panama to stop the revolt and protect North American interests. The railroad reopened after United States troops fitted out two flatcars with a Gatling gun, cannon, and a howitzer behind a shield of boiler iron. The rebels understandably refused to duel with this moving fortress. Cleveland successfully completed the largest landing operation undertaken by United States forces between the Mexican War of the 1840s and the War of 1898 against Spain.[26] Colombia's authority further deteriorated. Equally important, Panamanian rebels learned they needed the United States with them, not against them.

Colombia tried to recoup its losses by imposing a new constitution that theoretically placed Panama directly under Bogotá's rule. The theory dissolved between 1899 and 1902 when Colombian liberals, exiled in Nicaragua, attacked the Bogotá regime in the "War of a Thousand Days." More than 100,000 Colombians died, guerrilla warfare terrorized the country, and amidst the ruins Panamanian nationalism blossomed. In 1902 Colombia finally was reduced to asking the United States for help in reclaiming the Isthmus. A truce was worked out

24. Ricaurte Soler, *Pensamiento Panameño y Concepción de la Nationalidad durante el Siglo XXIX* (Panama, 1954), pp. 99–101, 120, 125.

25. Kenneth J. Hagan, *American Gunboat Diplomacy and the Old Navy, 1877–1889* (Westport, Conn., 1973), p. 144.

26. *Ibid.*, pp. 170–188.

aboard the *U.S.S. Wisconsin* in the Bay of Panama at the same moment, ironically, that the Colombian government was beginning to tell Hay that its control over Panama allowed it to demand better terms from the United States.

Colombia's claim had been proven wrong throughout the nineteenth century. Indeed the Bogotá government itself had admitted failure. At least four times (some historians say six) between 1846 and 1903 Colombia asked the United States to restore order on the Isthmus. The settlement of the Thousand Days' War aboard a United States warship in November 1902 was only the last in a long line of North American interventions into affairs between Colombia and its raucous, hell-bent-for-independence province. A distinguished Panamanian diplomat later remarked that his country emerged as an independent nation because of its geography, economy, history, and "the interest and the sentiments of the people of Panama"—not "the arbitrariness of Theodore Roosevelt."[27] And Panamanian historian Ricaurte Soler has observed that by 1903 "a nation already existed and a Panamanian consciousness had already been formed."[28]

That was an important lesson to be drawn from four hundred years of Panamanian experience. There were others. Panama's prosperity historically depended on traffic through the Isthmus. When the Spanish Empire prospered or the new railroad flourished, so did Panama, but at other times the country stagnated. Without vast arable lands or mineral wealth, the people's fortunes rose and fell with the use outsiders made of the major resource—geographical location. The Panamanians have been historically conditioned to think of this as the key to their welfare. That perception has been sharpened by the nationalist, anti-imperialist ideology that began to take hold in the mid-nineteenth century. In the end, Colombia could not control a nationalism that was rooted in the historical memory of four centuries and expressed in the demands of a revolutionary elite.

As Colombia's grip slipped, Roosevelt's hand began to close around the Isthmus. A long list—Balboa and Spain, Drake and England, de Lesseps and France, as well as many Colombian leaders—tried to claim this crossroads of the world. All failed. Roosevelt and the United States, with the confidence peculiar to expanding empires, now determined to try their luck.

27. Ricardo J. Alfaro, *Media Siglo de Relaciones entre Panama y los Estados Unidos* (Panama, 1959), p. 14.
28. Soler, *Formas Ideológicas*, p. 125.

2

Roosevelt, Bunau-Varilla, and Taft

With an isthmian canal virtually within his grasp, Roosevelt refused to allow those "contemptible little creatures" in Colombia to frustrate his grand plan. But TR could not decide how to deal with the Colombians. He apparently held little hope the deadlock would be broken by a successful Panamanian revolt. As the President searched desperately for alternatives, Bunau-Varilla and the Panamanian nationalists were devising a solution. That solution, together with a 1904 agreement negotiated between Washington and Panama City by Secretary of War William Howard Taft, created the framework for sixty years of relations between the two countries and shaped the crisis of the 1970s.

Bunau-Varilla, with considerable help from top State Department officials, took the lead in solving Roosevelt's dilemma. During September and October 1903, the Frenchman held a series of talks with Hay, Assistant Secretary of State Francis B. Loomis (whom Bunau-Varilla had known since a meeting in Paris two years before), and John Bassett Moore, a former Assistant Secretary of State, renowned international lawyer, and confidant of TR. Out of the conversations grew Bunau-Varilla's conviction that if the Panamanians tried to declare their independence the United States would use force, ostensibly to uphold its

1846 commitment to maintain transit rights across the Isthmus, but in reality to prevent Colombia from quashing the revolution.

As early as August, Moore sent a memorandum to Roosevelt arguing that the 1846 pact gave the United States the right to construct a canal. Loomis, who spent many hours with Bunau-Varilla, apparently inspired the memorandum; in any case, it completely reversed Moore's previous opinion of the 1846 treaty.[1] Later in the autumn Bunau-Varilla asked Loomis how the United States would respond to an outbreak on the Isthmus. The Assistant Secretary of State said he "could only venture to guess that this Government would probably do as it had done in the past under like circumstances." Bunau-Varilla agreed, hoping that the North Americans "might freely do more rather than less." The Frenchman received the same reply from Moore and on October 10, 1903, probably heard similar words from the ultimate authority, Roosevelt. As the President later remarked, Bunau-Varilla "would have been a very dull man had he been unable to make such as guess."[2] The Frenchman was many things, including devious, scheming, ambitious, and money-hungry, but he was certainly not dull.

And if he had been, Bunau-Varilla needed no more hints after a candid talk with Hay in the privacy of the latter's home. "I expressed my sentiments on the subject some days ago to President Roosevelt," the Frenchman began, "the whole thing will end in a revolution. You must take your measures. . . ." Hay played the game perfectly: "Yes, that is unfortunately the most probable hypothesis. But we shall not be caught napping. Orders have been given to naval forces on the Pacific to sail towards the Isthmus." As Bunau-Varilla later editorialized, "It only remained for me to act."[3]

He first contacted the head of the revolutionary junta, Dr. Manuel Amador Guerrero, a physician closely associated with the Panama Railroad, now owned by the New Panama Canal Company. Amador happened to be in New York City to obtain money and support for the plot. Bunau-Varilla contacted Amador none too soon, for the Panamanian had just discovered that Cromwell, the New Panama Canal Company's lawyer, was growing fearful that the revolution would abort and his company's concessions seized by a vengeful Colombia. The story of Cromwell getting cold feet has been embroidered by Bunau-Varilla and

1. Stanford University Libraries, *Francis Butler Loomis and the Panama Crisis* (Stanford, 1965), p. 6.
2. *Ibid.*, p. 7; an account of the Roosevelt conversation is in Philippe Bunau-Varilla, *Panama: The Creation, Destruction, and Resurrection* (London, 1913), pp. 311–312.
3. Bunau-Varilla, *Panama*, 317–319.

so is highly suspect; in his memoirs the Frenchman, with spectacular condescension and malice, always calls him "the lawyer Cromwell." Much of the malice doubtlessly resulted from Bunau-Varilla's fear that Cromwell would someday receive as many lines in history texts as he. But it does seem that his report to Amador of the TR and Hay conversations revived sagging Panamanian hopes.

Plans again moved forward on the Isthmus. The revolutionaries comprised an odd but not illogical assortment, for a number of them had one association in common. Other than Amador (the Panama Railroad's physician), the group included José Agustín Arango (the railway's attorney), James R. Shaler (superintendent of the railway), and James R. Beers (the railway's freight agent). It might have been Beers who first assured Arango that a Panamanian revolt would be supported by the United States. Amador and Arango were joined by the oligarchy's leaders: C.C. Arosemena, Ricardo Arias, Federico Boyd, and Tomás Arias. Once free of Colombian control—once they could develop their already extensive economic and political power according to their own interests and without concern for Bogotá—these oligarchs, their sons, and grandsons dominated Panama for sixty years. The motives varied, but for good reasons the railway officials and the Panamanian nationalists remained closely allied. As Roosevelt understood, "You don't have to foment a revolution. All you have to do is take your foot off and one will occur."[4]

As the zero hour approached, however, TR displayed more optimism than did people in Panama. In early October the commander of the *U.S.S. Nashville* visited Colon, then reported to Washington that although three-quarters of the people would support a leader who would build a canal, "such a leader is now lacking, and it isn't believed that in the near future these people will take any initiative steps."[5] The junta was preparing to provide the leadership, but the timing would be crucial. Closely following ship movements in the newspapers, Bunau-Varilla learned on October 30 that the *Nashville* was leaving Jamaica for an unspecified port. He correctly guessed it was heading for Colon and would arrive in two or three days. Given the intimacy between the Frenchman and Loomis, this was perhaps a mere deduction, not a lucky guess. Bunau-Varilla wired this news to Amador, who had returned to the Isthmus to lead the revolt. Both men now believed the United States

4. Charles D. Ameringer, "Philippe Bunau-Varilla: New Light on the Panama Canal Treaty," *Hispanic American Historical Review*, XLIV (February 1966), 30–32; Liss, *The Canal*, p. 19; Miles P. DuVal, Jr., *Cadiz to Cathay* (Stanford, 1940), pp. 273–276.
5. Richard D. Challener, *Admirals, Generals, and American Foreign Policy, 1898–1914* (Princeton, 1973), pp. 154–155.

was moving into a position to support their revolution. Loomis, however, jumped the gun and the result was nearly farce. "Uprising on the Isthmus reported," the Assistant Secretary anxiously cabled the United States Consul in Panama on November 3. "Keep department promptly and fully informed." Maintaining his composure, the Consul replied, "No uprising yet. Reported will be in the night. Situation critical."

Late that day the Panamanian rebels moved to seize control of the Isthmus. The governor appointed by Colombia to rule the province, José Domingo de Obaldía, had long been sympathetic to Panamanian autonomy and gladly joined the revolutionaries. For his understanding he became one of Panama's first Vice-Presidents. Colombian army detachments were apparently bought off by Cromwell and the New Panama Canal Company; the commander received $30,000, other officers $10,000, and rank-and-file $50 each in gold.[6]

Commander Hubbard aboard the *Nashville* received no orders regarding the uprising until late on November 2. Roosevelt and Loomis apparently did not trust the navy with their plans. Thus when 2500 Colombian soldiers appeared off Colon on November 2 to prevent the rumored revolution, a confused Hubbard allowed them to land. Shaler, the superintendent of the railway, saved the situation. He first moved his cars to the Pacific side of the Isthmus, 48 miles from Colon, so the Colombians could not use the railway. Then he talked the Colombian officers into traveling to Panama City, assuring them that their troops would soon follow. In reality, the soldiers next saw their commanders when all were packed aboard ships for the return trip to Bogotá.[7] The next day U.S. sailors finally landed to ensure that the Colombian troops behaved. An independent Panama had already been proclaimed by Amador. A new nation the size of South Carolina was born, and the labor pains had been easy. None of the belligerents was killed. The only deaths were a Chinese citizen who had gotten trapped in some desultory shelling, a dog, and, according to some reports, a donkey.

The Rewards of Revolution

Roosevelt justified his aid to the revolutionaries by citing the 1846 commitment, a justification that had no legal or historical basis. The treaty

---

6. William Henry Harbaugh, *Power and Responsibility: The Life and Times of Theodore Roosevelt* (New York, 1961), pp. 208–209.

7. Ameringer, "Philippe Bunau-Varilla," pp. 33–34; Ernesto J. Castillero Reyes, *Episodios de la Independencia de Panama* (Panama, 1957), pp. 102–105, 110–118.

certainly did not give the United States the right to use force against Colombia, with whom the pact had been made, in order to build a canal. Nor did it require Colombia to allow a canal to be constructed. The treaty indeed justified United States intervention in order to preserve Colombia's sovereignty on the Isthmus. TR intervened, however, to destroy that sovereignty.

But Roosevelt clung to the 1846 pact since he had little else. He was consequently interested when Oscar Straus, a New York lawyer and adviser of the President, suggested the 1846 treaty required the United States to intervene because it was not made merely with Colombia, but was "a covenant running with the land"—regardless of who happened to control the land. With delight, and doubtless a sense of relief, Roosevelt immediately ordered Hay to use this argument. The United States held to this interpretation even though John Bassett Moore (certainly the State Department's most distinguished lawyer) exploded Straus's sophistry and suggested that in TR's hands it actually amounted to a "covenant running (away!) with the land!!"[8]

The President later argued that the seizure had been for the sake of "civilization," thereby adopting the proposition that since North American actions were justified morally they were justified legally. His Attorney-General, Philander C. Knox, offered the appropriate reply: "Oh, Mr. President, do not let so great an achievement suffer from any taint of legality."[9] Knox's caustic advice was better than he knew, for soon Roosevelt began a campaign, backed by force, to compel Latin American governments to uphold their own legal obligations as he defined those obligations.

In one sense, TR acted quite uncharacteristically: he aided a revolution. For a man whose central political tenet was stability, and for a nation that had fought revolutionaries and secessionists at least since 1861, unleashing revolution marked an abrupt change. It was also a short-lived change. Roosevelt possessed his canal territory and recognized the new Panamanian government led by Amador, Pablo Arosemena, and Obaldía on November 6. But when the Panamanian army attempted to land at Colon to claim the city, TR stopped it.[10] A little revolution was sufficient. Washington needed time to sort things

---

8. Quoted in David S. Patterson, *Toward a Warless World: The Travail of the American Peace Movement, 1887–1914* (Bloomington, Ind. 1976), pp. 124–125.

9. The best discussion is Munro, *Intervention and Dollar Diplomacy,* pp. 57–58; and Albert K. Weinberg, *Manifest Destiny* (Baltimore, 1935), pp. 155–156.

10. Liss, *The Canal,* pp. 18–19.

out. The Panamanian government would have to wait a while before its army could enter the country's second largest city. In the first moments after recognition, Panama and the United States were at loggerheads.

Nor did Roosevelt try to reconcile the Colombians. On November 6 he told them he had intervened because "treaty obligations" and the "interest of civilization" required that the Isthmus not endure "a constant succession of . . . wasteful civil wars." TR urged Bogotá to recognize the new government. Colombia responded by sending to Washington its most distinguished citizen and former president, General Rafael Reyes, in an attempt to revive the Hay-Herrán treaty—the same pact which the Colombian Senate unanimously rejected several months before. Reyes was not prepared to lower the price. The welcome in Washington was cool. Hay advised Roosevelt that "the sooner you see him, the sooner we can bid him good-bye." But Reyes was a forceful, popular figure, and hired one of the most adept lobbyists in Washington to fight against a treaty with an independent Panama. Hay wrote TR, "I told [Secretary of War Elihu] Root I was going to see Reyes. He replied, 'Better look out. Ex-Reyes are dangerous.' Do you think that, on my salary, I can afford to bear such things?" Hay need not have worried. As Roosevelt later noted, he viewed Colombians as similar to "a group of Sicilian or Calabrian bandits. . . . You could no more make an agreement with the Colombian rulers than you could nail currant jelly to a wall."[11]

TR and Hay focused on arranging the canal treaty with the Panamanians, or, more precisely, the Frenchman who had taken the opportunity to represent Panama. Bunau-Varilla engaged in a mini-power struggle with Arango, Tomás Arias, and Federico Boyd for control over negotiations in Washington. Since the three Panamanians were not yet in the United States, and because Bunau-Varilla convinced them he knew the political situation and financial channels, the Frenchman was empowered to initiate talks with Hay. Amador and Boyd left Panama on November 10 to join Bunau-Varilla.

The new government meanwhile instructed the Frenchman that the negotiations were to be guided by three principles. First, no deals could be made that affected "the sovereignty of Panama, which [was] free, independent, and sovereign." Second, the United States should pledge to uphold the new nation's "sovereignty, territorial integrity, and public

11. Thayer, *Hay*, II, 319–327.

order." That clause would place North American troops, if necessary, between Panama and a vengeful Colombia. Third, a canal treaty would be drafted, but only after consultation with Amador and Boyd. "You will proceed in everything strictly in agreement with them," the Frenchman was told.[12]

The instructions did not reach Bunau-Varilla in time, nor did Amador and Boyd. The minister made certain of that. On Friday the 13th of November he began talks with Roosevelt and Hay. Bunau-Varilla emphasized that time was all-important. If the treaty was not rushed to completion, he argued, a number of events would occur, all of them bad: a restless United States Senate, under Morgan's lashing, might turn back to Nicaragua; Colombia might seduce Panama back into the fold (the suave Reyes was on his way to Panama City); and isthmian politics might turn chaotic, forcing delays in the talks. Implicitly, but obviously, Bunau-Varilla also wanted to pocket the $40 million for his New Panama Canal Company as quickly as possible. Nor would he mind going down in history as the lone negotiator of the Panamanian side who signed the epochal pact.

Heartily sharing the Frenchman's mistrust of the Senate, Hay quickly prepared a treaty draft. It was largely the Hay-Herrán agreement that Colombia had rejected. The draft explicitly recognized Panamanian sovereignty in a canal zone, and even went further than the Hay-Herrán agreement by increasing Panama's judicial authority in a zone. Panamanian troops would protect the canal, and United States forces would be used in the area only with Panama's consent. The proposed treaty would run 99 years, or until about 2002.

Then, in what proved to be one of the most momentous twenty-four-hour periods in American diplomatic history, Bunau-Varilla worked all night and all day on November 16 to rewrite Hay's paper. The minister was afraid that the draft would not sufficiently appease the Senate, at least not enough to have the body act quickly on the treaty. Bunau-Varilla also wanted to complete the treaty before Amador and Boyd arrived. They were in New York City, but Cromwell, for purposes of his own, had detained them. On November 17, Bunau-Varilla told the two Panamanians to remain in New York for another day, then rushed to the State Department to consummate the deal.

---

12. This and the following discussion of the negotiations rely upon unpublished State Department documents and the excellent discussions in Ameringer, "Philippe Bunau-Varilla," especially pages 36–44; and Munro, *Intervention and Dollar Diplomacy,* pp. 45–47.

Hay could hardly believe his eyes. Bunau-Varilla's treaty ensured the canal's neutrality, proposed payment to Panama of an amount equal to that which the United States would have paid Colombia, and guaranteed Washington's protection of Panama's independence. The United States was to assume a virtual protectorate over the new country. But in return, the treaty gave the United States extensive powers in the Canal Zone, for Washington would have "all the rights, power, and authority within the zone . . . which the United States would possess and exercise if it were the sovereign of the territory within which said lands and waters are located to the entire exclusion of the exercise by the Republic of Panama of any sovereign rights, power, and authority."

That was the most radical change, a change that has caused continual crisis in U.S.-Panamanian relations for the next three-quarters of a century. But there was more. Bunau-Varilla surrendered Panamanian judicial power in the Zone, widened the zone area from ten kilometers (or six miles) to ten miles, and lengthened Hay's 99-year lease to "perpetuity." The astonished Secretary of State made only one change (the United States "leases in perpetuity" phrase was tranformed into the more direct wording that Panama "grants to the United States in perpetuity the use, occupation, and control" of a canal zone). At 6:40 p.m. on November 18, the treaty was signed by the two men. Amador and Boyd arrived in Washington three hours later. Bunau-Varilla met them at Union Station, showed them the pact, and Amador nearly fainted on the train platform.

The Panamanian government angrily protested "the manifest renunciation of sovereignty" in the treaty. That protest echoed down through the years, becoming ever more magnified. If the new government rejected the pact, however, it faced bitter alternatives: the United States might seize the canal area without either paying for it or undertaking to protect the new republic, or Roosevelt might build in Nicaragua and leave the Panama City revolutionaries to the tender mercies of the Colombian army. In truth, the Panamanians had no choice.

They had leaped across an abyss to gain their independence, were hanging on the other side by their fingertips, and the United States held the rescue rope. Having helped put them in that position, Bunau-Varilla dictated the terms under which they could be pulled up to safety. Hay and Bunau-Varilla were too powerful and sophisticated to allow Panama to claim it accepted the treaty under duress, a claim that if declared legally valid could void the acceptance. Panama, however, did accept under duress. Having a French citizen disobey the Panamanian government's instructions, and then having no choice but to accept the French-man's treaty, compounded the humiliation. In the 1970s a documentary film made in Panama about the 1903 affair was entitled, "The Treaty that No Panamanian Signed."

The Debate in the United States

For the revolutionaries humiliation was nevertheless preferable to hang-ing. Throughout the negotiations Bunau-Varilla had kept them informed of rising indignation in the United States over his and Roosevelt's man-agement of the affair. The President soon had another revolt on his hands; this one was in the Senate and the country at large.

It was not a massive revolt, but a surprising number of Senators and important newspapers condemned TR's action. The division was par-tially along party lines. William Randolph Hearst's Democratic papers attacked the President's action as "nefarious." Hearst's Chicago *American* called it "a rough-riding assault upon another republic over the shattered wreckage of international law and diplomatic usage." Such widely circulated urban dailies as the *New York Times*, New York *Evening Post*, Philadelphia *Record*, Memphis *Commercial Appeal*, and *Springfield Republican* agreed with Hearst's assessment.

In the Senate the powerful Maryland Democrat, Arthur Pue Gorman, organized opposition to the treaty. That Gorman was an avowed candi-date for the 1904 presidential run against Roosevelt made his opposition doubly significant. Holding 33 of the 90 Senate seats, the Democrats could theoretically prevent the necessary two-thirds of the Senate from ratifying the pact. And with Senator Morgan holding out for the Nicara-guan route, Gorman's chances for success seemed reasonable. Even the newspapers and public spokesmen who supported TR refused to justify his action on moral grounds. Instead, as *Public Opinion* noted, since the majority of the country wanted "an isthmian canal above all things," it was willing to overlook moral issues in order to justify taking the canal as strictly "a business question."[13]

Roosevelt refused to take that approach. As have most rulers who aggressively used naked force, he wanted it masked with morality. In an outspoken special message to the Senate on January 4, 1904, the Presi-dent submitted the treaty and justified his actions in November on the

13. *Public Opinion*, XXV (Nov. 19, 1903), 643.

grounds of the 1846 pact, "our national interests and safety," and the usual Rooseveltian claim of "the interests of collective civilization." He suffered no doubts that the United States had "received a mandate from civilization" to build a canal, although he could not tell exactly how that mandate had been expressed. One problem, of course, was that "the interests of collective civilization" had never been seen or defined (was Colombia, for example, a part of "collective civilization"?). Like many Rooseveltian phrases, the term better fit the President's prejudices than any international legal or moral standard.

Yet TR won and Gorman lost. The prospects of a United States-controlled canal caused flutters of patriotism in too many hearts and the prospect of rich satisfaction in too many pocketbooks. In the Senate the Democrats split, with many southerners, who had long sought the project, joining the President. Led by the prestigious Atlanta *Constitution,* southern papers crossed party lines formed during the Civil War in order to back the treaty. Even Gorman admitted he wanted a canal constructed; he simply disliked Roosevelt's methods. Some skeptics were won over by the President's message. Noting that he had denied any wrong-doing, the Detroit *Free Press* believed that the word of a United States President "is as good as anybody else's word." The *New York Times,* the New York *Evening Post,* and the *Washington Post,* however, never surrendered, and the Chicago *Chronicle* (a Democratic paper) summarized their feelings by calling Roosevelt's appeal to "civilization" a "pitiful and alarming chapter in American government," a "tyrant's plea of necessity." The opponents were equally bitter over the South's defection to the President's side. As the *New York Times* editorialized, "This is the southern spirit of the slavery days," for like slavery, the canal to the South is "purely a question of profit in dollars and cents."[14]

As Roosevelt and the Senate Republican leadership intensified the pressure, Gorman admitted his effort had "ended in smash." On February 23, 1904, he watched sixteen, or nearly half the Senate Democrats, join the Republicans to sweep the treaty through 66–14. Opposition came almost entirely from the Northeast, the Middle States, and pockets of the South. The Midwest, West, and much of the South supported the President. Gorman's presidential hopes sunk with his effort to stop the treaty.[15] Running eight months later against the colorless Democrat, Alton B. Parker, Roosevelt understood how the opposition had been

14. *Ibid.,* XXVI (Jan. 7, 1904), p. 6.
15. John R. Lambert, *Arthur Pue Gorman* (Baton Rouge, 1953). pp. 297–308.

silenced. "Can you not tell our speakers to dwell more on the Panama Canal?" he wrote a campaign manager. "We have not a stronger card."[16]

After early 1904, politicians who opposed United States control of the canal were committing political suicide. Bunau-Varilla had triumphed. Although, as the *Pittsburgh Post* remarked, TR's methods in Panama "were subversive of the best principles of the republic,"[17] the Frenchman had made the treaty so attractive that the United States, as he hoped, quickly chose power over principle.

"Titular Sovereignty": What Did the Treaty Mean?

The Senate ratification marked a beginning, not the end, of the struggle over the treaty. With Article I placing them under Washington's protection ("The United States guarantees and will maintain the independence of the Republic of Panama"), the Panamanians immediately began protesting the mushrooming North American control over their country. A first clash occurred in early 1904 when the State Department insisted that Panama must acknowledge in its new constitution (and not merely in the treaty), the United States right of intervention. William Buchanan, the U.S. Minister, wanted the widest possible power to control "pests" inside Panama, and brought great pressure to bear on the Panamanian constitutional convention.[18] Finally, Article 136 gave the United States the right to "intervene, in any part of Panama, to reestablish public peace and constitutional order." The North Americans could apparently unilaterally determine when public peace and order were jeopardized. But this Article squeaked through the convention 17–14; leading Panamanians were already trying to contain United States influence. As Buchanan told Hay, "The fact that fourteen . . . voted against it," together with the appearance on the streets of handbills and newspapers condemning Article 136, "amply justified the wisdom of our having secured" it.[19]

Article III of the treaty, however, has most disrupted relations. It gave the United States the rights, powers, and authority in the zone "as if it were the sovereign of the territory." From the outset Panama argued that it remained the actual sovereign in the area. Bunau-Varilla agreed,

16. Roosevelt to Senator Nathan Ray Scott, Oct. 9, 1904, in Morison, ed., *Letters of Theodore Roosevelt,* IV, 978.

17. *Public Opinion,* XXXVI (March 3, 1904), 260–261.

18. Buchanan to Hay, Jan. 4 and 5, 1904, Dispatches, Panama, NA, RG 59.

19. Buchanan to Hay, Jan. 28, 1904, Dispatches, NA, RG 59.

perhaps out of conscience. "The United States, without becoming the sovereign, received the exclusive use of the rights of sovereignty," the Frenchman wrote, "while respecting the sovereignty itself of the Panama Republic."[20]

Such an arrangement was not unprecedented in 1903, although from the United States point of view the precedents were not happy. When Germany, France, and Russia forcibly took territory from an enfeebled China during the late 1890s, the treaties stipulated (to quote the words of the German-Chinese pact), that "in order to avoid the possibility of conflicts, the Imperial Chinese Government will abstain from exercising rights of sovereignty in the ceded territory during the term of the lease, and leaves the exercise of the same to Germany."[21] The precedent was not a happy one, for Washington had vigorously opposed those treaties.

Yet the United States wanted to compromise none of the vast powers Bunau-Varilla wrote into Article III. Attempting to placate the Panamanians while retaining all the power, in 1904 John Hay coined the phrase "titular sovereignty" to describe Panama's rights in a canal zone.[22] The phrase became a widely used and condescending description of Panama's sovereignty in the zone, but on October 18, 1904, Roosevelt recognized the limitations of United States rights in the canal area when he instructed Secretary of War William Howard Taft:

> We have not the slightest intention of establishing an independent colony in the middle of the State of Panama, or exercising any greater governmental functions than are necessary to enable us conveniently and safely to construct, maintain and operate the canal, under the rights given us by the treaty. Least of all do we desire to interfere with the business and prosperity of the people of Panama. . . . In asserting the equivalent of sovereignty over the canal strip, it is our full intention that the rights which we exercise shall be exercised with all proper care for the honor and interests of the people of Panama.[23]

Roosevelt's term, "the equivalent of sovereignty," and the limitations placed upon United States power before and after the phrase, indicated that the President interpreted his nation's rights in the Canal Zone to be short of sovereignty itself.

20. Quoted in Helen C. Low, "Panama Canal Treaty in Perspective," Overseas Development Council Monograph Series, #29 (1976).
21. Lyman M. Tondel, Jr., ed., *The Panama Canal: Background Papers and Proceedings of the Sixth Hammarskjold Forum* (Dobbs Ferry, N.Y., 1965), p. 12.
22. *Ibid.*, p. 13.
23. Instructions to Taft, Oct. 18, 1904, Morison, ed., *Letters of Theodore Roosevelt*, IV, 986.

After looking into the matter in Panama, Taft, who possessed a notable judicial mind, thought the issue inconsequential. His report to Roosevelt of December 19, 1904, became the standard view of the question:

> The truth is that while we have all the attributes of sovereignty necessary in the construction, maintenance and protection of the Canal, the very form in which these attributes are conferred in the Treaty seems to preserve the titular sovereignty over the Canal Zone in the Republic of Panama, and as we have conceded to us complete judicial and police power and control of two ports at the end of the Canal, I can see no reason for creating a resentment on the part of the people of the Isthmus by quarreling over that which is dear to them, but which to us is of no real moment whatever.[24]

Taft thus admitted the United States did not have full sovereignty over the new Canal Zone. It had "complete judicial and police power and control" at the vital points, but the "titular sovereignty" or residual sovereignty resided with the Panamanians. Some North Americans who insisted on total control over the Zone during the 1960s and 1970s argued that their country was "sovereign" in the Zone. They were wrong, if Hay, Roosevelt, and Taft, the three Washington officials who constructed the Panamanian-United States relations, are to be believed. From the start, the question was not whether Panama had residual sovereign rights in the Zone, for it did, but what would happen in the distant future if the Panamanians tried to exert those rights against the full control exercised by the United States.

The North Americans, of course, never had sovereignty over the Canal Zone as they do over Alaska or Texas. They must pay an annual fee to Panama for the use of the Zone, and children born of non-North American parents in the Canal Zone are not automatically United States citizens as they are if born in Texas or Alaska.[25] The $10 million paid to Panama in 1903 was for treaty rights, not the purchase of territory as in the Louisiana acquisition of 1803 or the Alaskan purchase of 1867.

The clash over sovereignty initially occurred because the United States acted as if it were sovereign throughout parts of Panama *outside* the Canal Zone. Article II of the treaty gave the United States the right "in perpetuity" to occupy and control any lands outside the Zone which it thought necessary for building or maintaining the canal. Related provisions in the treaty were breath-taking in their sweep of power granted Washington.

24. Quoted, with good commentary, by Ralph E. Minger, "Panama, the Canal Zone, and Titular Sovereignty," *Western Political Quarterly,* XIV (June 1961), 544–554.
25. *Wall Street Journal,* April 29, 1976, p. 14.

Article IV gave the United States "in perpetuity" the right "to use rivers, streams, lakes, and other bodies of water" for any purpose relating to the canal. Article V granted the United States a "monopoly" over "any [sic] system of communication" in Panama. Article VII provided the power to take by right of eminent domain needed lands, buildings, or water rights in Panama City and Colon, and to intervene in those cities, if necessary, to preserve public order. The same article granted the United States the authority to create and enforce sanitary regulations in the two cities, a power which actually gave Washington the dominant voice in their political and financial affairs. Article XII surrendered to the Canal Company control over Panama's immigration.

These provisions made Panama a potential colony of the United States. Article II—giving Washington officials the right "in perpetuity" to occupy and control any lands outside the Zone which, in their own opinion, they needed—was a virtual blank check. The cost of the lands would be determined by a joint U.S.-Panamanian commission, but under no circumstances could it delay canal construction while deliberating. The North Americans seized large chunks of Panamanian territory. Numerous requests for additional land were made between 1908 and 1930. Fourteen military bases were ultimately established, ostensibly to protect the Canal although some were for purposes outside Panama; several of the bases occupied land outside the Zone. Panamanian protests grew with the development of the military complex, particularly when United States-owned land later prevented orderly growth of Panama City and Colon.

Panama officials also objected to the $10 million fee and the $250,000 annual annuity. They noted that in contrast with their $10 million, the redoubtable Bunau-Varilla and his company received $40 million, and they further observed in the 1920s that the United States apologetically paid Colombia $25 million (although, admittedly, Congress found the courage to pacify the Colombians only after Roosevelt died). The $250,000 annuity merely equaled the amount Washington paid Colombia for the railroad rights alone before 1903. Panamanians interpreted each North American demand for additional land as fresh evidence they were being cheated.

As the Twig Is Bent

In May 1904 Roosevelt created an Isthmian Canal Commission to build the canal. The Commission was placed under the supervision of Secretary of War Taft. Within three months, the military members of the Commission clashed with the State Department representatives in Panama. In Panama the questions of sovereignty and the right of United States intervention coalesced to create the first major crisis between the two countries. The events of 1904 were not only a portent. They left an indelible mark on Panamanian political life.

The initial controversy involved policy-making within the Washington bureaucracy. The State Department has continually battled with the War Department (after 1947, the Department of Defense), and the military officers who operated and defended the Canal Zone. A first clash occurred in 1904 when the Panamanian government strongly protested the United States use of its ports as if they belonged to the North Americans. U.S. Minister John Barrett attempted to dampen the dispute and believed he was making progress until Admiral J. G. Walker of the Isthmian Canal Commission arrived in Panama. When the Panamanian Foreign Minister invited both Walker and Barrett to discuss the port problem, Walker bluntly told Barrett not to come along. As did later military officials, the Admiral viewed Panama more as a North American base than a sovereign country. He wished to handle the talks alone. He did, and despite the Minister's warnings, Walker insisted in undiplomatic language that Panama totally yield on the port issue. The Foreign Minister was enraged. Forced to clean up after Walker's indiscretions, Barrett then started again from scratch to settle the issue.[26]

He made little headway, especially after the problem was complicated by a host of disputes. In August 1904 Panama protested that within the Canal Zone United States post offices accepted mail at rates lower than those in Panama. In Colon and Panama City, moreover, the North Americans were collecting unfair tariff rates on goods coming into the Zone from Panama itself. Businessmen from the United States escaped payment of tariffs by setting up shops in the Zone, then underselling Panamanian merchants. Hay initially wanted to claim the United States could do whatever it pleased. Roosevelt, however, took the longer view. He instructed Secretary of War Taft to work out the problems in Panama. Before Taft could board ship for the Isthmus, the Panamanian situation suddenly approached a flash point.

Soon after independence, the nation's politics divided into two parties, the Conservatives, led by Amador who controlled the government, and the Liberals, a group convinced that it represented a majority of the country. In certain respects that conviction was probably true. The Con-

26. Barrett to Hay, Aug. 16. 1904, Dispatches, Panama, NA., RG 59.

servatives included the white minority of Panama, but the Liberals were closer to the mulattoes and mestizos who comprised most of the population. Elections were due in late 1904, but neither party was experienced in the compromises and delicacies of democratic politics. The Liberals hoped to overcome such shortcomings by working with General Esteban Huertas. The general was now a national hero; during the revolution he and his troops had joined the junta rather than remain loyal to Colombia. The Liberals considered putting him into power through a *coup* if necessary. Huertas needed little convincing. He was highly susceptible to flattery, alcoholic beverages, and money. As the moment of the rumored *coup* arrived in November, the frightened Amador locked himself in his house. United States officials then took matters into their own hands.

When they talked with Amador he called his own army a "Frankenstein," and declared that only the North Americans could control it. The officials told the State Department that the "Panama Army of about 250 men is a continual menace to the peace of the Republic. It will always be a handy tool to be used by either party and a continual source of unrest until it is paid off and disbanded. Among the 250 soldiers there are from 20 to 30 small boys, many of whom are not more than eleven years old." The "more substantial element" was scared of such an irresponsible and unpredictable force.[27] Several weeks later the Legation added, "It would be far better for Panama if the army could be disbanded and four or five good brass bands established in this city so that there might be plenty of music every day. This would amuse, interest and occupy the minds of the people and also save much money for the Panama Treasury."[28]

Several days before Taft was due to arrive, Minister Barrett and the Canal Zone Governor, George W. David, decided to short-circuit Huerta's presidential aspirations. They demanded that he resign from the army and the force be disbanded. Barrett later gave a fascinating account of how he single-handedly dismissed the Panamanian army. A later Panamanian historian claimed that Tomás Arias played an important role in subduing the army. Perhaps, but Barrett's dispatch nevertheless illustrated the colonial control which the North Americans were beginning to exercise over Panama:

> It was finally arranged that the soldiers were to report at the Government house at one o'clock Saturday, to be paid off upon the terms of the Government. By two o'clock, they had not put in an appearance and

27. Lee to Hay, Nov. 1, 1904, Dispatches, Panama, NA, RG 59.
28. Lee to Hay, Nov. 14, 1904, Dispatches, Panama, NA, RG 59.

President Amador sent for me to know what was the best thing to do. He was afraid the army might have decided to resist his terms. Upon my arrival at Government house I advised the President to wait half an hour more. . . .

Just before the half hour expired the first detachment of some fifty soldiers came marching, unarmed, to the Government house, followed by a great crowd. When they halted, they sent up word to the President, evidently not knowing that I was there, to the effect that they would not accept the Government's terms of two payments [of cash for their dismissal], but they demanded the whole pay at that moment. The President was naturally much disturbed at this ultimatum, and asked me what he should do. I immediately told him to be absolutely firm and yield in no way to their demands, emphasizing that they had already been guilty of gross insubordination and that, if they were soldiers in the United States, they would be shot or court-marshalled [sic], and that it was no time now for temporizing. This word was sent to them but they still persisted in their position and muttered threats against the President.

When this word came up from the street, I saw that there must be no further delay, in bringing matters to an end, and taking General Guardia, the Minister of Foreign Affairs and War, with me, I went down stairs and out upon the sidewalk in front of the soldiers who were there assembled. In brief words I told General Guardia to say to them that the United States, with its forces, stood back of the Government in this crisis, and that they must accept the terms of the Government, or accept the consequences. They were warned that if they did not accept these terms, and engaged in any acts of insurrection, riot, or mutiny, they would be dealt with in a most summary way, and that if necessary, the naval forces in the Bay, and the marines at Ancon and Empire [in the Canal Zone] would be used to maintain order, with the severest punishment for those who were responsible for disorder. This warning had the desired effect and the soldiers immediately declared that they would accept the terms of the Government. . . .

The business community, and the Government, are most grateful for the attitude and action of the Legation during this crisis.[29]

Panamanian arms and ammunition were placed in the Canal Zone under U.S. control. For the next quarter-century, the country depended on a 700- to 1000-member police force and the United States military for its internal security.

Taft approved this action when he landed. His decision was hardly surprising. He earlier wrote his brother that since the 1903 treaty "per-

---

29. Barrett to Hay, Nov. 22, 1904, Dispatches, Panama, NA, RG 59; Arias's role is described in Ernesto J. Castillero Reyes, *Historia de Panamá* (Panama, 1955), p. 162. The issue of "colonial control" is defined and discussed in chapter III below.

mits us to prevent revolutions," he would "advise them that we'll have no more." Panama, after all, was only "a kind of Opera Bouffe republic and nation." Since "we have four hundred marines and a fleet on one side and three naval vessels on the other," the Secretary of War thought matters could be arranged satisfactorily.

For Taft the top priority was tranquility so canal construction would not be interrupted. The Conservative was therefore the preferred party, he told Roosevelt, for it included the propertied white families which had a stake in maintaining order. The Liberals, on the other hand, depended on blacks and mixed races who were "much less worthy" than the Conservatives. If the Liberals grasped power, a "large Negro influence" would appear, and since Taft believed Panamanian blacks less intelligent than North American blacks, the Isthmus could become a festering, unsettled trouble spot similar to Haiti.[30]

With the military and political situations in hand, the Secretary of War turned to tariff and postal disputes. Refusing to wilt in the damp Panamanian heat, the three-hundred-pound Taft energetically worked out a compromise that limited the Zone's imports to items needed only for the Canal or Canal employees. He quickly settled the postal problem to Panama's satisfaction while keeping the post offices in the Zone under United States direction. The series of agreements between Taft and the Panamanians became law in December 1904 when Roosevelt issued Executive orders and Panama announced decrees to put them into effect.[31]

Taft's mission was a landmark. By maintaining the Zone's right to a wide range of economic privileges, including selling goods to Panamanians working in the Zone, Taft only scotched, not ended, the complaints of Panamanian merchants outside the Zone. Those complaints later led to important modifications of the 1903 treaty. In stopping the ridiculous Huerta, the United States crippled the opposition political party, destroyed the Panamanian army, and made the government reliant upon Washington for protection against external enemies. More important, the United States assumed responsibility for protecting the government against internal enemies. If, for example, the Conservatives urgently asked for help, Washington had some obligation to respond—that is, to maintain the oligarchy in power.

In a country possessing little experience in democratic politics, but of

30. The notes to Taft's brother and to Roosevelt are quoted in Minger, "Panama, the Canal Zone, and Titular Sovereignty," pp. 546–547, 550–554.
31. The text of the agreements, as well as the texts of other major reports and treaties of the 1826 to 1954 years, can be found in Diogenes A. Arosemena, *Documentary Diplomatic History of the Panama Canal* (Panama, 1961), pp. 303–316.

which democratic procedures were somehow expected, the United States placed an elite white oligarchy firmly in control. Washington officials helped create the conditions for an economically bipolarized, undemocratic, and potentially unstable country. When Panama later appeared as bipolarized, undemocratic, and unstable, North Americans could not understand why.

"Police the Surrounding Premises"

The implications of Bunau-Varilla's treaty were out-running even Roosevelt's fertile imagination. It should be stressed, however, that the implications made a greater impact on Panama than on United States policy. Roosevelt was extremely active in the Caribbean region during these years, but his activity was not due solely to the newly acquired canal area. TR's policy was the logical continuation of a century-long North American involvement that was turning Washington into a self-appointed policeman in the Caribbean.

Since the eighteenth century the United States had been driving southward, first to conquer a continent, then, after the Civil War, to seize economic and strategic prizes. Its financial power increasingly penetrated the Caribbean area after the 1870s. Victory in the War of 1898 brought Puerto Rico and the Cuban naval base of Guantanamo. The Caribbean was becoming a North American lake, and obtaining the Canal Zone marked one more step in that direction.

Within a year after construction of the Canal began, however, Roosevelt announced a new policy, the so-called Roosevelt Corollary to the Monroe Doctrine. In his Annual Messages to Congress in 1904 and 1905, the President hoped that Latin American nations would be happy and prosperous, but he believed they could not share such joys "unless they maintain order within their boundaries and behave with a just regard for their obligations towards outsiders." To help them, the United States would become the policeman throughout the area. (Roosevelt privately understood that the primary police work would be in the smaller Caribbean and Central American countries, not the large nations on the South American continent.) The policeman, TR proclaimed, would ensure that the countries met their "obligations," so the "outsiders" would have no excuse to intervene.[32] The "outsider" most

32. James Daniel Richardson, ed., *Messages and Papers of the Presidents* (New York, 1897–1914), XVI, 7375–7376.

feared in Washington was Germany, whose businessmen, diplomats, and naval officers seemed overly ambitious in the Western Hemisphere. Great Britain possessed a greater fleet, but it apparently had made its peace with North American expansion southward, most notably by agreeing to the second Hay-Pauncefote treaty.

The Roosevelt Corollary triggered the most ignoble chapter in United States-Latin American relations. Believing, as TR said, that "a civilized nation" such as the United States possessed the right to stop "chronic wrongdoing," North Americans sent troops into a half-dozen Caribbean nations during the next twelve years, and within two decades dominated at least fourteen of the twenty Latin American countries through either financial controls or military power—and, in some instances, through both.

Officials at the time argued that the Roosevelt Corollary was necessary to protect the new canal. As John Hay's successor in the State Department, Elihu Root, wrote a friend in 1905, "The inevitable effect of our building the Canal must be to require us to police the surrounding premises."[33] It became an early version of the domino theory: if unfriendly, powerful Europeans settled in one part of the Caribbean, their influence could spread until the Canal would be endangered.

Root's explanation of the Roosevelt Corollary cannot withstand historical analysis. That the Canal increased United States interest in the Caribbean cannot be disputed. But the Corollary's principles were formed long before the Isthmus was seized—as early as the 1870s, 1880s, and 1890s, when such Washington officials as Ulysses S. Grant, "Jingo Jim" Blaine, and Richard Olney bluntly told Europeans that the Caribbean should be considered a North American lake. And the Corollary evolved quite independently of Canal Zone policy. To misunderstand this relationship is to misunderstand a most important chapter in United States-Latin American affairs.

TR's inspiration to act as a "civilized" policeman occurred before the Canal Zone was seized, and quite independently of events on the Isthmus. In 1900–1901, for example, the United States imposed on Cuba the Platt Amendment, giving Washington the right to intervene any time at its discretion to maintain order in the newly independent island. The provision established a precedent and a rationale for the later Corollary. In 1902–03 Germany and Great Britain intervened in Venezuela to collect overdue debts. An uproar resulted in the United States, and the

33. Quoted in William Everett Kane, *Civil Strife in Latin America: A Legal History of U.S. Involvement* (Baltimore, 1972), pp. 66–67.

British shrewdly suggested to Roosevelt that if he did not want the Europeans to protect their legal rights in the Western Hemisphere, he should do it for them. Grumbling that "These wretched republics cause me a great deal of trouble," TR believed a second foreign intervention "would simply not be tolerated here. I often think that a sort of protectorate over South and Central America is the only way out."[34]

His opportunity finally arose in Santo Domingo. For over five years New York City bankers had fought French and German financiers for control of the country's resources. By early 1904 Santo Domingo seemed to be moving toward a state of permanent revolutionary instability. Roosevelt ordered the navy to seize the country's customs houses, pay off the foreign debt, and under no circumstances allow any revolutionary activity to interrupt the country's development. He publicly rationalized the seizure by announcing the Roosevelt Corollary.

These affairs in Cuba, Venezuela, and Santo Domingo had little or nothing to do with the Isthmus. Taking the Canal Zone by no means led to the Roosevelt Corollary. Instead, Roosevelt's Panama policy can be interpreted as fitting into a larger Latin American policy that was evolving long before the Panamanian revolution. To confuse the Canal as the cause of the Corollary, therefore, is to confuse fundamental motivations of American foreign policy.

Two motives shaped Roosevelt's Corollary. First, he hated disorder, especially disorder that might lead to political bipolarization or an opportunity for European economic and/or political intervention. The Monroe Doctrine might act as a shield for Latin Americans against European imperialists, but Roosevelt would not allow the Doctrine "to be used as a warrant for letting any of these republics remain as small bandit nests of a wicked and inefficient type."[35] That premise of the Corollary was easily extended to Panama. Taft's intervention in 1904 (and again in 1908), rested in part on that premise, and both the President and his Secretary of War would have agreed with a leading naval strategist in Washington who argued that "so-called revolutions in the Caribbean are nothing less than struggles between different crews of bandits for the

34. Dexter Perkins, *Hands Off: A History of the Monroe Doctrine* (Boston, 1941, 1963), pp. 232–234. My interpretation of the Corollary is taken from Lloyd Gardner's work in Lloyd Gardner, Walter LaFeber, and Thomas McCormick, *Creation of the American Empire* (Chicago, 1976), chapter 14. For the long pre-1904 development of the Corollary, see the important essay by J. Fred Rippy, "Antecedents of the Roosevelt Corollary of the Monroe Doctrine," *The Pacific Historical Review,* IX (September 1940), 267–279.
35. Roosevelt to Cecil Arthur Spring Rice, July 24, 1905, Morison, ed., *Letters of Theodore Roosevelt,* IV, 1286.

possession of the customs houses—and the loot."[36] A second motivation was Roosevelt's belief that the United States had been entrusted with a "civilizing" mission which it should bear proudly. This belief seemed particularly applicable to the Caribbean, including Panama, where the people were largely a mixture of Indian, Spanish, and black. This motivation, of course, had its ironies. As sociologist William Graham Sumner observed at the time, "We talk of civilizing lower races, but we have never done it yet. We have exterminated them."[37]

If Taft and Roosevelt were so concerned about the Canal Zone's security (instead of their "civilizing mission" of imposing order on Latin America), they might have allowed the United States Navy to build a chain of bases in the isthmian area. They did not. After the Panamanian revolution, naval officials asked for three bases around the Zone, bases they had long sought from Colombia. Roosevelt rejected the request. When fortifications were planned for each end of the Canal, two military boards concluded that these, along with the Guantanamo base in Cuba, sufficiently protected the passageway. As President, Taft later upheld this decision and refused to spend $4 million on army barracks in Panama. If war began, he reasoned, troops could move to the Isthmus quickly enough from the United States. Taft thought the fortifications along the Canal primarily useful for stopping any unhinged Latin American dictator who might try to seize the waterway.[38]

Building the Panama Canal did not cause the announcement of the Roosevelt Corollary. TR instead used the Isthmus as one of several areas for the exercise of his police powers. The President's Panama policy was a symptom, not a cause, of his larger Caribbean plans. The evolution of United States policy in Panama can consequently be interpreted as another manifestation of his racial, economic, and military views. How such perceptions affected Panamanians and helped create their growing animosity toward North Americans should be considered separately, not filtered through a supposed preoccupation on Roosevelt's part to provide security for a canal.

The failure to understand the demands, dynamics, and confusions of nationalism is hardly peculiar to TR, yet historical circumstances made him President precisely at the point when the European-dominated

36. Quoted in Challener, *Admirals, Generals, and American Foreign Policy*, p. 20.
37. Quoted in David Healy, *U.S. Expansionism; the Imperialist Urge in the 1890s* (Madison, Wis. 1970), pp. 151–153, also 237–238.
38. Challener, *Admirals, Generals, and American Foreign Policy*, pp. 324–327.

world system, which he so admired, was disintegrating.[39] In 1904–05 Japan's dramatic victory over Russia surprised the white races and encouraged non-whites, especially those who lived in Asian and African colonial areas. The Chinese, Turkish, and Russian revolutions formed roots in those years. Roosevelt prided himself on his understanding of historical change and his sensitivity to the nuances of a global balance of power, but he never comprehended the significance of these shattering events. TR was unable to see that the world was comprised of more than simply the "civilized" versus the "wicked and inefficient types."

After he intervened in Panama in 1903, Roosevelt painstakingly explained his actions to the Cabinet, then demanded to know whether the explanation would silence his opponents. "Have I defended myself?" he asked. "You certainly have," replied a brave Elihu Root. "You have shown that you were accused of seduction and you have conclusively proved that you were guilty of rape."[40] Roosevelt never understood how his policies and explanations worsened the problems in the Caribbean area that he tried to stablize. He, Taft, and Bunau-Varilla were making Panama as well as the Canal Zone a virtual colony of the United States, but the North American leaders refused to assume even the responsibilities of enlightened colonialism, save that of using force or the threat of force to maintain order. That solution worsened, not ameliorated, Panama's problem and, consequently, Panamanian relations with the United States.

---

39. See the pioneering discussion by Geoffrey Barraclough, *Introduction to Contemporary History* (New York, 1965), pp. 101–103.
40. Richard W. Leopold, *Elihu Root and the Conservative Tradition* (Boston, 1954), p. 178.

3

Wilson, Arias, and Roosevelt

During the post-1964 crisis, Panamanians picked out two targets for attack: the oligarchy which had long manipulated the country's politics while exploiting its resources, and the United States which dominated Panama through informal colonialism. Both the oligarchy and the colonial power were firmly established by 1914 when the Canal opened. But tensions were developing. Within a generation the oligarchs and the colonial authority were challenged by a new middle class that revitalized Panamanian nationalism. The 1905 to 1939 years served as the spawning ground for the tensions that exploded in 1964 and after.

Man's Greatest Liberty with Nature

The tensions were not apparent until World War I. In August 1914 world attention focused on Austria-Hungary, where a political assassination was leading to war among Europe's greatest powers. The opening of the Panama Canal that month nevertheless commanded headlines. It was "the greatest liberty Man has ever taken with Nature," Great Britain's statesman-historian James Bryce remarked. The builders, as Roosevelt prophesied in 1904, had completed "the most important and also the more formidable engineering feat that has hitherto been attempted."

In a decade the North Americans had finished what others merely dreamed of for four hundred years. The result was a waterway equal to a channel dug ten feet deep and fifty-five feet wide from Maine to Oregon.[1] While engineers commanded by George W. Goethals bisected the Isthmus, North American medical teams under the direction of Dr. William Gorgas conquered yellow fever and tamed malaria, the two destroyers of de Lesseps' enterprise thirty years before.

The engineering and the materials were of such quality that the mechanisms controlling the locks in 1914 remained in perfect working order sixty-four years later. ("It is a splendid antique, a Zonian noted with pride in 1976.) Ships passed through six huge but delicate locks which raised vessels eighty-five feet above sea level at the Continental Divide before lowering them at the other end of the Isthmus.

A ship entering from the Pacific side passed by the present site of Balboa (now the Canal Zone's main city), and Panama City before Miraflores Locks' two-step mechanism raised it fifty-four feet. Sailing through Miraflores Lake, it entered Pedro Miguel Lock and its one-step chamber for the remaining thirty-one-foot rise. The ship then moved through narrow Gaillard Cut, the channel which posed the greatest engineering problems since the deep cut and sheer mountain sides created sudden landslides that could close the waterway. That problem was not satisfactorily solved until the 1930s. But as late as 1974, 250,000 cubic yards of dirt slid into the Cut, reducing the Canal to one-way traffic and costing $2 million for removal.[2]

Moving from the Cut into Gatun Lake, the ship began the downhill side of the journey. Gatun Lake, created by a gigantic dam, was a key to the Canal's success. Its water, captured from Panama's heavy mountain rainfall, allowed the locks to fill with water. The dam creating the lake became one of the waterway's most sensitive points, for if it were destroyed by nature or sabotage, Gatun Lake would empty into the sea and at least two years of rain would be required to refill the lake and make the Canal usable. After passing through Gatun Lake, a vessel was lowered through Gatun Locks, sailed seven miles into Cristobal Harbor, and at Colon entered the Atlantic.

1. Morris, "A Terminal Case of American Perpetuity," p. 47.
2. U.S. Congress, House, 93d Cong., 2nd Sess., *Report on the Activities of the Merchant Marine and Fisheries Committee* (Washington, D.C., 1975), p. 143; an excellent analysis of the passage and the toll problem is Norman J. Padelford and Stephen R. Gibbs, *Maritime Commerce and the Future of the Panama Canal* (Cambridge, Md., 1975).

The lock systems were miracles of engineering. One thousand feet long and one hundred and ten feet wide, the locks could handle anything that sailed until the 1930s. Water from the lakes filled each chamber in the lock system by force of gravity. No pumps were installed, thereby saving parts and fuel. If a malfunctioning chamber refused to open while the water continued to flow in, a control tower operator had approximately one minute to rush down next to the locks and turn the huge valves of the chamber by hand to release the water. If the operator did not move quickly enough, he and the operators of the "mules" (the engines which guided the vessel through the locks), could be drowned. That has never happened; indeed, serious problems of any kind have been rare, although each ship passing through the entire system requires fifty-two million gallons of fresh water, about the amount used each day by a city of a half-million people.

Not only is passage through the locks highly delicate, but at points the channel is breathtakingly narrow. Those obstacles, together with the islands that dot the passage through Gatun Lake, make the Canal pilots the Zone's aristocracy. Because of the navigational hazards, the Canal is one of the few waterways on earth where the pilot has authority over the vessel's own captain. Despite the hazards, in the 1980s the system can handle a ship that has a 975-foot length, 106.9-foot beam, 39.5-foot draft, and 65,000 long tons of cargo.

Ship tolls are based on tonnage. The cheapest voyage was paid for in 1928 by adventurer Richard Halliburton who swam the Canal and paid 36¢ toll. In a conscious policy of subsidizing North American shipping, the United States did not raise tolls between 1914 and 1973. Expanding costs were absorbed by increased tonnage passing through the Canal. The low tolls and the nearly 8000 miles cut from a trip between New York City and San Francisco enabled a ship's owner to spend for Canal charges only one-tenth the amount required to move the vessel around the tip of South America.[3] Most important in 1914, the Canal allowed the growing United States Navy to sail easily from one ocean to the other, while putting the gigantic industrial complexes in the Northeast thousands of miles closer to the mineral wealth of South America's western coast and the supposedly bottomless markets of Asia.

Theodore Roosevelt, who needed little encouragement, could justifiably feel proud. Characteristically, however, he overdid it. Speaking at the University of California stadium in 1911, TR bragged: "If I had followed traditional conservative methods," the Canal debate "would

3. Billard, "Panama," p. 414; Liss, *The Canal,* p. 26.

have been going on yet; but I took the Canal Zone and let Congress debate, and while the debate goes on the Canal does also." For an out-of-power politician, particularly a Republican positioning himself to challenge the incumbent Republican President for the White House in 1912, the words were not wise, although they were accurate. The House of Representatives ordered a full investigation of the 1903 revolution. The inquiry revealed in detail for the first time the roles played by Bunau-Varilla, Cromwell, and Roosevelt.

Roosevelt's speech produced one other notable and rather embarrassing result. In 1914 Woodrow Wilson's administration indirectly tried to apologize for TR's bragging by expressing "sincere regret" to Colombia and offering to pay a $25 million indemnity. The treaty was on its way to congressional passage when Roosevelt emerged from a safari in Brazilian jungles where he had nearly died from fever. Wilson's apology acted as a wonderful tonic for the self-righteous TR. In full throat, he attacked this "crime against the United States" with typical Rooseveltian energy. Wilson's handiwork, TR cried, could "only be justified upon the ground that this nation has played the part of a thief or of a receiver of stolen goods." He used the treaty as a springboard for an all-out attack upon Wilson—whom he condemned as a "pacifist"—and the President's overall foreign policy which, TR was convinced, "meant the abandonment of the interest and honor of America."[4]

The Senate quickly backed off. In 1921, however, the State Department reopened negotiations in order to smooth the way for North American oil companies which sought concessions in Colombia. The apologies were implicit, but $25 million did change hands. This time the Senate ratified the treaty. Theodore Roosevelt had died two years before.

Oligarchs—and Others

The country surrounding the new Canal held about 400,000 people in its seven provinces. The racial composition was complex and potentially dangerous. At the top of the socio-political-economic ladder stood approximately 51,000 "whites" whose largely Spanish ancestry made them whiter than most other Panamanians. The leaders of this group came from several dozen, often interrelated families that comprised the oligarchy. They not only traced their lineage to the 1903 revolutionary leader-

4. Harbaugh, *Power and Responsibility,* pp. 464–465; Henry F. Pringle, *Theodore Roosevelt, a Biography* (New York, 1931, 1956), p. 407; Arciniegas, *Caribbean,* p. 444.

ship, but to the early Colombian and Spanish eras. Sometimes this required mighty efforts. One family even tried to claim Pedrarias the Cruel as an ancestor. Such genealogical detective work was necessary since Panamanian sensitivity to skin color helped determine the power hierarchy. According to popular sayings, the rule was that "White is right," and "Blacks go to the back." Although the mass of Panamanians sarcastically referred to the leading families as *rabiblancos*, or white-tails, the oligarchy made white, Spanish-speaking ancestry the key to social acceptance, and what it termed "kinky hair" the sign of the outcast. In reality few Panamanians could legitimately claim pure white bloodlines. The oligarchy could not profit from living at the world's crossroads without coming in close contact with many races.

Panamanian social status consequently became determined not only by bloodlines (real or supposed), but by economic power. The oligarchy remained relatively small, but it was open to new members who possessed wealth. Among the oligarchs the ubiquitous Chiari family grew rich from sugar growing; the Boyds from cattle, dairy, and import businesses. Arnulfo and Harmodio Arias came from a poorer family, yet Arnulfo's coffee plantations and Harmodio's legal and publishing businesses ultimately gave them social status.

Not accidentally, the same names dominated political life. Wealth was a prerequisite for political power. Panamanian politics have never organized around parties or issues, but around charismatic, rich men. Without a party apparatus, candidates were forced to pay political expenses themselves, and given the rampant corruption expenses ran high. But politics, in turn, became the key to preserving wealth against competitors and expanding landholdings or concessions. Few Panamanians left high office without having piled up large bank accounts to cushion the pain of retirement.

More than 200,000, or well over a majority of the population, were mestizo (Spanish and Indian blood) or mulatto (black and Spanish blood). The vagueness of the figures indicates the racism of the society, for while outside experts could estimate mulattos outnumbering mestizos two to one, the ratio was reversed when the Panamanians themselves were asked about their racial background. Few claimed black blood if they could pass for mestizo. It remains difficult to challenge them since mestizos and mulattos have married the whiter Panamanians and each other ever since Spanish soldiers first impregnated Indian and black women some four centuries ago.

Panamanian racial discrimination thus cuts fine. Just how fine has been demonstrated by the experience of the blacks. In 1914 about 50,000 of them occupied the bottom of the socio-political scale, but some were more unequal than others. Those who entered as slaves during the Spanish era learned the native language and became more easily assimilated than later arrivals. Several of the Spanish-speaking blacks later became Vice-Presidents of Panama. The late arrivals were brought from the British West Indies by de Lesseps or the American engineers to do the backbreaking work on the Canal. Since they spoke English, immigrants won preferred status in the Zone at the expense of Panamanians who wanted those jobs. For seventy-five years, the English-speaking blacks, or *chombos* as they are called, have been the most visible targets of racial discrimination in Panama.

Several thousand Asians and Jews congregated in urban areas. The Jews prospered and generally became assimilated in the society. Many of the Asians also did well; by the 1960s they were among the most astute of Panamanian businessmen. But their racial differences made them so conspicuous that they were often victimized as scapegoats, particularly during times of economic or political tension. At least 35,000 native Indians lived in such inaccessible areas that census-takers could not find them.

Since political-economic power divided racially, it also tended to divide geographically. The *rabiblancos* dominated urban centers, while the mixed races and Indians peopled the outlying provinces. In 1910 one-third of the population lived in twelve towns. Panama City contained 38,000, and another 18,000 lived at the other end of the Canal in Colon. David, the capital of wealthy Chiriqui Province (site of the United Fruit Company's expanding banana plantations and many oligarchical land holdings), had more than 15,000 population.[5] The urban oligarchy controlled the country for 60 years, and a striking aspect of post-1969 Panama has been the attempt of the Torrijos government to reduce the cities' political power in order to help the impoverished peasants in the interior. The attempt has not been overly successful.

Panama's racial sensitivities needed no honing, but they were sharpened to a fine point by the Canal Zone's policies. The blacks earned twenty cents an hour, and they were bossed by men who had experience with black labor—that is, whites from the Gulf States who in the words

5. This section has in part been drawn from material in Willis J. Abbot, *The Panama Canal: An Illustrated Historical Narrative.* . . . (New York, 1922), pp. 273–274; Thomas E. Weil, *et al., Area Handbook for Panama* (Washington, D.C., 1972), especially pp. 195–200; John and Mavis Biesanz, *The People of Panama* (New York, 1955), pp. 208–210.

of one scholar "were sent to the Canal Zone with instructions to make an inter-racial society work as well as it did in our Deep South."[6]

While the Canal was being built, some 5300 United States citizens and a few Panamanians received wages in gold coin. The remaining 31,000 laborers, including most Panamanians and all the blacks, were paid in lesser silver coin. The gold and silver payroll made the aristocracy instantly recognizable. Soon the labels—and the segregation—spread to drinking fountains, toilet facilities, and nearly every other public service. The discrimination was hardly surprising since Jim Crow laws (segregating whites and blacks on transportation, in schools, etc.) were sweeping through the United States, and as many as a hundred blacks were being lynched annually in the South. But when Jim Crow laws and lynching gradually disappeared in the United States after World War II, the gold and silver distinctions remained entrenched in the Canal Zone (although the terminology officially disappeared). The racially sensitive Panamanians never forgot or forgave the United States, for they had not joined the blacks in the silver lines by choice.

The United States Colony, or Nabobs in Panama City

Panamanians have been quick to condemn what they termed the "colonial presence" of the United States in the Canal Zone. But they tended to miss—or, particularly if they were oligarchs, were reluctant to confront—the larger problem: although their country was legally sovereign and independent, in reality it was a United States colony. That colonial relationship helps us understand both the hatreds that developed and why many North Americans and some Panamanians considered Panama unfit to run the Canal in the 1970s. That relationship was also why the Canal could be described as "a body of water entirely surrounded by trouble."[7]

Rupert Emerson, an authority on colonialism, has defined it as "the establishment and maintenance, for an extended time, of rule over an alien people that is separate from and subordinate to the ruling power." The term no longer refers only to colonies formed by settlement abroad of people from a mother country, as it did in eighteenth-century England. Emerson sees colonialism as "white rule over peoples of different race inhabiting lands separated by salt water from the imperial center,"

6. Mercer D. Tate, "The Panama Canal and Political Partnership," *The Journal of Politics,* XXV (February 1963), 119–120.
7. E. J. Kahn, Jr., "Letter from Panama," *The New Yorker,* Aug. 16, 1976, p. 66.

and a rule "asserting racial and cultural superiority over a materially inferior native majority." But "more particularly," he concludes, "it signifies direct political control by European states or states settled by Europeans, as the United States . . . over peoples of other races."[8]

All of these relationships, and especially the last, have characterized Washington's ties with Panama. The colonial ties were informal; that is, they were not systematically designed as a colonial system to be operated (as it was in London) by a Colonial Office. Panama ostensibly retained independence and sovereignty. Yet the North American control

8. Rupert Emerson, "Colonialism: Political Aspects," in David L. Sills, ed., *International Encyclopedia of the Social Sciences,* Volume III (New York, 1968), pp. 1–5. "Informal colonialism" seems to be a more accurate description of United States-Panamanian relations, particularly through the 1930s but beyond as well, than "dependency." Theotonio Dos Santos has defined dependency as "a situation in which the economy of certain countries is conditioned by the development and expansion of another economy to which the former is subjected. The relation of interdependence between two or more economies, between these and world trade, assumes the form of dependence when some countries (the dominant ones) can expand and can be self-starting, while other countries (the dependent ones) can do this only as a reflection of that expansion, which can have either a positive or a negative effect on their immediate development." This is a widely accepted definition of the term. Dependency has received much attention from Latin American scholars, and several of the elaborations are applicable to U.S.-Panama affairs. C. Richard Bath and Dilmus D. James, for example, note how scholars agreee that development and underdevelopment are two components "of *one unified system.*" That approach provides some insight into Panamanian underdevelopment. Dependency is less useful than "informal colonialism" in understanding the Panamanian case, however, because it does not go far enough in describing the extent of United States control. As the Dos Santos definition indicates, dependency revolves around economic factors, but Washington's power in Panama allowed the use of direct political and military intervention. That power, moreover, was legitimized by treaty and did not depend on "free trade imperialism," as does Dos Santos's dependency relationship. The United States integrated Panama into its system not through trade, but through treaties, including an agreement that made the dollar interchangeable with Panamanian currency. If dependency is used to analyze United States relations with large Latin American nations (Chile seems to be a favorite example), it is doubtful it can be used to explain adequately the wholly different type of relationship between Washington and Panama City. The following recent studies have been especially useful in enabling a non-Latin Americanist to understand the dependency concept: Theotonio Dos Santos, "The Structure of Dependence," in K. T. Fann and Donald C. Hodges, eds., *Readings in U.S. Imperialism* (Boston, 1971), pp. 225–236; Ronald H. Chilcote and Joel C. Edelstein, *Latin America: The Struggle with Dependence and Beyond* (New York, 1974), especially pages 26–32, 40; and C. Richard Bath and Dilmus D. James, "Dependency Analysis of Latin America:Some Criticisms, Some Suggestions," *Latin American Research Review,* XI (Number 3), pp. 3–36, particularly their suggestion of considering dependency in terms of "linkage politics." Most valuable have been the continued and often unavailing efforts of Professor Thomas Holloway of Cornell to initiate me into the mysteries of dependency theory.

of Panama fit Emerson's criteria, with the relationships developing less formally, less systematically, and handled by the State Department rather than a Colonial Office. As a foreign affairs expert observed in 1932, "The relations of the United States with Panama are in many respects similar to those of the British Empire with Egypt and Japan with Manchuria."[9]

The colonial relationship began when the 1903 treaty gave the United States power over Panama's economy, immigration, city services, and foreign policy. In 1904 the Panamanian currency was tied to the dollar (change in Panama still has to be given in North American coins). That same year the U.S. Minister disbanded the Panamanian army, thereby making the government dependent on North American military units for maintaining order. In 1905 the Liberals, whom Taft had carefully kept out of power in 1904, argued that United States policy was contradictory. If Washington guaranteed public order, they claimed, "it is strictly logical and just that it should guarantee the existence of an absolutely lawful system of government."[10] Panamanian opposition groups might have thought such a position logical, but North Americans equivocated. On the one hand they demanded cooperative Panamanian regimes, but on the other they wanted no formal, long-term responsibility for publicly policing Panama's elections.

Washington consequently embarked on a search, still in progress in the late twentieth century, for a method of shaping isthmian politics without ostentatious interference in Panama's affairs. The search seemed initially successful. In 1908 a United States commission of fourteen members publicly cooperated with Panamanians to ensure that the election would be orderly (if not incorrupt). The Liberals won, but this time Taft and Roosevelt did not mind. The Conservative oligarchs had fought among themselves until the party split. Former Conservatives moved into the Liberal party and it also became factionalized. So began the era of fragmented, personalized political parties that lasted until 1969.

United States participation in the elections profoundly influenced Panamanian politics. In 1908, for example, the acting President, José Domingo Obaldía, could control the election process and, not surprisingly, decided to be a presidential candidate. The opposition hoped the United States would either guarantee a free election by cracking down on Obaldía's manipulation of the voting, or stand aside while the opposi-

9.   R. L. Buell, "Panama and the United States," *Foreign Policy Reports*, VII (Jan. 20, 1932), 409.
10. *FRUS, 1905*, p. 718.

tion overthrew Obaldía with a coup. Washington naturally rejected both alternatives. The latter could cause a disruption in canal construction, and the former would result in a blatant, bothersome intervention. After all, Taft sighed, one must expect "the use of government aid to secure the fradulent election of a government candidate." The United States consequently did not intervene directly to ensure a fair election, only indirectly to guarantee order and, not entirely coincidentally, the continuance of a cooperative regime.

Four years later 180 North American election supervisors ineffectively attempted to reduce vote fraud as another Liberal candidate, Belisario Porras, triumphed. In 1916, however, Porras asked Washington to stay out. The opposition pleaded for more United States supervisors to prevent the President from fixing the results. The Woodrow Wilson administration cooperated with Porras and his party easily won.[11] Washington's adherence to the status quo was best demonstrated in the 1918 local elections. Faced with increasing opposition, the government simply cancelled the election. It reversed itself only after the United States moved troops into Panama City and Colon, promised to supervise the balloting, and acted as an arbitral commission to judge disputed results. The North Americans decided that indeed the government's candidates won a majority of the provinces.[12] The Panamanian electoral process had become unrepresentative and a farce. Dedicated above all to maintaining order and cooperative regimes, the North Americans helped shape that process.

In retrospect, Washington's sensitivity to isthmian politics was amazing. In these elections, as in most others held since, the leading candidates belonged to the oligarchy, showed equal commitment to close ties with the United States, and were prepared to pledge their property, lives, and honor to preservation of the status quo. To tell the top candidates apart required the splitting of political issues with a precision that taxed even Taft's legalistic mind. In reality, Washington cared little about supposed differences between Conservatives and Liberals after 1908. It worried only that the supporters of each candidate might take their cause so seriously that violence could erupt, then spread into the Canal Zone and hinder operations. Efficient functioning of the Canal took precedence over the political development of Panama. Debates over meaningful political issues not only became irrelevant, but dangerous. The waterway consequently flourished, but Panamanian political

---

11. Porras's great abilities and personality are described in Ernesto J. Castillero Reyes, *Historia de Panamá* (Panama, 1955), pp. 169–170.
12. Buell, "Panama and the United States," p. 416.

life became corrupt and stagnant. As in India, where the native nabobs remained in power by working within the rules of the British colonial empire, in Panama the oligarchy retained power by acknowledging the supremacy of the Canal's needs, as Washington defined those needs.

The "Outlying Possession"

In Washington's view, those needs, and its power to fulfill them, were becoming ever larger. Supervising elections constituted one method of protecting United States interests. Military intervention, control of Panamanian foreign policy, and domination of the country's economy were other methods.

Under the 1903 treaty and Article 136 of Panama's Constitution, the United States possessed the right to intervene to "reestablish public peace and constitutional order." In return, the North Americans guaranteed Panama's independence. By World War I, however, the Panamanians were having second thoughts about this arrangement. Their independence was secure. The threat of a Colombian invasion vanished years before. Panamanians began to argue that Washington could intervene only when they asked for help.

The United States nevertheless continued to intervene at will. In 1912 riots occurred in the red light district of Cocoa Grove, which the city fathers had placed, with considerable foresight, between the hospital and cemetery and adjacent to the Canal Zone. Anti-Yankee in origin, the rioters killed a U.S. sailor and wounded nineteen others. Panama City police ended the fracas, but the government stalled when Washington demanded an explanation and assurance of future protection. In 1915 riots again erupted in Cocoa Grove, spreading this time to Colon before they were extinguished.

The State Department dressed down the Panamanian government, warned that such disorders would not be further tolerated, and—to make the point clear—demanded that the Panamanian police surrender their high-powered rifles which, the State Department claimed, threatened unarmed North Americans. Panama angrily told President Woodrow Wilson that such demands infringed upon its sovereignty. Wilson did not push the issue until Panama unwisely threatened to appeal to other Latin American nations for mediation. The State Department then sharply defined Panama's rights: any proposal to have Latin Americans interfere in United States-Panamanian relations was "unworthy of serious consideration."[13] The police were left with pistols. The rifles were taken to the United States for sale.

U.S. troops intervened periodically in Panama during these years. The interventions exemplified a policy being followed throughout the Caribbean and must be understood within that larger context.

The Wilson administration cited the need to defend the Canal as a justification for many of those interventions, much as Roosevelt had justified his Corollary. Because of the Canal, Secretary of State Robert Lansing wrote the President in late 1915, European political control should be excluded from the region. Since the "small republics of America . . . have been and to an extent still are the prey of revolutionists, of corrupt government, and of predatory foreigners," the United States needed the right to create "stable and honest government, if no other way seems possible to attain that end." Caring little about "our humanitarian purpose" or the "benefit which would result to the peoples of those republics by the adoption of this policy," Lansing urged only the protection of his nation's "national interests."[14]

Wilson and Lansing consequently sent United States troops into Mexico, Santo Domingo, Cuba, Haiti, Nicaragua, and Panama. The motivations were complex, differed from one case to the other, and most—contrary to Lansing's note—bore little relationship to the Canal's defense. The policy usually resulted from the desire to stop or contain revolutions (as in Mexico, Cuba, and Nicaragua), or protect United States investments threatened by either default or European competition (as in Santo Domingo, Haiti, and Nicaragua). Defending the Canal became just one more reason for intervention, not a primary or sole justification. As Lansing's letter illustrated, it was a reason that nicely fit into a policy of creating a Caribbean political system that was non-revolutionary and under United States control. The Canal became a symbol of North American expansionism, but it was by no means the primary cause of the expansion.

In Panama the first major military intervention occurred in Chiriqui Province, site of the banana plantations owned by the Boston-based United Fruit Company. Chiriqui was also the country's richest agricultural area, although its income was perhaps the most inequitably distrib-

---

13. *FRUS, 1915*, p. 1236.
14. Lansing to Wilson, Nov. 24, 1915, "Personal and Confidential Letters," Robert Lansing Papers, Library of Congress, Washington, D.C. (Microfilm); Wilson's interventionist policies in Latin America are analyzed by Lloyd Gardner in Gardner, LaFeber, and McCormick, *Creation of the American Empire*, chapter XVI, from which the interpretation in this section is drawn.

uted of any Panamanian province. The intervention was triggered by riots which erupted after a fixed election in 1918. One North American was killed in fighting which the rifleless Panamanian police could not prevent. United States troops moved in and remained for two years. As the weeks, then months, passed, the Panamanian government strongly protested. It argued that, under the 1903 treaty, troops could land only at Panama's request and be used only in Panama City and Colon. Washington flatly rejected that argument.

The troops left Chiriqui by 1921, but the debate continued. If the United States possessed blanket right to intervene "without the authorization of our government," the Panamanians argued, "the guarantee in the treaty [in which the United States promised to protect the country's independence] would not be of independence but of absolute subjection."[15] Washington did not budge an inch. In 1918, without waiting for Panama to ask, it had landed troops in Panama City and Colon to cool election fevers. Three years later, at President Porras's personal request, United States soldiers protected him from mobs besieging the Presidential Palace. Only in 1925 did the Panamanian government use Article 136 to justify calling in North American aid. When rent riots erupted in the capital, Marines with fixed bayonets stopped the uprising. They were also used later in the year to guarantee peace during elections.

Landing the Marines was the most spectacular but not always the most important display of Washington's colonial authority over Panama. Beginning in 1911, the U.S. Navy sought a monopoly of Panamanian wireless stations. The State Department agreed that since radio control was essential to Canal defense, Panama did not even have to be consulted. In 1914 the Wilson administration abruptly demanded an "immediate monopoly," and after the usual strong and ineffective protest, the Panamanians surrendered "complete and permanent control" over their radio communications.[16]

If they could not control their own communications, or internal order, Panamanians would logically encounter difficulty in controlling their foreign policy. The country developed its own diplomatic corps, belonged to the League of Nations (which the United States refused to join), and proudly became a member of the elite League Council in 1931. All this, however, was window-dressing. Washington had laid down the rules in 1909 when the Taft administration announced that it possessed the "moral right to prevent Panama from getting into a contro-

15. Quoted in Buell, "Panama and the United States," p. 414.
16. *Ibid.*, p. 418; George W. Baker, Jr., "The Wilson Administration and Panama, 1913–1931," *Journal of Inter-American Studies*, VIII (April 1966), pp. 279–93, especially p. 281.

versy with any government which might eventually require the United States to take a part in the controversy and support Panama."[17]

In 1921 the Panamanians learned the meaning of this rule. They agreed to settle a long-disputed boundary question with Costa Rica by accepting the mediation of a commission headed by a justice of the U.S. Supreme Court. When the justice turned over the disputed land to Costa Rica, however, the Panama police prepared for war. Warren G. Harding's newly installed administration sharply instructed Panama to surrender the land, then sent a battleship and 400 Marines to ensure compliance. That same year Washington reversed a 1905 decision and announced that foreign diplomats acting as consuls in Panama required separate exequaturs to work in the Canal Zone. Panama naturally protested that the Zone was not separate from the surrounding country. The United States rejected the protest. Humiliation followed humiliation. In 1923, at the request of the Canal Zone government and the State Department, Congress suddenly repealed the 1904 Taft agreement. Panamanian merchants again faced competition from Zonian sellers who bought at prices subsidized by the United States.

Ricardo Alfaro, Minister to Washington, complained to Harding's Secretary of State, Charles Evans Hughes, that Panama understood Washington's need to control the Zone for Canal operations, "but when it comes to commerce and other sovereign rights [as the exequatur] it was a different matter." Hughes's reply was brutal. "This government could not and would not enter into any discussion affecting its full right to deal with the Canal Zone . . . as if it were sovereign of the Canal Zone and to the exclusion of any sovereign rights or authority on the part of Panama. . . . It was absolute futility," Hughes added icily, for Panama "to expect any American Administration, no matter what it was . . . ever to surrender those rights."[18] Hughes's prophecy left much to be desired, but the essential question was: who had the rifles? No one doubted the answer. The U.S. Navy went ahead to establish in the Zone a special squadron capable of quickly landing Marines anywhere in the Caribbean area.[19]

Hughes finally agreed to renew the Taft agreement of 1904, but he would not promise to stop seizing lands adjacent to the Canal Zone or reverse his policies on exequaturs. Washington indeed demanded that

17. *FRUS, 1909*, pp. 469–70.

18. *FRUS, 1923*, II, 684; Joseph Tulchin, *The Aftermath of War: World War I and U.S. Policy Towards Latin America* (New York, 1971), pp. 95–96.

19. Kenneth J. Grieb, "The United States and the Central American Federation," *The Americas*, XXIV (October 1967), 121.

Panama hand over part of New Cristobal (a section of the country's second largest city, Colon, and the Atlantic terminal of the Canal). The North Americans also requested further monopoly rights in radio communications, airways, and sanitation policies. To cap the negotiations, Panama, on the initiative of one of its own diplomats, promised to join the United States automatically whenever Washington decided to go to war. When the pact embodying these changes arrived in Panama City, it was attacked so viciously in the legislative Assembly and street rallies that the government refused to consider it.

The refusal was a brave act, but it changed nothing. As was sometimes the case, President Calvin Coolidge was inadvertently accurate in 1928 when he called Panama one of "our outlying possessions." As regards the Zone, Taft had defined the situation when he privately argued that the United States could agree Panama had "titular sovereignty," since the term was a barren scepter "that had a poetic and sentimental appeal to the Latin mind."[20]

"Spiggoties" and "Gringos"

Economically the country had long been an appendage of United States interests.[21] As early as the 1880s Colombia absorbed $14 million of North American investment, much of it in Panama. The United Fruit Company, which started banana plantations in Colombia's western provinces in 1899, owned 23,000 acres of land and 73 miles of railroad worth over $2 million when Panama declared its independence. In 1906 less than one percent of the country's land was cultivated, but one-third of the land under cultivation belonged to United Fruit. Investments flooded in, including the Central and South American Telegraph Company, a tobacco monopoly, large-scale sugar production, saw mills, distilleries, coffee plantations—all controlled by North Americans. They built Panama City's street railways, electric power company (later controlled by General Electric), telephone network, and ice service. By 1913 the total value of Panama's private property was about $33 million, and United Fruit alone owned $7 to $8 million.

The State Department closely watched the financial situation. When Panama went deeply in debt to finance internal improvements in 1916,

20. Quoted in Liss, *The Canal*, pp. 33, 35. A Panamanian view is given briefly in Ernesto J. Castillero Reyes, *El Canal de Panamá* (Panama, n.d. [1965?]), pp. 137–141.
21. Much of the following is based on the superb account by William D. McCain, *The United States and the Republic of Panama* (Durham, N.C., 1937), pp. 97–104, 106–118.

Washington insisted that a United States financial adviser be hired. The Panamanians protested, one claiming the demand meant the death of the young republic. In 1918 the first of a series of advisers nevertheless moved in to control the country's fiscal system. When Panama wanted to issue bonds for railways in Chiriqui Province, Secretary of State Lansing agreed in 1917 on the condition that the government cooperate fully with loan demands set down by National City Bank of New York. Panama refused, then, with no choice, finally agreed. But when Panamanians wanted to build feeder rail and wagon roads to tap the lucrative traffic in the Zone, Lansing turned them over to the War Department, which operated the Zone. Nothing was done.[22]

During World War I the United States suddenly became the world's richest nation. Loaning vast amounts to both the Allies and Central Powers, it moved to the center of the globe's money exchanges. Panama was one of several Latin nations targeted by capital-rich North Americans. The Isthmus possessed no regular banking services until 1910, but after the war Chase National and National City, both of New York, moved in. A decade later National City held immense power. It pressured the government, for example, to undertake a thorough survey of the country's resources. The survey would be headed by an executive of the bank. Panamanians loudly objected, but the government again gave in. United Fruit meanwhile built its holding to 250 miles of railways, 26,000 acres of bananas, and more than 20,000 acres of other food products.

This penetration was accompanied, indeed protected, by a 1929 State Department decision that North American airway companies would not be allowed to compete for the rich access routes to Panama. Instead, one company, Pan American, received a monopoly and mail contract subsidies. As the State Department argued, "it is certainly desirable and perhaps essential that the United States should, in so far as possible, control aviation in the Caribbean nations."[23] In some circumstances, marketplace competition was not to be trusted.

As the country began to slide into the morass of economic depression in 1930, Panama City and Colon were rapidly growing urban areas of 74,000 and 33,000 people respectively. The 40,000 people living in the

---

22. Baker, "Wilson Administration and Panama," pp. 288–289.

23. *FRUS, 1929*, I, 542–545, esp. 543. The best analysis of United States economic penetration into Latin America during the "Progressive" era (1906–29), and the role played by government in aiding that penetration, is Robert Neal Seidel, *Progressive Pan Americanism: Development and U.S. Policy Toward South America, 1906–1931*, Cornell University Latin American Studies Program Dissertation Series, Ithaca, 1973.

Zone on United States government salaries seemed a buffer against economic troubles. In some years the Zone provided as much as one-third of Panama's national income.

The Zone, however, gave the Panamanian economy a rosiness that hid a dangerous fever, not good circulation. By 1930, North Americans held nearly $29 million in direct investments and $18 million in Panamanian bonds. Panama's foreign trade was a misnomer; it was actually North American trade. In 1930 the United States provided more than two-thirds of the nation's $19 million of imports and took 94 percent of its $4 million in exports. Panama City depended on the Zone; so did Colon, whose economic health was at the mercy of the U.S. government-owned Panama Railroad. The company not only operated the city's main hotel, but owned a number of the most valuable land parcels and buildings. It frequently leased buildings to Panamanians. In this way Colon's red-light district, whose buildings belonged to the Railroad, paid rent to Panamanians. As a State Department official later noted, this arrangement put "an end to the incongruity of United States authorities collecting rent from prostitutes."[24] When the world's greatest economic power began to capsize in 1929, Panama was one of the passengers onboard. By 1932 United States investments stopped and Panamanian exports and imports were sliced in half.

As unemployment grew, race relations worsened between the Zone's inhabitants and the people of Colon and the capital city. The relationship had long been uneasy. In 1914 when the Canal opened, Panamanians believed the North Americans and black West Indians would shortly leave so the Zone's jobs would be open for them. The builders instead isolated the Zone and gave job preference to the English-speaking blacks who would accept low "silver" wages. Panamanian intolerance toward the blacks heightened along with a hatred of North American economic discrimination.

A United States visitor in the early 1920s observed that Panamanians thought the Canal brought them little but sanitation, and this convenience they had done nicely without before the Yankees appeared. Panamanians disliked North Americans, the visitor wrote, because of "their resentment at our hardly concealed contempt for them." The whiter, Spanish elite did not share these feelings, at least in such intensity, but "as for the casual clerk or mechanic we Americans call him 'spiggoty' with frank contempt for his undersize, his lack of education, and for his

24. Laurence Duggan, *The Americas: The Search for Hemisphere Security* (New York, 1949), pp. 32–33.

large proportion of Negro blood." He responds by calling North American " 'gringos' and hating [us] with a deep, malevolent rancor that needs only a fit occasion to blaze forth in riot and in massacre."[25]

The "Revolution" of 1931

Such simmering hatred would have been less dangerous if Panama had not been, as Coolidge described it, an outlying possession of the United States. By 1930 many Panamanians easily blamed their problems on Washington. Given the imbalance of fire power in the area, they seemed to have little chance of breaking the colonial ties. In 1931, however, Panamanians overthrew their elected government for the first time, and when this act led them into a dead end, they focused their discontent on the Canal Zone.

The events that led to the 1931 coup began in the mid-1920s. One dominant family, the Chiaris, controlled the presidency, and since President Rudolfo Chiari could not run for a second term in 1928, he transferred the office to a close associate, Florencio H. Arosemena. The triumph of the Chiari-Arosemena scheme angered the wealthy and politically ambitious Arias Madrid family. The Arias's determination to drive Arosemena from power received unexpected help from two sources. The first was the growing economic depression which sharpened political frustrations. The second was a new political organization, *Acción Comunal,* which United States Minister Roy T. Davis first suspected of links with the international Communist movement. Investigation soon revealed that it was an indigenous group whose program, in the Minister's words, seemed "semi-radical," and whose real concern was to become a player in the game of trying to evict Arosemena from office.[26]

Acción Comunal actually marked a milestone in Panamanian history. Formed in 1926 to fight the treaty made with the United States, it soon attracted members of a small, new Panamanian middle class who were searching for a political home that the oligarchy had no intention of providing. Its members were predominantly mestizo; included teachers, government employees, small businessmen, and some urban workers; and many had migrated from the provinces to find their fortune in Panama City and Colon. On racial, functional, and geographic grounds,

---

25. Abbot, *The Panama Canal,* pp. 233–236. Abbot speculates that "spiggoty" came from the attempts of hackmen to lure fares by shouting "Speaka-da-English."

26. This important story is best revealed in the dispatches and instructions in *FRUS, 1931,* II, 890–904, and especially Davis to Department of State, Jan. 6, 1931, pp. 894–902.

therefore, the oligarchy perceived the new arrivals as an enemy. That perception was accurate, especially since the middle class was extremely ambitious (its members often used the verb *luchar,* to struggle, in describing themselves),[27] and saw the oligarchy's control as oppressive. For these same reasons the new class was also highly nationalistic and anti-Yankee. In its view the United States-subsidized commissaries in the Zone robbed merchants of sales, discriminated against Panamanian workers, and humiliated their country's government. The teachers carried that message into the schools which, in turn, spawned the anti-oligarchical and anti-North American movements of the next half-century.

Harmodio and Arnulfo Arias moved naturally into the leadership of the movement. The brothers were mestizo, made their fortunes in the provinces (where they built a large political following, especially among peasants), and were initally disliked by the oligarchy. In 1911 while a student at the London School of Economics, Harmodio published a widely noticed book arguing that the United States had issued the Monroe Doctrine not for purposes of self-defense, but as the first step of an imperialistic policy. From this premise, as well as numerous legal arguments, he concluded that Washington's expansion must be checked at the Isthmus and the Canal neutralized by international agreement.[28] By the late 1920s the brothers were fighting a two-front war against the United States and oligarchical control. The new middle class appeared to be their natural ally.

For the next five decades Arnulfo was a perennial candidate for the presidency and Harmodio the most accomplished political schemer in Panama. The latter's first move to gain power wonderfully displayed his talents. On the night of January 2, 1931, *Acción Comunal* seized the Panama City telephone company and the Presidential Palace. However, it wisely allowed Davis, the U.S. Minister, to pass its guard around the Palace to talk with Arosemena. The President hoped Marines would be sent to restore order, but, according to Davis, "did not insist on it." The Minister decided not to employ troops since news of their landing might lead the opposition to kill Arosemena. The ensuing battle could then spread into the Zone. Most important, Davis discovered the Arias group to be quite cooperative, perhaps in part because Davis carefully refused to indicate whether or not Marines would be summoned.

Arosemena resigned and Harmodio Arias became Acting President until Arosemena's Vice-President, Ricardo Alfaro, returned from Wash-

27. Biesanz, *People of Panama,* pp. 210–215.
28. Harmodio Arias, *The Panama Canal: A Study in International Law and Diplomacy* (London, 1911).

ington to assume the top office. By working with those whom he termed the "responsible and representative" opposition members, Davis preserved the semblance of constitutional procedure. Of equal significance, he resolved the crisis before troops had to be landed. Throughout, Harmodio Arias appeared responsible and cooperative.

Washington deeply appreciated such moderation. During 1930–31, a half-dozen revolutions in depression-ridden Latin America threatened the area with political chaos. Secretary of State Henry Stimson declared himself "very blue" over the upheavals, particularly since he and President Herbert Hoover were sharply turning United States policy away from Roosevelt's and Wilson's gunboat diplomacy toward a more peaceful, cooperative policy. Although it started down the uncharted path, Panama, at least, had turned back. The oligarchy, Arias, even the "younger element" of "semi-radical tendencies," to use Davis's phrases, proved to be "responsible." After luncheon with Davis in Washington, Stimson happily recorded in his diary that "what he had done . . . was really very fine, for he had virtually stopped the revolution there."[29]

But of course the sores of economic depression and political frustration continued to fester. Alfaro could do little to remedy them during his two years in office. In the 1932 election Harmodio Arias returned as a Liberal candidate to win the presidency on his own. During the electioneering he encountered no difficulty whipping up support for his commitment to create a new relationship with the North Americans. All three of the leading candidates indeed joined Harmodio in attacking the United States. The 1932 campaign marked perhaps the first time none of the parties considered asking the United States to supervise the elections.[30]

Roosevelt Revises Roosevelt

Economic conditions worsened in 1933 until 50,000, or about a quarter of the workforce, were unemployed. President Arias tried a range of remedies, including a reduction in civil service salaries and a moratorium on the national debt. He focused relief efforts on the rural provinces where two-thirds of all Panamanians lived, most at subsistence levels. Arias was the first President to extend such state help to the

29. Diaries of Henry L. Stimson, Vol. XIX, Nov. 6, 1931, pp. 15–16, Papers of Henry L. Stimson, Yale University (microfilm).
30. McCain, *United States and Republic of Panama*, p. 77.

impoverished countryside.[31] To finance the spending, Arias tried to increase governmental bond issues, but credit sources dried up. By 1934
governmental issues totalled $18.7 million; $14.5 million of those were
in default because interest could not be paid.[32] When the country's
national bank defaulted, bankruptcy seemed near.

Arias's only hope was to draw more revenue and employment from the
Canal Zone. It became not merely the country's greatest, but apparently
its only resource. Yet Panama had no control whatever over the Canal. As
a foreign policy expert drily remarked in 1932, the relationship between
the Zone and Panama "would have been simplified had Panama been
annexed to the United States."[33] Panamanian sensitivity to the Zone's
affairs was illustrated by the uproar that resulted when the United States
began selling beer along the Canal. Panamanian merchants had profited
since 1920 from the peculiar North American refusal to make or sell beer,
but to drink large amounts of it. After Prohibition ended in November
1933, the merchants lost one of their few remaining sources of profit.
Several months before, a Panama City newspaper warned that the nation
might cut diplomatic relations with Washington if the Zone became
"wet." Arias denied the threat, but speeded plans for a direct talk with the
new United States President, Franklin D. Roosevelt.

As a guest at the White House for a week in October 1933, Arias got
along well with Roosevelt. Noting that "misunderstandings" between
the two nations "had become intensified by the continued economic
depression," FDR smoothly agreed that two of the provisions Panamanians found most obnoxious in the 1903 treaty should be terminated: the
explicit right of the United States to intervene in Colon and Panama
City, and the implicit right of freewheeling merchants in the Zone to
compete with Panamanians in selling to tourists or in Panama itself.

Roosevelt further understood that the black, English-speaking West
Indians could serve as a lightning-rod for Panamanian unrest. (Perhaps
that understanding occurred when, as FDR recalled years later, Arias
warned "that the Jamaicans in Panama were dangerous; that each Jamaican man slept with three women every week.")[34] The President conse-

31. Castillero Reyes, *Historia de Panamá*, p. 188.
32. J. Fred Rippy, *Globe and Hemisphere; Latin America's Place in Postwar Foreign
Relations of the United States* (Chicago, 1958), p. 62.
33. Buell, "Panama and the United States," p. 409; McCain, *United States and Republic of
Panama*, p. 245 contains the material relating to the Panama City newspaper warning.
34. "Top-secret Memorandum, Annex to Memorandum of March 15, 1945," FDR-
Taussig conversation, Box 52, Papers of Charles Taussig, Franklin D. Roosevelt Library,
Hyde Park, N.Y.

quently urged Congress to appropriate funds for repatriating "some of the aliens," who "constitute a serious unemployment problem for Panama," to their home islands.[35]

The famous phrase of the 1903 treaty—that the United States could act "as if it were sovereign"—was not restated. The joint statement issued by Arias and FDR declared only that "the provisions of the Treaty of 1903 . . . contemplate the use, occupation and control by the United States of the Canal Zone."[36] Nor did the statement repeat the 1903 clause that the United States could hold its rights "in perpetuity." Roosevelt, however, left no doubt about his feelings when he visited Panama in July 1934. He noted proudly that his "interest in Panama may be said to be of a historical character" since his great-uncle, William H. Aspinwall, built the Panama Railroad in the 1850s. "It was this railroad which began to restore the Isthmus" as the "crossroads of the Americas," Roosevelt announced, and the United States would continue to act as "a trustee for all the world" in maintaining the Canal.[37] While revising part of his cousin Theodore's work in Panama, FDR retained full power over the Zone so the United States could charitably protect "civilization," as TR called it.

Arias and Roosevelt turned the detailed negotiations over to their diplomats. The talks did not go smoothly. Between 1934 and the signing of the treaty on March 2, 1936, 110 conferences were convened. In Panama, Arias was pressured to obtain a more explicit repudiation of the 1903 sovereignty clause. In the United States the War Department took the lead in demanding that FDR reiterate "all rights of sovereignty" granted in 1903, that control over Panama's ports at the Canal terminals be retained, and that Marines be allowed to maintain public order in the ports.[38] The War Department won support for its demands from a powerful group of Senators led by William Borah (Rep., Idaho), Hiram Johnson (Rep., Calif.), and Claude Pepper (Dem., Fla.). Perhaps not coincidentally, Borah and Johnson fondly remembered campaigning for Progressivism in 1912 with Theodore Roosevelt.[39]

Roosevelt fortunately rejected the War Department's proposals. He

35. Samuel J. Rosenman, ed., *The Public Papers and Addresses of Franklin D. Roosevelt,* 13 vols. (New York, 1938–1950), II, 407–410.

36. *Ibid.*

37. *Ibid.,* III, 348–349.

38. Secretary of War George Dern to Roosevelt, Jan. 11, 1935, in Edgar B. Nixon, ed., *Franklin D. Roosevelt and Foreign Affairs,* 3 vols. (Cambridge Mass., 1969), II, 351–352.

39. Lester D. Langley, "World Crisis and the Good Neighbor Policy in Panama, 1936–1941," *Americas,* XXIV (October 1967), 140–142.

understood, as the military did not, that the political and economic concessions made the Canal more secure, not less. They could also be granted because recent Panamanian presidential campaigns demonstrated that foreign troops were not necessary to assure victory for the "responsible" element. A concern for order underlay the rising nationalism. Such concern could be encouraged, the nationalism contained, the Canal's security therefore enhanced, by overruling the more blatant, less sophisticated policy of the War Department.

FDR's position paralleled his highly publicized "Good Neighbor" approach toward all Latin America. The blunt tool of military intervention, used by TR, Wilson, Harding, and Coolidge, was replaced by political friendship and economic leverage. Roosevelt's Secretary of State, Cordell Hull, launched a massive economic offensive southward, attempting to tie together the Hemisphere through reciprocal trade agreements rather than the irritants of military occupation. As the last United States occupation troops left Central American countries, Hull moved to integrate the area peacefully and economically: Latin American raw materials received favored position in the United States, while U.S. manufactured products and some farm exports benefited from preferred treatment in southern markets.

The Panamanian-United States economic relationship again served as a case study. Events in the Isthmus between 1934 and 1936 demonstrated why those relations had to be tightened. In early 1934 Hull told FDR an unusual number of Japanese had recently arrived in Panama, some of whom had been evicted as spies from the Philippines. Both the Nazis and Japanese initiated trade offensives in Latin America, including Panama. As Hull recalled in his memoirs, he was shocked during a visit to Latin America in 1936 to see how "Axis penetration had made rapid, alarming headway under various guises."[40]

With Axis pressure intensifying, in March 1936 the two sides finally signed the Hull-Alfaro treaty that marked a significant, if short step toward recognizing Panamanian rights. The treaty's first sentence abrogated Washington's guarantee of Panamanian independence. The isthmian nation was no longer to be a legal protectorate under the United States. The North Americans next renounced the right to seize additional lands or waters without Panama's consent. (Within five years that issue threatened again to rip apart relations between the two countries.) A number of economic concessions lessened competition

---

40. Nixon, ed., *FDR and Foreign Affairs*, II, 33–34; Wallace to FDR, June 5, 1936, *ibid.*; Cordell Hull, *Memoirs of Cordell Hull*, 2 vols. (New York, 1948), I, 495.

between the Zone and Panama's businessmen, theoretically allowed the latter to bid on supply contracts in the Zone, and gave the Panamanian government the right to tax many of its own citizens who worked on the Canal. After thirty-three years Panama regained control over most of its immigration by being able to prevent aliens from entering Panama through the Zone.

Contrary to the War Department's wishes, the right of United States intervention for the maintenance of order in Colon and Panama City was terminated. Finally, the United States agreed to increase the annual annuity from $250,000 to $430,000. The increase was illusory. In 1934 Roosevelt had devalued the dollar, cutting deeply into the worth of the payment which Panama received. The new 1936 figure merely restored what FDR had earlier taken away unilaterally.

Panama's National Assembly immediately ratified the treaty 27–4. The United States Senate, however, refused to accept it for three years. Panamanian anger grew, but the Senate continued to stall. If Roosevelt's overriding of the War Department was far-sighted policy, it was also dangerous politics. The military's friends in Congress shared its concerns about surrendering any rights. The anti-treaty forces were especially apoplectic over FDR's promise to include Panama when making plans (such as the timing for seizing additional Panamanian lands), to protect the Canal "in case of an international conflagration." Actually no one should have doubted that in an emergency the United States would move first and consult Panama later, particularly since Panama had no army, navy, or air force. Yet the War Department continued to be unhappy, and FDR finally issued sharp orders to the military leaders regarding what to say and not say when the Senate called them to testify. He warned them that ties with Panama must be examined in proper context: "It is highly important to the relations of this Government with all the other American republics that this treaty be ratified."[41]

Roosevelt's prompting did not work. The Senate and the War Department finally accepted the pact in 1939 when intimations of a Second World War pushed Washington to put western hemispheric affairs in order. Even then FDR was forced to mollify the Senate through a further exchange of notes with Panama that gave the United States the right to react without consulting Panama if a military emergency occurred.[42] On the urging of military officers, moreover, the Senate refused to act on another agreement that gave Panamanians jurisdiction over two ra-

---

41. FDR to Hull, March 29, 1936, in Nixon, ed., *FDR and Foreign Affairs*, III, 276.
42. A. R. Wright, "Defense Sites Negotiations Between the United States and Panama, 1936–1948," *U.S. Department of State Bulletin*, XXVII (Aug. 11, 1952), 213.

dio stations, even though the pact provided that Washington would retain ultimate control of the stations. Panama remained without its own radio frequencies.

Obviously the Senate did not display undue sensitivity for Panamanian concerns. Any doubt about the Senate's feelings disappeared when it dealt with FDR's promise, expressed in a note of March 2, 1936, which accompanied the treaty, to provide equal opportunities for Panamanians who sought jobs in the Zone. At the request of Canal Zone authorities, Congress passed a measure in 1939 directly contradicting Roosevelt's promise. The bill placed high-paying jobs at the disposal of United States citizens only. The President protested, but he signed the legislation since its proponents had the foresight to attach it to legislation providing for enlarging the Canal through a third set of locks. The third-lock system was never completed. A few approach channels dug during the World War became swamp homes for alligators. Panamanians remained excluded from the better jobs along the Canal far into the future. The Zone commissaries, moreover, refused to carry through in good faith the economic concessions promised to Panamanian merchants.

As the two nations prepared for world war, Panamanians were embittered that they had received less than had been promised in 1936. Their hopes for the treaty were finally reduced to the belief that at least the United States recognized their sovereignty over the entire Isthmus. Article III contained the magic words: "The Canal Zone is territory of the Republic of Panama under the jurisdiction of the United States." A Panamanian historian later justifiably claimed that this provision, along with two other parts of the agreement, "confirmed" his country's sovereignty over the Zone.[43] The North Americans meanwhile simply assumed they held total control; Article III was of little significance in their debates between 1936 and 1939.

The United States view of the pact's importance suddenly appeared in 1940 when it was used not to improve relations, but as a lever to seize more Panamanian territory. Another crisis resulted and another government was overthrown—but this time by legitimately armed Panamanian police. A new era was beginning.

43. Castillero Reyes, *El Canal de Panamá*, p. 157.

4

Arias, Remón,
and Eisenhower

With war approaching from both east and west in 1938, Roosevelt and Hull desperately sought Latin American support. But despite the Axis threat, six years of the Good Neighbor, the Panama Treaty of 1936, and several successful Inter-American conferences, the southern neighbors remained suspicious. When Hull attempted to create a collective security agreement, the Latin American delegations at the Lima Conference pointedly amended his motion so that it condemned intervention by either a "continental or extracontinental power." Memories of Wilson and the earlier Roosevelt remained fresh. At the 1939 Panama City Conference, however, Hull finally obtained a security zone around the hemisphere which was declared out-of-bounds for any belligerent. The Americas also pledged to follow strict neutrality, denying, for example, bases to warring powers.

Panama fully supported the United States. Not that the Panamanians had much choice; on matters of peace and war they were bound to Washington by geography and treaty. Relations between the two nations nevertheless seemed improved. Roosevelt raised the United States legation in Panama City to embassy level, pleasing status-conscious Panamanians while signifying the importance FDR placed on the area.

Underneath the diplomatic protocol, however, tensions were building, tensions that became noticeable even after Hitler suddenly brought the Low Countries and France to their knees in June 1940. For regardless of Nazi triumphs, the same inexorable problems divided Panama and the United States. The isthmian economy, for example, remained unhealthy and unbalanced. With only primitive communications linking east and west Panama (and the Zone posing the greatest barrier), no national market existed. Populous urban areas suffered from high unemployment and the poor farmers were isolated in the provinces. With little incentive and less responsibility, the oligarchical families invested much of their capital overseas. To make matters worse, Washington not only refused to grant Panamanian demands that the black, English-speaking West Indians be sent home, but as planning began on the new third-lock system in 1939, the United States shocked the Panamanians by bringing in more Jamaican labor.[1] The 1936 treaty seemed little more than a deception.

In late 1939 the War Department leased a huge area from private citizens for building the Rio Hato air base. Washington next demanded ten one-acre base-sites for air tracking facilities. The leases would run 999 years. That seemed an inordinately long time to most Panamanians, and they further objected that these "little Canal Zones," as they called them, would pockmark their country. Refusing to agree to the demands, they nevertheless watched passively as the United States moved into some of the sites. Washington argued that possession was justified by the 1936 treaty. Legally the action was questionable; politically it was irresponsible. In October 1940 the United States approached the newly elected Panamanian President to legalize the occupation and obtain as many as one hundred more sites. The new President was Arnulfo Arias.

The Rise and Temporary Fall of Panameñismo

Arias was a phenomenon in Panamanian politics. In 1940–41 he disrupted a political process caked with tradition and corruption. Since Taft's intervention in 1904 a small group of oligarchs had controlled affairs, with the possible exception of 1932 to 1936 when Harmodio Arias ran the country. But even he proved to be "responsible." Although the governmental structure resembled the three-branch North

1. A. R. Wright, "Defense Sites Negotiations Between the United States and Panama, 1936–1948," *Department of State Bulletin,* XXVII (Aug. 11, 1952), 217.

American system, the President actually dominated a rubber-stamp legislature (the National Assembly), and used his powers of appointment and patronage to control the Supreme Court. The presidency had carefully been kept within the club, in this case the posh Union Club of Panama City which commanded a magnificent view of the Pacific. Within the Union Club gentlemen made deals ensuring that no political faction would be burdened with either suspicious foreign ideologies or simple promises to distribute wealth more equitably. Factions formed, but along personal and kinship lines. Since party programs were meaningless, a member was known less as a Liberal or Conservative or one of the many other formal titles, than as a follower of "The Fox," "The Rifle," or "The Cripple." Party labels carried less clout than nicknames.

Doubly ensuring stability, oligarchical leaders devised voting procedures that tended to guarantee electoral triumphs. Ballots, for example, were counted by an election board under the President's control. The government was so democratic in distributing *cedulas* (or identity cards needed for voting), that even friendly aliens received them. The President obtained support from remote provinces by working with the *cacique,* or provincial political boss, who used methods not unfamiliar to the ward machines in Memphis, Chicago, or Kansas City.[2]

In light of his cooperation between 1931 and 1936, Arnulfo Arias (or "El Hombre"—"The Man"—as he was better known on the streets), apparently posed no danger to the Union Club's *grandes.* Quite unlike the oligarchy's leaders, Arnulfo came from a poor family living in the interior. It was not related to the rich, aristocratic Arias clan that had been influential throughout the nineteenth century (and was again in the 1950s). Through luck and skill Arnulfo received training as a physician at the University of Chicago and Harvard. Returning to Panama he gained a reputation for ministering to the poor and quickly turned it to advantage, for his real talent lay in politics.

In 1940 United States Intelligence reported that Arnulfo had remained "friendly to Americans" until he became Minister to Italy in 1934; there he served intermittently until 1938. When he returned home he led campaigns against United States- and Canadian-owned businesses in Panama, forcing National City Bank and Chase National, among others, to move their offices into the Canal Zone. Some observers linked his change to an audience with Hitler in 1937. "Those who have known him for years can offer no explanation to the change of sentiment

2. John Biesanz and L. M. Smith, "Panamanian Politics," *Journal of Politics,* XIV (August 1952), 394.

towards the United States," the Intelligence report concluded, "other than that he has reached some understanding with the Berlin and Rome Chancellories."[3]

Returning to economically devasted Panama, the charismatic "El Hombre" pieced together a political coalition, including some oligarchs with fascistic tendencies and the growing, nationalistic middle class. He swept into power by a vote of 107,750 to 3,022. The supporters of his opponent, the distinguished diplomat Ricardo Alfaro, decided to protest Arias's certain victory by boycotting the polls. So began a political career that continued after two more short but dramatic terms as President. Arias made it an interesting half-century.

His political genius lay partly in his ability to tap the country's centuries-old nationalism and its more recent anti-Gringo feelings. Breaking with oligarchical tradition, he advanced a highly ideological program called *panameñismo* meaning, in the words of a sympathetic Panamanian historian, "government by Panamanians for the happiness of the Panamanian people."[4] The United States Embassy's report of his Inaugural speech, however, presented another side to *panameñismo*. Arias, in the Embassy's words, rejected "as biologically without justification the 'demogogic concept' that 'all men are born free and equal,' " then "referred to the desirability of improving the nation's racial strains by selected immigration and criticized the entrance of large numbers of negroes." Arias reiterated the need for friendship with the United States, but he also advocated constitutional reforms.[5] The last point appeared ominous, given Arias's racial views.

The new President moved quickly to implement his program. English signs were replaced by Spanish, English newspapers could only be supplements inside Spanish journals, government officials talked only Spanish to North Americans, West Indians faced deportation, and in the provinces Arias confiscated Chinese and Hindu businesses, turning them over to political cronies (who, in most instances, soon lost or sold them). Beginning his own New Deal, Arias planned a social security system and initiated some agricultural reforms. Meanwhile the Axis presence grew in Panama until it influenced newspapers; Germans and Italians obtained quick citizenship rights through easy provisional natu-

3. Memorandum by Military Intelligence Division, Oct. 7, 1940, 819.00/2106, Box 3728, NA, RG 59.

4. Ernesto J. Castillero Reyes, *Historia de Panamá* (Panama, 1955), p. 201.

5. Memorandum by Willard F. Barber, Oct. 9, 1940, attached to 819.001/Arias, Arnulfo/42, Box 3729, NA, RG 59. This memorandum noted the dangerous aspects of Arias's program.

ralization. By July 1941, Harmodio complained to the American Ambassador that his brother was using racketeering methods to gain control of his newspaper so it could be used for totalitarian purposes. Harmodio begged the United States to make no agreements with Arnulfo's administration that would "increase its prestige."[6] The story doubtless lost little in the telling. Jealous and fearful of his younger brother, Harmodio, in one of his typical political schemes, plotted to have the embassy act as front-man in bringing down Arnulfo.

Harmodio spoke to a receptive audience. Washington tempers were growing short. At a Cabinet meeting Secretary of War Henry Stimson detailed Arias's refusal to cooperate with United States defense preparations. Roosevelt, Stimson wrote in his diary, "appreciated this fully—told me of his troubles with Arias and told Hull to try some strong arm methods on him."[7] Nor were the State Department's fears lessened when the popular journalist, John Gunther, returned to inform North American foreign policy experts that "Panama has the closest thing to a totalitarian government—Paraguay excepted—that is to be found in the Western Hemisphere. It is ruled by a Harvard-trained neurotic." In 1967 a careful scholar offered an assessment at least equally accurate: "Arias was a logical product of the decades of anti-American antagonism on the isthmus."[8]

In retrospect, 1940–41 marked a radical turn in Panama's politics. A fascistic charismatic leader of middle-class background appealed across class lines to confront the oligarchs and United States officials with an explosive political program; indeed to their eyes it appeared doubly dangerous since it appealed to so many Panamanians. For the first time, demands for radical social change linked up with Panamanian nationalism. That nationalism, particularly its anti-Gringoism, had ironic aspects, for it came mainly from a middle class created by North American dollars and jobs. The economic impact of the Canal Zone turned the small, pre-1903 middle class into a large and vocal group of office workers, professionals, and teachers whom Harmodio and Arnulfo Arias first utilized to gain power in the early 1930s. Arnulfo received strong support in Panama City and Colon, where most of the middle class lived, when he attacked blacks. The new class was the most anti-black of all

6. Edwin C. Wilson to Sumner Welles, Personal, July 2, 1941, 819.00/2134 1/2, Box 3729, NA, RG 59.

7. Diaries of Stimson, Stimson Papers, XXXII, 9 Jan. 1941, p. 94.

8. "Study Group Reports," John Gunther, March 13, 1941, *Records of Meetings*, VI, Council on Foreign Relations, New York City; Langley, "World Crisis and the Good Neighbor policy in Panama, 1936–1941," pp. 147, 152.

Panamanian groups, due partly to fears of economic competition, partly to a proud nationalism that feared outsiders might mistake their country for a "Black republic." The very success of the Canal Zone, and its thousands of West Indian laborers, had created a middle class whose anti-Yankeeism and dislike of blacks formed the basis of Arnulfo's burgeoning power.[9]

Not surprisingly, negotiations involving the 100 new military sites did not progress. Arias refused to agree until the United States dropped the 999-year lease demand, promised $25 million of economic aid, and built a bridge over the Canal to connect eastern and western Panama. He also required that the West Indians be returned to their island homes, the Panama City and Colon water and sewer systems be given to Panama, and rent on Rio Hato be raised to $30 million a year (the annual lease was then $2400). Roosevelt refused to meet most of the demands, threatening instead to occupy the bases. Arias then approved leasing one small site. When Winston Churchill and FDR announced the Atlantic Charter's promise of freedom and self-determination in August 1941, Arias announced his delight that Roosevelt finally recognized "the right of all people to adopt that government which is most in accord with their idiosyncrasies and their needs, and with the desire of their own people."[10]

A month before, United States Ambassador Edwin C. Wilson had reported rumors of a coup, although he discounted them since Arias supposedly controlled the police. On October 7, however, Wilson received "reliable information" that Arias's attempt to curb the Guard's powers was making it restless. That morning Arias suddenly left for Cuba, ostensibly for medical reasons, actually to spend a few days in Havana with his mistress. On October 9 a dissident Cabinet member and the second-in-command of the Guard asked Wilson how the United States would regard the overthrow of Arias. Could they count on immediate recognition? Wilson replied he could give no "indication whatsoever on these points," since under the Good Neighbor the United States did not involve itself in the internal affairs of other nations.[11] Wilson

9. The Panamanian middle class was thoroughly studied during the 1940s, especially in essays by John Biesanz, Georgina Jiménez de López, and Carolyn Campbell and Ofelia Hooper published in Theo R. Crevenna, *Materials para el estudio de la clase media en la America Latina,* Volume IV (Washington, D.C., 1950); see especially pp. 8–10, 20, 66–68; also for general background, Eric Wolf and Edward C. Hansen, *The Human Condition in Latin America* (New York, 1972), p. 196.

10. Donald Marquand Dozer, *Are We Good Neighbors?* (Gainsville, Fla., 1959), pp. 102–103.

11. Wilson to Secretary of State, Oct. 9, 1941, 819.001/Arias, Arnulfo/90, Box 3729, NA, RG 59.

thus signaled that Washington would not try to stop the coup, but also would not directly encourage it. The anti-Arias group, however, did not need further encouragement, only a sign of United States intention to abstain benignly when the coup occurred. This they received.

National Guard officers announced that Arias was deposed and First Vice-President Ernesto de la Guardia was the new President. The Panamanian Supreme Court gave the proper constitutional blessing to the overthrow by declaring that de la Guardia's ascension was legal since Arias had "abandoned" the presidency.[12] The new President quickly rescinded many of Arias's policies: newspapers were again delivered with the English language sections outside, the National Bank recalled newly issued Panamanian paper money which Arias had hoped would break the country's tie to the dollar, and the government confiscated games of chance, especially slot machines, which were a highly profitable racket for the Arias faction. When the "traganiqueles," or nickel swallowers, were hauled away, the U.S. Ambassador reported, supposedly with a straight face, that crowds cheered.

Reports circulated widely that the United States engineered the overthrow of Arias. Hull denied any involvement "clearly and uncategorically." Stimson nevertheless observed the coup was "a great relief to us, because Arias has been very troublesome and very pro-Nazi."[13] Adolf Berle, a top State Department official and FDR "brain-truster," believed the United States "had absolutely nothing to do with" the coup, yet welcomed it since Arias was "pro-Nazi" and a nuisance." Berle then defined a dilemma which increasingly confronted Washington policymakers: "I don't like revolutions on principle," but this one was "probably all to the good."[14] Significantly, this marked the first time U.S. officials faced such a problem in Panama. It would not be the last.

Washington's leverage in Panamanian affairs remained strong. In 1944 the U.S. Chargé in Panama candidly discussed his nation's domination of isthmian politics. "As a matter of fact," John Muccio told the State Department, "there has never been a successful change of government in Panama but that American authorities have been 'consulted' beforehand—remember 1931 and 1941!"[15]

12. Wilson to Secretary of State, Oct. 14, 1941, 819.001/Arias, Arnulfo/98, Box 3729, NA, RG 59.

13. Diaries of Stimson, Stimson Papers, XXXV, 9 Oct. 1941, p. 123.

14. "Memorandum," Oct. 10, 1941, Diary, Papers of Adolf Berle, Franklin D. Roosevelt Library, Hyde Park, N. Y.

15. John J. Muccio to Phillip W. Bonsal, June 6, 1944, 819.00/6–644, Box 3729, NA, RG 59.

Another First: The Riots of 1947

A former student at Dartmouth, de la Guardia was warmly disposed toward North American interests. He acceded to most of Washington's demands for 134 base sites, although he limited the lease-duration to the war plus one year after the signing of a peace treaty. For its part the United States turned the sewer and water systems of the two major cities over to Panama and granted new economic assistance, but refused to deport the West Indians or pay high rents for the sites. Panama, moreover, was one of only two Latin American nations that received no Lend-lease help from the United States. (The other country was Argentina, which Hull considered pro-Nazi, an outcast, and a personal obsession.) The State Department sent no Lend-lease since it wished no large arms supplies given to the National Guard.[16] The United States remained not just the largest, but the only important military force on the Isthmus.

As an economic stimulus, Lend-lease would not have been important. The Panamanian economy boomed as military traffic tested the canal's capacity. With its usual North American imports going to European or Pacific war theaters, Panama's domestic production rose rapidly. Production of milk, sugar, electricity, and slaughtered cattle nearly doubled between 1939 and 1946. The government accelerated the take-off by increasing its expenditures fourfold, but the real catalyst was the influx of dollars: wartime savings drove up bank deposits nine times and bank loans rose four times.

Dollars poured in also through direct investments. Between 1930 and 1943 United States capital investments dropped sharply in every Latin American country except Venezuela (where oil was found) and Panama. The latter enjoyed the higher percentage increase of the two as investment multiplied three times to $154 million, mostly in banking and utilities. Controlling twenty-two enterprises in Panama in 1929, by 1943 United States corporations owned at least seventy-nine. This influx was part of a massive invasion by North American businessmen; between 1940 and 1943 they nearly doubled the number of their enterprises in Latin America.[17]

16. "Memorandum" by Emilio Collado, July 21, 1941, *FRUS, 1941,* VI, 142.
17. United Nations Economic Commission for Latin America, "The Economic Development of Panama," *Economic Bulletin for Latin America,* IV (October 1959), 48–49; Rippy, *Globe and Hemisphere,* pp. 43–45. The mass of Panamanians made real sacrifices for the war effort; see Laurence O. Ealy, *The Republic of Panama in World Affairs* (Philadelphia, 1951), pp. 116–118.

The United States thus fueled hemispheric prosperity, but also made itself an obvious target if the economy deteriorated in peacetime. Growth did decline in Panama during 1946–47, and nowhere was the United States presence more obvious, or, because of the base agreement, more exposed to a new type of nationalism.

In 1946 Washington asked to renew the leases on base sites occupied since 1940–41. President Enrique A. Jiménez, flatly refused. The United States returned over 100 installations, but asked to retain Rio Hato airbase and thirteen of the one-acre sites. The State and War Departments fought bitterly over the terms. The military insisted on leases of thirty or more years and refused to consider any joint control with Panama. The State Department, considerably more sensitive to (and, as it turned out, more realistic about) Panamanian nationalism, wanted a shorter lease period. It also was willing to meet Jiménez's demand for economic aid, but only after he delivered the leases.[18] Finally in December 1947 an agreement appeared on the fourteen sites. Rio Hato's lease would run ten years with an option for another ten, and leases on the thirteen remaining sites would last for five years. The United States would enjoy total control. Jiménez sent the pact to the National Assembly for ratification.

Between December 11 and 17 the streets of Panama City erupted in violence. On the 11th Ricardo Alfaro, the distinguished Panamanian who negotiated the 1936 treaty and the early portions of the 1947 agreement, suddenly resigned to organize opposition to the new pact. Jiménez had refused to listen to Alfaro's warning that if the President did not obtain a concrete United States promise of economic assistance *before* signing the agreement, "he could whistle for it after."[19] With the government split and the treaty's terms public, students started to riot against the agreement. In clashes with the National Guard, one student was killed, dozens hurt, and at least seventeen police sent to hospitals. On December 16, 10,000 women and children staged anti-Yankee demonstrations outside the Assembly. Professors and students went on strike.

Not only the treaty was in danger. On December 18 the Embassy cabled the State Department that the "Amazing development is actual physical fear which had seized most deputies. President of Assembly spoke of '10,000 boys with knives' which might await them." Several Colon deputies had promised Jiménez their votes, but reneged since they did not promise "to allow themselves to be shot at."[20] In Colon a

18. *FRUS, 1947,* VII, 887, 905.
19. *Ibid.,* 942.
20. For a description of the rioting see *ibid.,* 943–946.

U.S. soldier was stabbed. At the last minute the State Department tried to salvage the situation by offering to discuss specific economic aid.[21] The message arrived too late. On December 22, surrounded by screaming galleries, a motion rejecting the treaty passed 51–0. Three months later the North Americans evacuated all the sites occupied after 1940.

The 1947 upheaval marked a number of firsts. It was the first time a massive nationalist movement successfully thwarted United States policies in Panama. It was also the first time students were pivotal in the protests. After President Harmodio Arias founded the National University in 1935, it quickly became what he no doubt intended it to be, an institution of learning for middle-class Panamanians. (Most oligarchs sent their children abroad for education.) In this sense the students' nationalism directly descended from events set in motion by the Arias brothers in the 1931 coup. In 1944 the highly politicized Federation of Panamanian Students was organized at the university. The university, and especially the Federation, became ladders for middle– and lower–class students who determined to succeed economically, were willing to challenge the government in the streets, and advocated a political program that was to the left. The oligarchy's politics followed kinship lines, but the students based theirs on reform programs, institutional ties, and a multi-class base.[22] When, for example, they protested the 1947 agreement, lower-class Panamanians gave visible support.

The oligarchy appreciated none of this. Its political power had been severely shaken. Nor did the National Guard welcome student rioting. Since the overthrow of Arias in 1941, if not since the 1931 upheaval, the Guard had acted as the arbiter of Panamanian politics. When the students challenged the Guard's power, the 1947 clashes marked another first that was portentous for United States–Panamanian relations. By the 1960s and 1970s those relations had to be worked out in a Panamanian political context shaped by Guard-student animosity.

Guard strongman José Remón blamed Communist and Socialist leaders for the rioting. Celso Selano, Secretary General of the Communist People's Party (the Partido del Pueblo), indeed directed some of the student activity. The Communist involvement, however, was minute compared with the students' role. Communism held little attraction for the students, at least as long as they could hope for some security within the present system. Harmodio Arias understood this. After the clashes,

21. Wright, "Defense Sites Negotiations," p. 219.
22. Biesanz and Smith, "Panamanian Politics," pp. 401–402.

his influential newspaper vigorously attacked Remón's police for embarrassing Panama internationally by beating up students. (Since the police suffered more casualties than the students, Harmodio's sympathies seemed misplaced.[23]) Arias, with some help from Arnulfo, was trying to group the students and lower classes in a political coalition against Remón and the Guard. Out of the 1947 treaty protests, therefore, emerged the two main protagonists—the students and Guard—who would shape the nation's politics as oligarchical power declined.

The intensity of the hatred between the Guard and students hinted at a deeper problem. The National Guard recruited many blacks and mestizos from the interior provinces. The students were mainly urban and included whiter Panamanians as well as mestizos. Not only a political conflict impended, but class, ideological, and perhaps racial struggles. The dimensions of this confrontation could not be forgotten in the future, not even when National Guard leaders tried to coopt the students by calling them natural allies in opposing United States policy. Underneath any pretended alliance lurked political divisions and personal hatreds rooted deep in history.

Depression Amidst Gold and Silver

The 1947 riots were also significant because the United States played no direct role in restoring public order. One part of its colonial rule, Theodore Roosevelt's "big stick," was apparently discarded. But the other part of its control remained, for its economic leverage—indeed its dominance—increased. As Washington's wartime spending sharply declined, Panamanians entered a depression that sharpened their nationalism and shaped future clashes with the United States.

Panama again served as a case study of broader hemispheric relations. During the war the Latin Americans sacrificed for the Allies' war effort by sending more than 50 percent of their exports to United States war industries. In some cases entire production of a raw material moved north, despite shortages and growing inflation in the producing countries. After the war ended, the Latins possessed some dollar reserves for developmental purposes, but they needed, and believed they richly deserved, United States help. They particularly wanted access to financial sources and the limited number of North American manufactured

23. Larry LaRae Pippin, *The Remón Era: An Analysis of a Decade of Events in Panama 1947–1957* (Stanford, 1964), pp. 17–19.

goods. Washington turned down both requests, bluntly announcing that Western European reconstruction enjoyed first preference. Latin America, it turned out, was far down the list. As the price of manufactured goods skyrocketed in the late 1940s, raw material prices slumped. Latin American economies entered a crisis period. The United States offered no systematic response, only advice that the Latins ask private investors for help. Those financiers doubled United States investments in Latin America between 1946 and 1955 from $3 million to $6.6 million. Most went into raw material production, especially Venezuelan oil.[24]

In 1947 the Rio Treaty brought South America and Central America into a military alliance with the United States. The following year these nations upgraded the old Pan American movement by forming the Organization of American States. The Rio pact and the OAS, however, rested on sand. No economic foundation existed. With appropriate symbolism, the OAS was born at Bogotá, Colombia, as rioters besieged the city demanding employment and food.

The Good Neighbor seemed to have deserted the neighborhood. Poverty and dictatorship threatened to fill the void, but the United States appeared undisturbed. At a Council of Foreign Relations meeting in 1949, men experienced in hemispheric affairs, including Nelson Rockefeller and Adolf Berle, gathered to discuss the problem privately. The chairman of the group, investment banker Franklin Adams Truslow, outlined a central assumption that henceforth shaped United States policy toward Latin America:

> A distinction should be made between totalitarianism and dictatorship. A dictatorship involves autocratic rule. But totalitarianism is autocratic rule plus total, absolute control of economic life, as, for example, communism. . . . Totalitarianism we refuse to cooperate with . . . ; with dictatorship we will.[25]

When the Korean War broke out, however, and Washington asked for help, not even many of the "dictators" responded as the United States hoped. The continent was moving to a "third force" position between

---

24. Duggan, *The Americas,* pp. 123–126; Rippy, *Globe and Hemisphere,* p. 72. The best discussion is David Green, *The Containment of Latin America* (Chicago, 1971), chapters 7–11.

25. "Study Group Reports, Inter-American Affairs," Feb. 7, 1949, *Records of Groups,* XVI-D, Council on Foreign Relations, New York City. Truslow graduated from Yale in 1928, attended Harvard Law School, and formed his own Wall Street law firm before working during World War II in Peru as Special Representative from the U.S. Government's Rubber Reserve agency. In 1947 he became president of the New York Curb Exchange.

the United States and Russia. As Panama's leading newspaper explained in early 1950, North Americans should not expect help against Communism "from those [in Latin America] who have not yet learned the exact significance of the benefits of liberty and democracy which involve their very existence."[26]

Panama's only alternative was to work with the United States during the Korean War. The cooperative efforts did not go smoothly, however, nor did they stop the Panamanian depression. As Canal Zone spending dropped sharply after 1946, Panama searched for help. The nation could not manipulate its money supply because the balboa, the paper currency, was tied to the dollar. Tax sources proved inadequate, for revenues dropped as imports declined. The wealthy oligarchy refused to tax itself for national development; many members invested in real estate or kept accounts in the United States and Switzerland. Canal Zone revenues were held tightly by the United States.

A fourfold increase in public spending between 1946 and 1950 kept the economy from collapse. The only tangible benefits were a huge Panama City tourist hotel and Tocumen Airport which soon became, like the Canal, an international crossroads. Otherwise unemployment and governmental deficits rose to dangerous levels. Between 1945 and 1955 per capita income actually dropped 2 percent as capital investments barely rose and the population increase accelerated. It was one of the worst of a bad lot of economic records in Latin America.[27]

The Zone provided less help than Panama needed. A high United States official explained in 1947, "The heart of the problem is the Gold and Silver rolls," through which "discrimination is practiced administratively." North Americans on the gold roll enjoyed a $1.07 per hour minimum wage, but the silver roll averaged 44¢ to 66¢. Gold teachers received three times the salary of silver teachers, and the silver teachers did the better jobs.[28] The United States continued breaking its 1936 promise to equalize opportunity. The former chief of the State Department's Latin American desk blamed the American Federation of Labor. In order to protect North American workers, he argued, the AFL "browbeat the War Department into setting up two scales of pay, one for United States citizens and one for 'foreigners.'"[29] By the 1940s, most of the "foreigners" were Panamanians.

26. Quoted in Dozer, *Are We Good Neighbors?* pp. 322–325.
27. Pedro C. M. Teichert, *Economic Policy Revolution and Industrialization in Latin America* (Oxford, Miss., 1959), p. 31.
28. *FRUS, 1947*, VIII, 950–956.
29. Duggan, *The Americas*, p. 171.

Conditions were worsened by urban housing—or lack of it. By 1950 one of every four of the 800,000 Panamanians lived in Panama City. Another 100,000 lived in Colon or David. The two Canal cities, Panama City and Colon, contained slums of unbelievable squalor, where the unemployed and underpaid existed in *barriadas brujas,* or "witch quarters." Since the "witch quarters" and the Zone were separated only by a roadway, the situation was highly combustible.

Arnulfo's Return

The economic chaos was mirrored in the political chaos. A power struggle between Presidents and the National Assembly prevented regular elections in 1944 and resulted in a new constitution of 1946. The document proved once again that by themselves, and when surrounded by economic crisis, written constitutions can be irrelevant.

For the 1948 campaign the reigning Liberal Party chose seventy-three-year-old Domingo Díaz as its candidate. Arnulfo Arias rose from the political dead, dusted off his *panameñismo* nationalism, and in an initial count by the National Elections Board apparently won the presidency by 1500 votes. Díaz supporters thereupon attacked the Board, wounding two members. Arias's backers prepared to move into the streets to ensure his election.

At this point José Remón, head of the National Guard, took charge. Under his protection the Elections Board magically made enough of Arias's votes disappear so Díaz became President. (Remón watched approvingly; in 1941 Arias had tried to emasculate the Guard's power and send one of its young officers, José Remón, out of the country.) The Guard then smashed a pro-Arias student rally. When Arias tried to start an uprising, Remón disgustedly threw both Harmodio and Arnulfo Arias in jail. During the next four years Panamanian presidential politics resembled a game of musical chairs, with Remón and the National Guard stopping and starting the music. The political system, the constitutional order, and the oligarchy's power would never be the same.

The country was in transition from the solid oligarchical control of the pre-1931 years to the hard-fisted National Guard domination that emerged full-blown after 1968. In early 1949 the United States Ambassador pointed to deeper fissures that threatened a political earthquake unless they were somehow checked. "All too frequently the [political] cleavage comes along racial and class lines," Monnet B. Davis warned the State Department, "a tendency that the subversive elements are at some pains to augment by constant propaganda designed not only to arouse race and class hatred," but to associate the United States "with the now distrusted and hated upper governing class in Panama."[30] For nearly a half-century Washington and the oligarchy had worked hand-in-hand, so both were threatened by the riptide of changes. Panama was no longer the obedient, manipulated-from-the-top country of 1903 or 1930.

Diáz faced an additional problem since he was also fighting a losing battle against senility. To buttress his power he devised a new system for cattle slaughtering, one of the most lucrative businesses in the country still under Panamanian control. Diáz granted a monopoly over the slaughter-houses to his son, Temistocles ("Temi"), and Remón. That seemed to ensure a long honeymoon with the National Guard and keep "subversive elements," as Ambassador Davis called them, in their place. When, for example, Harmodio Arias plotted a coup, the police smashed it and Diáz suspended constitutional guarantees so Harmodio could be jailed until evidence was collected. Remón's force worked with special effectiveness on this occasion because the U.S. Army's G-2 Intelligence had uncovered the Arias scheme and given the information to the National Guard. Relations between the Army and the Guard, the U.S. Embassy told Washington, "have never been better."[31] It might also have been one reason why, as Davis later noted, Panamanians associated the United States with the "now distrusted and hated upper governing class in Panama."

Unfortunately for this cozy arrangement, Diáz suddenly died in August 1949. First Vice-President Daniel Chanís assumed power, but he was hardly settled in the Presidential Palace before the Panama Supreme Court, in a fit of legality, declared the Diáz-Remón cattle monopoly unconstitutional. With a sure sense for self-destruction, Chanís decided to uphold the ruling. When Diáz and Remón accompanied their cattle to the slaughter-houses (with pistols cocked so their property would enjoy special consideration), Chanís summoned Remón to dismiss the Guard's chief and break up the clique. The National Guard promptly surrounded the Palace and rescued their leader. Chanís resigned.

Again, the United States appeared to be an accomplice to the coup. Diáz's body was still warm when "Temi" Diáz, his close and incredibly corrupt friend "Baby" Jiménez, and Remón began plotting against Chanís. They ostentatiously associated with North Americans so it would appear the Embassy and military were on their side.[32] The North

30. *FRUS,* 1949, II, 706–707.
31. E. W. Clark to Secretary of State, April 28, 1949, 819.00/4–2849, NA, RG 59.
32. Memorandum by Sowash, Nov. 22, 1949, 810.00/11-2249, NA, RG 59; Hall to Secretary of State, Aug. 31, 1949, 810.00/8-3149, NA, RG 59.

Americans happily cooperated in order to gain information. Although they played no active role in Chanís's overthrow, United States citizens were again perceived by Panamanians to be working with the most corrupt elements, this time to destroy a Supreme Court decision through the use of the National Guard.

The Embassy, moreover, was present at the kill. When the National Guard surrounded the Palace, Chanís entertained the idea of resisting. The foreign diplomatic corps immediately warned both the President and the Guard it wanted no bloodshed. Ambassador Davis insisted upon what he called, with perhaps unconscious humor, "our traditional policy observance [of] constitutional and democratic procedures."[33] Chanís graciously upheld such procedures by abdicating power at the point of National Guard rifles. In reality, Davis followed the traditional Roosevelt-Taft approach of choosing order over potential chaos, even if order meant the destruction of whatever small amount of constitutional legality remained in Panama.

But the game of musical chairs was not finished. Chanís was replaced by the Second Vice-President, Roberto Chiari, a wealthy oligarch who also happened to be Remón's cousin. The new President lasted a week. Chanís materialized before the National Assembly, delivered a blistering attack on Remón, and with Harmodio Arias pulling the strings, the Assembly supported Chanís, condemned Chiari's usurpation of power, and prepared to move into the streets against the police. Having no stomach for such a confrontation, Chairi was about to call for Chanís's reinstatement as President when Remón learned of his cousin's betrayal. The Guard chief gave the new President ten minutes to pack his belongings and leave the Palace. Remón then stunned everyone by putting Arnulfo Arias into power.

Davis and the State Department could not believe it. That Panama, with direct United States help, endured three Presidents within a week in November 1949 was of less concern to the Ambassador than Arnulfo ending the game with the only remaining chair. "What had happened," Davis phoned Washington, "was a complete challenge of democracy and represented extraordinary double-crossing in every respect." Davis was furious that he had stressed the need for "democratic processes," and ended with Arias, "Remón[,] and his gangster associates." He was convinced that Arias would remove Remón, "by fair means or foul. His dictatorship can be expected to be absolute and I am confident he will cooperate with our enemies to our embarrassment." Davis even called it "a misuse of force which should be challenged."[34] No longer, however, could U.S. Ambassadors so easily correct their errors by calling in the Marines.

Davis bravely suggested that Washington should continue to recognize Chanís as President. Washington equivocated, however, finally settling on a watch-and-wait non-recognition policy. Strikes spread in Panama, gasoline was in short supply, and a key State Department official, perhaps hoping that economic chaos would lead to Arias's overthrow, announced that "the best policy was for Americans not to interfere in any way with strikes."[35]

The non-recognition policy did not work. Remón consolidated Arias's power, even calling in the Elections Board to recount the 1948 results so Arnulfo would win officially. In hours the Board found pro-Arias votes it had been unable to find in weeks after the 1948 balloting. The National Guard successfully moved to end the strikes and restore order. Ambassador Davis could not understand why such bitter enemies as Remón and Arias were suddenly allies. "Everyone very much confused," Davis told Washington. But he had already provided one explanation by noting that Arias, unlike Chanís, willingly accepted the cattle slaughtering racket of Remón, "Temi" Díaz, and "Baby" Jimenez, all of whom duly closed ranks around the President. Remón believed he could handle Arnulfo. Since the new President could not constitutionally succeed himself, moreover. Remón was in perfect position to win the presidency himself in 1952.

Remón and the State Department believed Arias had mellowed since 1941. After watching him for nearly a week, an impressed State Department official observed that he was "saying all the right things and influential sections [of] American business community now favor early recognition." Arias especially reassured Jewish merchants who worried about his fascism of 1940–41.[36] Arnulfo, Panama desk officer Murray Wise concluded, had seen the light:

> [Arias] may have been pro-Nazi earlier because he was convinced Germany would win the war. . . . In any event I believe Arnulfo was more fascist or totalitarian than Nazi. Arnulfo is intelligent and shrewd and can make himself one of Panama's strongest Presidents. It would not be too risky to predict if he can firmly establish himself . . . he might decide to cooperate

34. Phone call from Davis to Wise, Nov. 24, 1949, 819.00/11-2449, NA, RG 59; Davis to Secretary of State, Nov. 25, 1949, 819.00/11-2549, NA, RG 59.
35. Memorandum of phone conversations between Davis and E. G. Miller, Jr., Nov. 26, 1949, 819.00/11-2449, NA, RG 59.
36. Davis to Secretary of State, Dec. 1, 1949, 819.00/11-2849, NA, RG 59.

rapidly and effectively with the United States and take an aggressive initiative in endeavoring to settle many pending problems successfully.[37]

In the context of a Cold War abroad and an increasingly fragmented political system in Panama, the profascist of 1940–41 looked appealing. The appeal grew in December when, as the British Ambassador to Panama observed, Arias was even winning over the safe and solid members of the oligarchy, "the notoriously fickle, greedy and unscrupulous petit bourgeois who control the commerce and industry of this country."[38] Appeal led to seduction. The United States recognized Arias in December, convinced that "all indications are that he has completely changed his position."

Neither the State Department nor Remón knew their man. The chief characteristic of Arnulfo's story-book career was the man's uncanny ability to posture and persuade when out of power, and, once in power, his equally uncanny inability to control his ambitions. Whether dealing with Roosevelt in 1941, Remón in 1950, the National Guard in 1968, or Ronald Reagan in 1976, Arias seemed more interested in a game of political manipulation than retaining and effectively using political power.

Having obtained United States support in late 1949, Arias spent public funds lavishly to build a supposedly impregnable political base. The budget deficit reached $7 million. The Arias family naturally received its share. The President forced owners of choice coffee lands to sell out to him, then built a twenty-seven-mile highway and a bridge on the lands at taxpayers' expense. He put a similar squeeze on Panamanian bankers. A huge narcotics and gold-smuggling operation developed under the alleged leadership of his favorite nephew, Antonio "The Druggist" Arias. "The Druggist" died in 1956 in a mysterious plane accident.

Opposition that could not be bought or coerced was jailed, and Arnulfo established his own secret police independently of the National Guard. In 1951, he went too far. After suspending the 1946 constitution, Arias tried to destroy the National Assembly and Supreme Court. The Assembly retaliated by impeaching him and electing Alcibiádes Arosemena as President. Arias asked Remón for protection. Concluding that Arias could no longer be trusted, Remón sided with the Assembly. But when Remón's two top aides served the eviction notice on the President, Arias's support-

37. Memorandum by Wise, Nov. 28, 1949, 819.00/11-2849, NA, RG 59.
38. Enclosed in LaRue to Secretary of State, Dec. 23, 1949, 819.00/12-2349, NA, RG, 59. For Arias's unsuccessful attempt to weaken U.S. claims to the Zone bases during the Korean War, *see* Ealy, *Republic of Panama,* pp. 160–161.

ers killed both in cold blood. A shoot-out followed in which sixteen died before the President was captured. The Assembly brought Arnulfo to trial, stripped him of all political rights, and sent him off into exile. (Within a decade he returned with rights restored, ready for another go-round with Remón's successors.)

An interim President served while Remón and Chiari fought the 1952 presidential campaign. Aided by his politically astute wife, Cecilia, who organized the newly granted vote to women and tramped provincial jungles to gather support, Remón won an overwhelming victory.[39] Another reason for the triumph was the Guard's unremitting efforts in beating down student demonstrations.

Remón

José "Chichi" Remón resembled Arnulfo in at least one respect: he added a new dimension to Panamanian politics. Remón represented the force that replaced United States troops as the guardian of order—if not always law—in Panama, for he used the National Guard as the stepping-stone to ultimate power. And as the authority of the Guard (and Remón) rose, the oligarchy's power became more shaky. Remón thus set precedents followed by General Omar Torrijos in the 1970s.

Remón, like Torrijos, was a self-made man, rising out of a lower income family by joining the police ranks, gaining military education in Mexico and the United States, then nimbly avoiding the traps of Panama City politics until he headed the Guard in 1947. As a young officer "Chichi" upgraded police prestige through higher salaries and fringe benefits. After becoming President, Remón turned part of the Guard, then wholly a police force, into the Panamanian army.[40] He cared about prestige (in his travels "Chichi" noted that army officers received greater deference than police), but the change also allowed the force to receive large amounts of United States military supplies. Personally sensitive and politically astute, Remón repaired two splits within the Guard: a division between those schooled overseas and those unschooled, and differences between black and those of mixed blood.[41] Since the Remón

39. A fascinating illustrated story on her efforts is in *Life,* May 5, 1952 entitled "A Woman's Place Is . . . On the Stump."
40. "National Guard" has been used through the book instead of "police." The Guard developed directly out of the police, and the police now form part of the Guard.
41. Pippin, *Remón Era,* pp. 1–7, is the definitive treatment.

years, race relations within the Guard have been much better than within the whole of Panamanian society.

The oligarchy was declining, the small middle class (except for the students) unorganized, and the lower classes effectively disenfranchised or manipulated. Remón's Guard became the instrument for maintaining order and gaining power. No serious rival existed. The Guard maintained close watch on the students; Remón never forgot the humiliation suffered by his men during the 1947 riots. A 1000-member Communist Party appeared in the late 1940s, but when it tried to gain control of unions the American Federation of Labor dealt with it ruthlessly. So had Arias, who used the Communists as scapegoats to excuse the excesses of his presidency.

Nor did Remón have to be concerned with the unions. The AFL only cared about protecting its members from the dual threats of communism and Panamanian demands for equal job opportunities. The only other important union worked closely with the United Fruit Company on the banana plantations. Splits between blacks and mestizos, English-speaking and Spanish-speaking laborers, Jamaicans and Panamanians, paralyzed union organizers. High unemployment undercut bargaining attempts. Remón and his National Guard reigned unchallenged.

Eisenhower and the 1955 Treaty

Not surprisingly, "Chichi's" personal fortunes followed his political good luck. He accumulated several million dollars by monopolizing cattle slaughtering, selling the gasoline used in police cars, auctioning city bus routes to the highest bidder, and allegedly owning part of Panama City's most renowned brothel. He also collected farms, apartment houses, and race horses, while supposedly profiting from the South American narcotics traffic that moved through Panama on its way to United States street corners.[42]

Remón, however, was more than an Arias with a badge. He committed his administration to social reform and economic development, particularly in the agricultural provinces where his wife had developed strong political ties. Remón moved to equalize the tax structure; more important, to the oligarchy's amazement he began collecting taxes. Following up his success within the Guard, the new President sought to

42. *Ibid.*, p. 8.

raise the status of blacks, especially for jobs in the Canal Zone.[43] The 2½ years of Remón's presidency initiated the most important reform program in Panama's history. The changes, moreover, were supported by a political coalition that drew its strength from the National Guard and the lower classes. The oligarchy and students were isolated, or, in individual instances, brought into the government on the President's terms.

Remón knew his reforms would be written on the wind unless they could be anchored to a strong national economy. Through public spending programs he accelerated agricultural and industrial production. Panama's economic dependence on the Zone actually decreased temporarily. Those trends, nevertheless, proved misleading. The country lacked the internal market, investment capital, and governmental lending powers to lift itself by its own bootstraps. The only important growth industry was the Canal.

Remón's attention inevitably swung toward Washington. His economic needs, concern for equal job opportunities in the Zone, and personal political future demanded a reordering of relations with the United States. So did an ever-louder Panamanian nationalism. In 1953 a new voice appeared. Ernesto Castillero Pimental was the son of Panama's most productive historian. As Remón assumed power, Castillero Pimental published an historical analysis of Panama-United States relations which scathingly attacked the 1903 treaty and urged that the national holiday be moved from the treaty date of November 3 to November 10 or 18, when the 1821 uprisings began against Spain.[44]

Remón asked the newly elected United States President, Dwight D. Eisenhower, to discuss a new treaty. Eisenhower had spent three years on the Isthmus as a young army officer during the 1920s. He liked the Panamanians and doubted Zonian arguments that only North Americans possessed the talents needed to operate the Canal.[45] Eisenhower was open to Remón's suggestion, but only to a certain point.

That point was the traditional North American determination to maintain control over the Canal Zone. Eisenhower also insisted that any new treaty not be costly to the United States. As talks opened in 1954, he

43. Daniel Goldrich, "Panama," in Martin C. Needler, ed., *Political Systems of Latin America* (Princeton, 1964), pp. 137–138.
44. Castillero Pimental's own views can be found in summary fashion in *Politica Exterior de Panama* (Panama, 1961), especially pp. 50–55 where he lists eighteen United States violations of treaties made with Panama since 1903. A good analysis is Gatell, "Canal in Retrospect," p. 28.
45. Peter Lyon, *Eisenhower, Portrait of the Hero* (Boston, 1974), pp. 56–58, footnote on p. 738.

told Remón personally of these conditions. In a long reply, the Panamanian disclaimed any intent to "affect fundamental rights of the United States," but did hope to bring those rights "into harmony with the rights of Panama." As for the money, Remón unsubtly argued that instead of being a request for aid, new financial arrangements would be merely "a means of equitable adjustment of the situation in which Panama was placed by reason of the Canal enterprise." Finally, he claimed that Washington's proposals, contrary to Eisenhower's public statements, "do not provide for equality of opportunity" in the Zone. He was especially incensed that the United States wanted to include a pledge that neither party would ever reopen monetary questions.[46] Panamanians, after all, already had enough trouble with "in perpetuity" clauses; they did not care for what they cynically termed the "perpetual silence" provision.

When Panama asked that the $430,000 annuity be raised to 20 percent of the Canal's gross revenue or $5 million (whichever was larger), the United States counteroffered $1 million annually for ten years to be used specifically for housing. Panama rejected this out-of-hand. The discussions deadlocked. Remón's rallying cry, "Neither Alms nor Millions, We Want Justice," became political dogma, if not an accurate description of his demands. (Twenty years later the Torrijos government placed the slogan on the retaining wall of the National Assembly parking lot, near a striking bas relief mural featuring Torrijos himself. The area, a hang-out for shoeshine boys and vendors, was located only several hundred yards from the Canal Zone.)

The Panamanians were engrossed in the Canal negotiations, but U.S. Secretary of State John Foster Dulles tried to focus Latin American attention on a left-wing government in Guatemala which had seized United Fruit Company holdings. At the Caracas meeting of the OAS in early 1954, Dulles worked mightily to align the Western Hemisphere against Guatemala. Some Latin Americans cooperated, hoping (vainly, as it turned out), that Washington would reward political loyalty with economic preferences. The Panamanian delegation, however, was led by out-spoken Cecilia Remón who attacked United States policies in her country, then succeeded in attaching to Dulles's proposals an amendment condemning job discrimination in the Zone. In May, President Remón nicely followed up his wife's efforts by declaring that short-sighted United States policies in Latin America allowed Communist propaganda to have an "effect it would not have under ordinary circum-

---

46. Eisenhower to Remón, Aug. 23, 1954; Remón to Eisenhower, Nov. 8, 1954, both in Ann Whitman file, Panama, Dwight D. Eisenhower Library, Abilene, Kansas.

stances."[47] Dulles stood firm. In June 1954, a United States-sponsored counter-revolution overthrew the Guatemalan government, replacing it with a right-wing regime whose policies satisfied both the United States and United Fruit. Dulles concluded that the Soviets might have targeted Guatemala for special attention because it lay only 700 miles from the Canal.[48]

For nearly fifteen years the United States had ignored Latin American problems, many of which were shaped by unilateral North American economic and political policies. When the Latins were dealt with, it was largely through military agreements (as the Rio Treaty), or force (as in Guatemala). The concern of the 1930s with being a Good Neighbor gave way to a 1950s obsession with global Communism. Order, which to Washington usually meant the status quo, received highest priority.

In such an environment Panamanians had little chance of receiving either "millions" or what they considered "justice." In the final 1955 treaty draft they nevertheless received a number of economic concessions. Most notably, the annual annuity was raised to $1,930,000. The new figure misled, however, for in real dollars (that is, discounting post-1945 inflation), the rental fee was actually less than the amount paid by the United States in 1914.[49]

Panama received for the first time the right to tax Zone employees who were Panamanian, a provision that could be interpreted as significantly extending Panama's authority in the Canal area. The United States surrendered the monopoly rights granted in the 1903 treaty over all railroad and highway building (although not canal construction), but no third power could construct future routes without Washington's approval. The North Americans also gave up their authority to control sanitation in Colon and Panama City. Of considerable importance to Panamanian merchants, Zone commissaries were not to sell goods to anyone except United States citizens who worked in the Zone and Panamanian employees (mostly the West Indians) who worked for the Canal and resided in the Zone. The Canal government, moreover, promised to purchase as many supplies as possible in Panama itself—subject, as a carefully written escape clause provided, to the discretion of the Zone's purchasing agents.

The United States handed back some lands outside the Zone. In return, Panama granted a fifteen-year renewable lease for 19 thousand acres in Rio Hato for the exclusive use of North American military forces. The

47. Pippin, *Remón Era*, p. 114.
48. Lyon, *Eisenhower*, p. 627.
49. *New York Times*, Jan. 13, 1964, p. 34.

Panamanians received no percentage of the Canal's revenue or any recognition of their sovereignty within the Zone. When the United States considered the pact, a citizen association (representing the North Americans living in the Zone) and some union representatives complained that Eisenhower was surrendering too much. Assistant Secretary of State Henry Holland assured the Senate that Washington still exercised "one hundred percent of the rights of sovereignty in this area."[50]

A "Memorandum of Understanding Reached" was also negotiated. Although it was an informal agreement and not submitted to the Senate for ratification, the Panamanians considered the Memorandum equal in importance to the treaty itself. Eisenhower pledged to create equality of opportunity within the Zone. He also promised to ask Congress for a single wage level for Canal jobs, regardless of whether the worker was Panamanian or North American. (United States citizens, however, would continue to receive a "differential" of 15 percent for serving overseas, as well as leave benefits and income tax allowance.)

The U.S. Senate ratified the treaty 72–14, but only after shippers (who feared that the higher annuity would force a rise in tolls), Zonians (who did not want to share jobs with Panamanians), and the colonists (who urged that not a comma be changed in the 1903 treaty) bitterly fought the new pact. Unlike those who fought the 1936 treaty, few opponents worried over the Canal's security. The "antis" of the 1950s cared foremost about personal interests which were tied to the status quo. The United States did not return the long-held lands until 1957, and not until 1958 did Congress made an initial, highly ineffective move to create equal job opportunities. Contrary to the agreement, the Zone government continued to purchase food supplies from as far away as Australia when the same product was available from Panamanians.[51]

A Different Panama, a Different World

Remón did not live to see the new treaty. While attending horse races outside the capital on January 2, 1955, two men machine-gunned him to death. The motive remains officially clouded but, to some observers, all too clear. Remón apparently was fighting attempts by the king of organized crime in the United States, Charles "Lucky" Luciano, to take over Panama's vast narcotics traffic. A Cuban crime expert who investigated

50. Lester D. Langley, "U.S.-Panamanian Relations Since 1941," *Journal of Inter-American Studies,* XII (July 1970), 345–346.
51. *Ibid.,* p. 349.

the killing believed that a Luciano gunman was one of the two killers. The other gunman was apparently Ruben Miró, an eccentric Panama City lawyer. The Luciano henchman was given his freedom immediately after the assassination. Miró was brought to trial.

Then the story grew mysteriously complex. A clique led by Remón's brother and Ricardo Arias (the Second Vice-President and no relation to Harmodio and Arnulfo), implicated the First Vice-President in the killing, took over the government, began repealing Remón's reform program, and gathered up large personal fortunes. On the brink of bankruptcy in late 1954, Ricardo Arias was allegedly worth $2 million when he left the presidency less than two years later. Ruben Miró, meanwhile, turned out to be a nephew of Harmodio Arias, one of Remón's implacable enemies. The yacht of Harmodio's son, Roberto, was seen stealing away from Panama City the night of the killing when all escape routes were supposedly sealed by the National Guard. This coincidence led some investigators to conclude that Guard officers worked with Ricardo Arias and Harmodio Arias to kill Remón. These three groups (Ricardo Arias, the Arias brothers, and the Guard) might have differed among themselves—and with "Lucky" Luciano—why Remón had to be removed, but not at all that he should be removed. With his political connections, Miró was well protected. A jury found him not guilty. The killers were never convicted and for some reason the new Panamanian government did not seem to mind.[52]

With Remón and his reform program gone, the oligarchy moved back into power. The government's apparent need to hide a political assassination was one of many good reasons why the 1956 elections were kept under tight control. Ernesto de la Guardia won easily, and the Union Club members settled back for business-as-usual. But the 1947 student uprisings, the Guard's new role as political arbiter, and Remón's reform and Canal programs were the seeds of a new Panama which threatened oligarchical and the United States interests.

The status quo was indeed growing shaky not only in Panama but around the globe. In Southeast Asia the French finally surrendered their colonial empire in 1954. North Americans replaced France in Vietnam, but their future was not bright. In only five years a series of African independence movements replaced a vast European colonial empire with autonomous, self-governing states. The focus of world attention in mid-1956 was on Suez, where Egypt broke away from British tutelage to gain control of the great canal. Alert to the precedents being set, Pana-

52. The story is well traced out in Pippin's *Remón Era*, especially pp. 127–135.

manians were furious when Secretary of State Dulles specifically excluded them from a twenty-two-nation users' conference called to settle
the Suez crisis. With unfailing insensitivity, Dulles humiliated Panamanians, publicly announcing that the United States would represent their
interests at the conference. When the Secretary of State suggested inter-
nationalizing the Suez, Panama issued a public pronouncement of its
own: the United States did not speak for Panama, and under no circumstances would its Canal be placed under international control.[53]

Of course Washington agreed with the latter point. Internationaliza-
tion could be a substitute for the tottering British authority in Suez, but
never for United States power in Panama. That feeling became intense
in July 1956 when Egypt took affairs out of Dulles's hands and seized the
Suez Canal unilaterally. The British and French, with Israeli cooperation, tried to reclaim their old power through an unbelievably confused
invasion of Egypt. Much to their embarrassment, Eisenhower and
Dulles had to stop their inept allies before threatened Soviet intervention turned a fiasco into a world crisis.

As the Suez confrontation built to a climax, Dulles appeared inflexible
before Panama's demands for a more equitable interpretation of the 1955
pact. Eisenhower approved: "We should be generous in all small administration details," he told his Secretary of State. "Our firmness should be in
holding fast to basic principles and purposes of [the] treaty."[54] As Egypt
tightened its grip on Suez, a reporter asked Dulles whether the 1955 treaty
promises would be fulfilled. His answer: "I'm not such a Utopian as to
think there will never be any problems between us because of the nature
of the situation."[55] As global relationships transformed in 1956, Washington clung tightly to the status quo in Panama.

Warning signals were up everywhere. In a private conversation, President Arias tried to make Eisenhower understand United States power in
determining Panamanian affairs:

> [Arias] compared the relative positions of the two countries by pointing
> out that this morning he had been told by Dr. Milton Eisenhower [the
> President's brother] that the budget for Penn State College is $30 million
> per year; whereas, the yearly budget for the Republic of Panama is only
> $50 million.
>
> President Arias stated that despite our recent treaties, things were not
> going well and that we are "running into trouble."

53. Liss. *The Canal*, pp. 53–54.
54. Handwritten note on Dulles to Eisenhower, Sept. 28, 1956, Ann Whitman File, Panama, Eisenhower Library.
55. Press conference of Oct. 2, 1956, Papers of John Foster Dulles, Princeton University.

President Eisenhower responded by insisting on "justice" for Panama, and blamed the State Department for "not always [keeping] him as closely informed on the problem with Panama." Sitting nearby, Dulles aroused himself enough to say that he "kept up with Panamanian matters but necessarily not as to detail." After all, Dulles was a busy man: "I [am] constantly being confronted with international problems of grave import." Panama obviously did not qualify for his attention. Three months later, newly elected President de la Guardia wrote Eisenhower that he "almost despaired as to the present and future of our relations." Eisenhower privately expressed puzzlement at "what President de la Guardia had in mind."[56]

Puzzlement soon gave way to consternation. While on a supposed good-will tour through South America in early 1958, Vice-President Richard Nixon encountered a series of violent anti-Yankee demonstrations. In Caracas his car was stoned, spat upon, and nearly turned over. For a moment Eisenhower considered ordering a parachute drop to rescue Nixon.

Eight months later, on New Year's Day 1959, the forces of guerrilla fighter Fidel Castro marched into Havana to mark his final victory over the North American-trained and equipped armies of dictator Fulgencio Batista. For sixty-one years United States-Cuban relations were those between a colonizer and a colony, but within six months they were transfigured by Castro's agrarian reform program and increasingly bitter exchanges between Washington and Havana. If the United States could not create a prosperous, stable, and friendly Cuba after six decades of near-total control in an island less than one hundred miles from Florida, it was natural to wonder whether North American overseas interests were safe anywhere.

World history took an important turn between 1956 and 1960. The old bipolar Cold War power structure dominated by the United States and the Soviet Union fragmented into a more pluralistic global order, especially in the southern hemispheres. Whether the United States could navigate this turn remained an open question in 1958–1959. Eisenhower tried to make it, particularly by announcing a massive program of economic cooperation with Latin America. The region would have its own bank, the Inter-American Development Bank (IADB), through which United States and Latin American capital would be funneled into devel-

56. "Memorandum of Conversation," July 23, 1956, and Eisenhower to Acting Secretary of State, Oct. 10, 1956, both in Ann Whitman File, Panama, Eisenhower Library.

opment projects. The IADB initiated what the John F. Kennedy administration would glamorize as the Alliance for Progress.

The 1959 Riots

But Eisenhower's new policies hardly touched Panama. By early 1958
relations with Washington were deteriorating nearly as rapidly as the
economy. As Zone employment dropped from 30,000 in 1945 to
12,000 eleven years later, Panamanian unemployment correspondingly
rose. Colon became a devastated area, its slums among the world's
worst. The city's politics understandably produced Thelma King, the
most outspoken nationalist and revolutionary in the National Assembly. King sympathized with Castro, but she denied any Communist
affiliations.

Colon represented only an extreme. A United Nations team concluded that Panama's economic expansion was over. Projecting from
1956 to 1966, the UN economists believed the gross national product
would barely keep up with population growth; the general living standard would actually drop an incredible 7 percent. Only "dismal prospects of growth" existed. Then came the kind of phrase that haunted
Washington policy-makers: "Given the lack of dynamic stimuli for private investment and the demands made by a high investment rate, an
increment of about 90 percent would be required in government gross
investment. This in itself would imply a radical alteration in the traditional role of the public sector in Panama." If the United States did not
like the sound of "radical alteration," the UN team offered one alternative. Since governmental spending and private investment could not
revive the economy, only transit traffic and tourism linked to the Canal
held out "really dynamic prospects."[57] The United States, in other
words, had to choose between two distasteful alternatives: either allow a
radically different governmental involvement in Panama's private economy (an involvement that hinted of socialism or fascism), or give Panama much larger economic benefits from the Canal.

Panamanians would not allow Washington to escape that choice. In
May 1958, Panama City university students announced "Operation Sov-
ereignty." They entered the Zone peacefully and planted some fifty
Panamanian flags at strategic points, only to have the Canal police pull

57. UN Economic Commission for Latin America, "The Economic Development of Panama," pp. 50–56.

up the banners. During other demonstrations that month, several students were shot, supposedly by the Guard although individual snipers might have been responsible. The old hatreds re-emerged betweeen students and the Zone as well as between students and the Guard.

Disturbed by the outbreaks in Washington's backyard, President Eisenhower decided to send his brother, Milton, on a fact-finding trip through Latin America. Panama turned into a most important stop. A Panamanian official explained the situation: "You in the United States inherited vast mineral wealth. . . . Africa was given gold and diamonds. The Middle East is rich in oil. God gave Panama nothing but a waterway. We must make a living from our resources, as others have from theirs." Returning to Washington, Eisenhower recommended carrying out the promises of the 1955 treaty and "Memorandum of Understandings." A few provisions were finally fulfilled, but when he proposed a large program of low-cost housing, his brother's government seemed deaf. And when he urged that the flag controversy be solved by allowing the Panamanian emblem to be flown "in selected locations, at least on ceremonial occasions," Eisenhower ran into a stonewall of Pentagon opposition. The U.S. Army would suffer no gesture that might indicate Panama's "titular sovereignty" along the Canal.[58] The Pentagon decided to fight by standing still.

The strategy seemed appropriate when 1959 began with a comic opera staged by Roberto Arias, Harmodio's playboy son and the husband of British ballerina Margot Fonteyn. Arias led a group of Cubans ashore in northern Panama and straight into the arms of the waiting National Guard. The "Aquatic Ballet," as humorists quickly tagged it, climaxed with Arias fleeing into the Brazilian Embassy and Fidel Castro condemning the whole affair. The Cuban leader apparently was not involved. He publicly announced that Panama, unlike Nicaragua, was not a tyranny, then attacked Roberto's raiders for trying to involve Cuba in a conflict with the United States. [59]

The comic interlude was brief. Panamanians directly challenged the Pentagon's standstill strategy. In March 1959 President de la Guardia sharply told President Eisenhower that despite the promises of 1936 and 1955, the Canal's new wage system "perpetuates in essence the old system of discrimination against Panamian workers." De la Guardia threatened to take the question to an international court, then unsubtly

58. Milton S. Eisenhower, *The Wine Is Bitter. The United States and Latin America* (New York, 1964), pp. 214–225.
59. Herbert S. Dinerstein, *The Making of a Missile Crisis, October 1962* (Baltimore, 1976), pp. 43, 46, 278.

ended his message by telling Eisenhower that it was regrettable how the "deterioration in our relations appreciably encourages our common adversaries."[60] By autumn tensions over job discrimination and the possibility of a new flag incident forced the Pentagon to ask Milton Eisenhower what could be done. Once again, the military had waited too long.

On Independence Day, November 3, 1959, a group of Panamanian students moved into the Zone to plant flags. They were led by Ernesto Castillero Reyes, perhaps the nation's best-known historian, and Aquilino Boyd. A former ambassador to Mexico and delegate to the United Nations, Boyd was the descendent of Federico Boyd, a founder of Panama; the son of a former President; a wealthy businessman in his own right; and ambitious for the presidency in 1960. Some observers believed that like others of his class, Boyd hoped to focus the attention of Panamanian malcontents on the Canal and away from the oligarchy's failures. Boyd and his friends, however, thought it righteous nationalism.

As the group departed, several students broke away and tried to re-enter the Zone. The Zone police arrested one. Mobs formed. Fresh attempts were made to rush the police, who were now supported by United States infantry with fixed bayonets. As news of the clash spread, Panamanians moved into the streets. Rioting broke out in Panama City. United States-owned automobiles were burned, buildings operated by North American corporations sacked, windows broken in the U.S. Information Agency, the flag torn down in front of the U.S Embassy, and North American lives endangered in Colon. At least 120 Panamanians were wounded, 9 by birdshot fired by U.S. troops on students who tried to storm into the Zone. Rioting did not stop until National Guard units deployed to calm the city. This led to another student-Guard clash in which three students were shot.

On November 4, President Eisenhower told a press conference, "In a way it's a little bit puzzling to me," especially since each treaty modification gave "a greater degree or level of rights to the Panamanians." He decided the troubles could be traced to "an excitable group; people that are extremists."[61] Despite his confusion, Eisenhower tried to make changes. His brother's housing proposals were revived. The Governor of the Canal Zone was directed to buy all supplies in Panama or the United States instead of Australia or New Zealand. On December 2 Eisenhower discussed the highly delicate flag question: "I do . . . be-

---

60. De la Guardia to Eisenhower, March 7, 1959, Ann Whitman File, Panama, Eisenhower Library.
61. *Public Papers of the Presidents, 1959* (Washington, D.C., 1961), pp. 772–773, 775.

lieve we should have visual evidence that Panama does have titular sovereignty" in the Zone.

That was too much for the champions of the 1903 treaty. They were led, at least rhetorically, by Daniel Flood (Democrat of Pennsylvania), who traced his political lineage back to Theodore Roosevelt. Flood was so outspoken that Panamanians labeled him their "Public Enemy Number One." In February 1960, Congress voted 380–12 against allowing the Panamanian flag to fly in the Zone. The vote was only advisory; it did not tie Eisenhower's hands.

In April the President announced a nine-point program which for the first time opened some skilled jobs to Panamanians. He also dispatched a new ambassador, Joseph S. Farland. The Farland appointment was a master-stroke. The new Ambassador ordered the Embassy staff to stay in touch with all classes of Panamanians. He entertained schools and hospitals with demonstrations of his skill as a magician, proving to be a true magician in quieting anti-Yankee feeling among Panamanian officials.

In September, Eisenhower announced that both flags would be shown in part of the Zone. The statement was historic. The United States flag had not flown in the Zone between 1903 and 1906, but after 1906 the Panamanian flag disappeared. Now it was to return. The announcement was perfectly timed: Congress was in adjournment. Eisenhower, moreover, had removed the possibility of Panamanian riots on the November 3d Independence Day. They could endanger Richard Nixon's chances in the final hours of the United States presidential election.

The 1903 congressional contingent was enraged. Flood called the new policy "Munich in spades" and demanded Eisenhower's impeachment. Of some 180 letters received by the White House, only three agreed with Eisenhower.[62] But the importance of the flag question, while symbolic, was overemphasized. It threatened to take Washington's attention off the fundamental problem of the Panamanian economy.

Some North Americans understood the danger. United States officials in Panama had told Milton Eisenhower that a revival of the Panamanian economy "would relieve the pressures on the Zone and the Canal Company."[63] Congresswoman Leonore Sullivan arrived at the same conclusion. Head of the powerful Subcommittee on the Panama Canal (a part of the House Committee on Merchant Marine and Fisheries), Sullivan blasted Eisenhower for giving away "fundamental American rights." She believed such tactics never worked. As long as slum-ridden Pana-

62. Langley, "U.S.-Panamanian Relations Since 1941," p. 353.
63. Eisenhower, *Wine Is Bitter*, p. 216.

manians lived across the street from air-conditioned Zonians, as long as "economic deprivation . . . generated the political dream of great riches for all if only Panama owned the Canal," no peaceful relations could exist. Only "if Panama were truly prosperous—if it had resources other than this canal," could the Panamanians stop troubling the Zone.[64]

Sullivan's approach would underlie John F. Kennedy's Alliance for Progress program in Panama during the 1960s. But the question was whether enough time remained to test Sullivan's thesis. Nearly two decades of a policy that shunned economic cooperation and emphasized hemispheric military alliances had climaxed in a series of disasters. Panama particularly suffered. Booming in 1945, by 1960 its economy was a disaster area. Massive governmental spending failed to prime the system. Remón's reforms were dead. The economy depended on two stimuli. The first was exports, of which 68 percent were bananas. United Fruit, not Panamanians, controlled banana production.

The second stimulus was the Canal Zone—whose economy, along with Eisenhower's enlightened policies, produced a tragic irony. After some of the 1955 treaty promises were made real, Panamanian workers in the Zone received higher wages; merchants outside the Zone suddenly could sell goods to the North Americans. The Zone provided the major impetus to the country's economy in the late 1950s.[65] Panamanians therefore grew more dependent on the Zone for their own economic survival. Granting Panama concessions accelerated the country's need to break the colonial relationship and control the entire Canal area, or else face economic stagnation.

Meanwhile the political system deteriorated. The Guard reopened its struggle with the students. Oligarchs remained irresponsible. Two North American political scientists observed in 1960 that Panama contained "all the conditions for a nationalist revolution which will rival the recent upheavals in Cuba and Egypt."[66] Cuban and Panamanian history contained striking similarities. Castro's emergence raised the question of whether the similarities would continue.

64. *Cong. Record,* Feb. 1960, pp. 1645–1649, Central files, L.B.J. Library.
65. Robert E. Looney, *The Economic Development of Panama: The Impact of World Inflation on an Open Economy* (New York, 1976), p. 19.
66. Martin B. Travis and James T. Watkins, "Time Bomb in Panama," *The Nation,* CXC (April 30, 1960), 378.

5

Chiari, Johnson, and Robles

In 1903 the oligarchs established themselves in power and a colonial relationship began between Panama and the United States. During the 1960s the oligarchy cracked then fell from power, while the killing of Panamanians and North Americans in the 1964 riots led to fundamental change in the colonial ties. Washington entered a new, difficult relationship with a different Panama. Sixty years of isthmian history, like a long river kept carefully within its banks, had reached a watershed. Its future course would be less restrained, more unpredictable, and hence more dangerous. But it could no longer be easily dammed up.

The Alliance

Once again Panama was a microcosm. As Castro's triumph illustrated, the whole of Latin America approached an historic watershed. Understanding this in 1961, newly elected President John F. Kennedy set out to control and channel change within the Western Hemisphere. He wanted Latin American development to move in orderly evolutionary, not revolutionary, channels. His instrument was the Alliance for Progress, a projected ten-year, $100 billion program in which North and South, private and governmental capital, would cooperate to create a dynamic Latin America immune to Castroism.

Panama received special attention, for as Congresswoman Sullivan had explained, only when Panamanians enjoyed prosperity would they stop pushing for more control over the Canal revenues. In mid-1961 the first Alliance grant for Panama was to build 200 rural schoolhouses and 150 miles of farm roads. An agricultural credit system was planned. The Alliance obviously hoped to create a self-sufficient agricultural sector which, among other attractions, would slow the migration from rural to urban areas and thus stabilize, perhaps even reduce, festering unemployment in city slums which bordered the Zone.

Between 1951 and 1961 the United States had granted Panama only $7 million in economic assistance per year. From 1961 to 1963 the amount jumped to $41 million. The Peace Corps, another Kennedy innovation, sent 57 volunteers to help develop schools, health centers, and rural cooperatives. In addition the Canal Zone itself infused at least $65 million annually through wages, tourism, and purchases into Panama's economic bloodstream.

Panamanians, nevertheless, were not mollified. In 1963 the $100 million gross revenue from Canal operations produced a net income to the Canal Company of $5 million, but of that amount Panama received only $1.9 million. Many Panamanians also disliked the Kennedy administration's use of the Zone for shaping military aspects of the Alliance. The School of the Americas trained Latin American army and police officers (including Panamanian National Guardsmen) for the counterinsurgency warfare. Panama had no control over the school, nor did its complaints that the school had nothing to do with Canal operations (and hence lay outside treaty understandings) have any effect. Some of the Cuban exiles who waded ashore to be captured or killed at the Bay of Pigs invasion in 1961 were trained in part in the Zone. By 1963 the United States also used the Canal area for stationing anti-guerrilla paratroop units that on short notice could drop into trouble spots throughout Latin America. As both a test-tube for the Alliance and a base for the military, Panama nicely exemplified the two parts of Kennedy's Latin American policy. Not all Panamanians, however, fully appreciated their role.

The country's new President, Roberto Chiari, was necessarily restrained in cooperating with the Alliance. After winning a 1960 election that was relatively open and not determined by the Guard, Chiari emphasized the need for rapid but not over-extensive change. Without it, he warned his fellow oligarchs, he might be the last official elected from their select circle. The oligarchy's problem was to determine how much reform it could tolerate without losing power. Many in the ruling class refused to believe that slow strangulation through change was preferable to standing still. For example, when the government attempted to build low-cost housing for slum dwellers in the capital, wealthy owners of slum housing fought back with some success through anonymous letter-writing campaigns. Chiari displayed keen sensitivity to such feelings, for his family monopolized milk distribution in Panama City and nearly monopolized sugar. Unsurprisingly he moved slowly to implement reform laws that were to accompany the Alliance's dollars.[1]

The oligarchy also encountered a second trap. For several decades it had focused nationalist rage away from itself by directing it toward the Canal Zone. The 1959 riots, however, were a red flag signaling that such games could get out of hand. The oligarchy and the United States nevertheless fully agreed on the need to fight Communism. Chiari cut relations with Cuba in late 1961, launched an attack to quiet the 500 to 1000 members of the outlawed Panamanian Communist Party, and—acting more royally than the king—threatened to quit the Organization of American States unless Cuba was expelled.

Hatred, Destruction, and Death

Flagellating Communists was easy sport. Other problems seemed intractable, and time was running out for the oligarchy. Surveys revealed that students, who comprised the most effective political opposition, placed considerable hope in Chiari, especially after he promised housing and tax reforms. Above all, however, the students wanted an open system in which they could use their education to gain economic security. They were overwhelmingly anti-Communist, yet a sizable minority considered themselves "extremists." Wanting middle-class respectability and income, the students, Professor Daniel Goldrich believed, threatened Panama with "an increasing possibility of violence and repression, at least during a transitional period,"[2] unless the oligarchy expanded employ-

1. Daniel Goldrich, "Panama," Martin C. Needler, ed., *Political Systems of Latin America* (Princeton, 1964), pp. 143–144; Louis Harris, "Panama," in Ben G. Burnett and K. F. Johnson, eds., *Political Forces in Latin American* (Belmont, Calif., 1968), p. 180; the best detailed analysis of the Alliance for Progress is Jerome Levinson and Juan de Onís, *The Alliance That Lost Its Way* (Chicago, 1970).

2. Daniel Goldrich, "Requisites for Political Legitimacy in Panama," *Public Opinion Quarterly,*XXVI (Winter 1962), 664–668; Daniel Goldrich and Edward Scott, "Developing Political Orientations of Panamanian Students," *Journal of Politics*, XXIII (February 1961), 103–107.

ment rapidly enough to accommodate the well-trained (and Panama had one of the top seven literacy rates in Latin America.)

The oligarchy was singularly unresponsive. Political factions continued to be organized around the charismatic and the rich, not reform programs. The exceptions to the rule were the illegal Communists and a moderate Christian Democratic Party organized by highly respected professional men whom the oligarchy's leaders ignored. One percent of the landowners controlled half the privately owned land (while more than half the farmers subsisted on annual incomes of less than $100), and oligarchs monopolized Panamanian access to banks, coffee plantations, and sugar refineries. Ownership of newspapers, radio, and television was so centralized that six men enjoyed almost total control over the media. Oligarch families sent their children to universities overseas, away from the ambitious and often rowdy middle- and lower-class students in Panama City who seemed to divide their time between classrooms and street riots. Resembling Dr. Pangloss, the oligarchy lived in the best of all possible worlds. A leading scholar of Panamanian politics, Lester Langley, called the oligarchy "perhaps the most socially irresponsible [elite] in Latin America."[3]

Despite, or because of, Chiari's attacks on the Communists, a *Fidelista* movement appeared in Veraguas Province during late 1962. The United Fruit Company, which controlled the province's affairs, was an attractive target. The company's operations, according to one North American visitor, resembled antebellum slave plantations in the South.[4] In other parts of the country peasants seized estates. But the most dangerous outbreak occurred in Panama City, where university students went on strike. The National Assembly went through its ritual of blaming the troubles on the United States and demanding full jurisdiction over the Canal. Chiari visited Kennedy in Washington, and out of the talks emerged a Joint Commission to discuss outstanding issues.

The Commission proved to be a disaster. It started auspiciously by settling several labor disputes in the Zone. Then on January 10, 1963, it announced that Panama's flag would fly with the United States banner at civilian institutions throughout the Zone. North Americans who operated the canal loudly protested. The Commission appeared paralyzed. In mid-1963 Chiari angrily disbanded it. This was followed by Ambassa-

3. Lester D. Langley, "The United States and Panama: The Burden of Power," *Current History*, LVI (January 1969), 17; on the media, see Harris, "Panama," p. 184.
4. Liss, *The Canal*, p. 106.

dor Farland's sudden resignation. Elected by Panamanians as one of the ten most popular men in the country (an honor no other United States Ambassador had ever received), the Zonians were happy to see Farland leave. So, apparently, was the State Department, which publicly played down his resignation. The Ambassador announced he wanted to return to private life, but actually he had become embittered over the ineffectiveness and limitations of the Alliance, the insensitivity of Washington to the storm signals in Panama, and criticism from the Zonians. Tragically, the State Department tarried in sending a replacement. For the five months before, as well as during the 1964 riots, the United States had no ambassador in Panama.

With Farland's scalp on their belt, the Zonians moved to repeal part of the Commission's accomplishments. Understandably, they liked the pre-1959 status quo. As *Time* magazine noted in 1964, "Few Americans abroad lead a more comfortable life or are more self-consciously American." They live

> in model company towns with look-alike houses, bargain-priced groceries, liquor and clothing from Government commissaries, bowling and Hollywood movies at the service centers. They have their own schools (including a junior college), country clubs and well-kept golf courses; 1600 boats are registered at the yacht basin.[5]

Their average salary was triple the average United States wage.

On the other hand the Zonians believed they fully deserved such benefits. They made the Canal work. Some of them, particularly the ship pilots and tower operators, possessed unique skills from long training and experience. If they suddenly left Panama the Canal would shut down for years before replacements could be adequately trained. They lived far from the mainland in a tropical climate that required "neatly manicured lawns" (as critics delighted in pointing out), not simply for aesthetic reasons but to prevent pools of water in which malaria-causing mosquitoes could breed. Above all, the Zonians wanted little contact with the squalor and anti-Gringoism of Panama City and Colon. Only 20 percent of them spoke Spanish. "There are some people here," one Zonian remarked, "who haven't been to Panama for ten or twenty years. And they're proud of it."

Governor of the Zone was Robert J. Fleming Jr., a major general in the Corps of Engineers who liked to talk while pacing about his office, a swagger-stick in hand. In 1963, Fleming later recalled, he told Washing-

5. *Time*, Jan. 24, 1964, p. 18.

ton officials "things had never looked better between the two countries. We were about to reach the point where you blow the froth off the beer and get down to essentials." As he later lamented, those "essentials" would not be determined by a majority of Zonians who were "moderates" and passive, but by 300 or so who acted as "the radical right. They've been isolated so long they've developed a reactionary mentality." The Governor added, "It's the perfect situation for the guy who's 150 percent American—and 50 percent whiskey."[6]

Seizing upon the flag decision as their cause, parents and students at the Zone's Balboa High School took matters into their own hands. They determined that only the United States flag would fly at the school. On January 9, 1964, several hundred Panamanian University students marched peacefully into the Zone to protest the absence of their flag. Zone police finally agreed to allow a half-dozen Panamanians to exhibit their flag in front of the school. Four hundred to five hundred North Americans were waiting, and when police sighted them the Panamanians were asked to retreat. A scuffle broke out, the Panamanian flag was torn, rocks filled the air, windows and street lights were smashed. The riot had begun.

Rumors of the clash swept Panama City. As many as 30,000 Panamanians moved into the streets, many swarming down 4th of July Avenue, which bordered the Canal Zone. They were repulsed for a time by Zone police. Finally United States troops took up battle stations in hastily dug foxholes in front of the Tivoli Hotel. Late on January 9 the Tivoli began to receive sniper fire from buildings that bordered the Zone. The U.S. troops first tried to use birdshot to clear out the snipers without killing them, but this proved ineffective. Fire from the Panamanian side increased to 200 rounds an hour. Expert army marksmen moved into the Tivoli with orders to warn snipers first by firing nearby before shooting to kill. According to Washington officials, the sniper fire reached over 500 rounds an hour during the next several days. In response the marksmen in the Tivoli killed several Panamanians.[7]

The rioters demanded that the National Guard attack the troops. The Guard, wisely, not only refused to challenge the U.S. Army, but largely disappeared from sight after telling the demonstrators to go home.[8]

6. The quotations in this and the preceding paragraph are from T. Armbrister, "Panama: Why They Hate Us: More Than One Torn Flag," *Saturday Evening Post,* March 7, 1964, pp. 76–77.
7. Tondel, ed., *Panama Canal,* p. 54; International Commission of Jurists, *Report on the Events in Panama, January 9–12, 1964* (Geneva, Switzerland, 1964), pp. 16–18, 20–28.
8. Associated Press Dispatch, January 1964, Central Files, Panama, Lyndon B. Johnson Papers, Lyndon B. Johnson Library, Austin, Texas.

Instead of returning home, the mobs roamed through Panama City for 3½ days, burning the U.S. Information Agency building, Pan American and Braniff Airway offices, and the tire plants of Goodyear and Firestone. North American banks were stoned. The U.S. Embassy was beseiged. More than 2000 bullets were later taken from the Tivoli Hotel's walls. (The grand landmark of the Theodore Roosevelt era was later demolished by Zone authorities, partly because of outmoded and decayed facilities, partly because it stood directly across from Panama City's slums as a symbol of the Big Stick era.)

The riots spread to Colon, then deep into the interior. In David the Chase Manhattan Bank and an Esso station were burned. The United Fruit Company prepared to evacuate its North American families. Over $2 million of property was destroyed in all. Significantly, Peace Corps volunteers were not harmed, and when several were threatened they were protected by villagers.[9]

By January 13 both sides were worn down by four days of fighting. The National Guard then emerged to clear the streets. Four U.S. soldiers had been killed, 85 North Americans wounded, and several thousand refugees had moved into the Zone, often with the covert but friendly help of National Guard troops. Right-wing groups in the United States alleged that in addition five of their countrymen were hanged and another chopped to pieces by Panamanians; no evidence was ever provided to substantiate these charges. Twenty-four Panamanians lost their lives and more than 200 were wounded. The Chiari government renamed 4th of July Avenue; it became, and remains, Avenue of the Martyrs. Nearly 500 demonstrators were arrested, including five Communist leaders who, with their usual sense of timing, arrived at the scene too late to receive credit for the riots but early enough to go to jail because of them.

LBJ: Between "Deformities" and One-Third the Population of Chicago

The shooting erupted as Lyndon Johnson was settling into the White House as the successor to the assassinated John Kennedy. As a Texan, Johnson believed he knew something about Latin America, particularly Mexico, but his knowledge of Panama went little farther than a determi-

9. Minor, "U.S.-Panamanian Relations: 1958–1973," pp. 74–78.

nation that small countries would not be allowed to harm his chances to become President in his own right in the November elections.

On January 10, the first full day of rioting, Chiari broke relations with Washington and accused the United States of "unjustifiable aggression." A stunned Johnson ordered an aide, "Get me the President of Panama— what's his name—on the phone." "Mr. President," the aide implored, "you can't do that. It isn't protocol." "Why in hell can't I," Johnson roared. "Come on now, get him on the phone."[10]

With most of his National Guard in the barracks, Chiari could give LBJ few assurances. Johnson became convinced that "having failed through diplomacy with President Kennedy, Chiari was going to try to exact a new treaty from me by force." He sent Thomas Mann, his chief Latin American adviser, to confer with Chiari. A fellow Texan, Mann had helped plan the Central Intelligence Agency-sponsored invasion of Guatemala in 1954. He tended to summarize policy in such phrases as, "These people need the application of a little muscle and common sense." Mann bluntly told Chiari to restore order immediately. Secretary of the Army Cyrus Vance flew to Panama to announce that the two flags would fly together as the 1963 agreements dictated; he provided the sugar for Mann's salt. But in a news conference Vance indicated that Communist agents trained in Cuba were largely responsible for the riot, an allegation soon supported by Secretary of State Dean Rusk.[11]

Only Washington officials seemed to be able to find Communists who merited such attention. The Panamanian government publicly ridiculed Vance's claim. That some party members were in the streets could not be denied, but as Panama's Second Vice-President observed, "The Communists here are like firemen. They don't run until they hear the bell. But instead of pouring water on the flames, they pour gasoline."[12] An Organization of American States investigation denied that Castro was involved. It reached this conclusion despite strained relations between the OAS and Cuba. The Commander of the U.S. Army who defended the Zone had a better sense of the situation than either Vance or Rusk. United States views, he believed, were "probably overdominated by the Cuban situation. Too many of us fail to comprehend what lies to the south of us."[13]

10. Eric F. Goldman, *The Tragedy of Lyndon Johnson* (New York, 1968), p. 87.
11. Statement of Jan. 20, 1964, Central Files, Panama, LBJ Papers; Johnson's view of Chiari is in Lyndon Johnson, *The Vantage Point* (New York, 1971), pp. 182–184; Mann's quote is in Goldman, *Tragedy of LBJ,* p. 89.
12. Armbrister, "Panama: Why They Hate Us," p. 78.
13. Minor, "U.S.-Panamanian Relations: 1958–1973," pp. 96–100.

An unidentified State Department official was more specific. The "imperialist mentality" of the Zonians, he claimed, played into the hands of the "leftist agitators" who were then able to embarrass such dependable Panamanians as President Chiari.[14] The rioters called Zonians "deformities" and "bastards of the earth," among other things, so the official's perception was doubtlessly accurate, but it was also dangerous policy if carried to a conclusion. For it meant that either the Zonians or Panamanians would have to experience a miraculous transformation in their own attitudes, which was unlikely, or relations could become tranquil only after the Zonians left the country.

The Zonians received vocal support in the United States, support that threatened to trap Johnson politically. Representative Daniel Flood again took the lead, at least rhetorically. The Pennsylvania Democrat scolded Johnson that since the United States enjoyed total sovereignty in the Zone, the President must stop making "accessions to unjustified demands from the mob-dominated Panama government." Appeasement would only lead "to greater blackmail." Flood believed the Panamanian demands for control over the Canal were "part of the audacious, cunning, and far-reaching strategy of the Soviets." He even urged the President to take additional land from Panama for the defense of the waterway.[15] Former President Harry Truman and a Republican presidential candidate, Senator Barry Goldwater of Arizona, reached rare agreement that the Zonian children were correct in raising the lone flag. In the Senate, Republican Minority Leader Everett Dirksen of Illinois intoned, "We are in the amazing position of having a country with one-third the population of Chicago kick us around. If we crumble in Panama, the reverberations of our actions will be felt around the world."

In the fifteen or so years before and after the 1964 riots, observers often claimed that Panamanian politics prevented cooperation with the United States, even when it was in Panama's interest to do so. That criticism applied to both sides, however. As early as 1936, and particularly after the 1964 riots, United States Presidents frequently developed a conciliatory policy only to discover that their hands were tied by special Canal interests (shippers, Zonians, labor unions), and vocal groups who loved the Canal Zone as a symbol of that happier past when Big-Stick diplomacy kept Panamanians in their place.

In late 1964 these political realities were explained in detail to Johnson by Richard Scammon, director of the Commerce Department's Bureau

14. *Wall Street Journal*, Jan. 13, 1964, p. 4.
15. Flood to Johnson, Jan. 14, 1964, Central Files, Panama, LBJ Papers.

of the Census (and then, as well as in the 1970s, a well-known political analyst). Although "more than a little concerned with the potential trouble which Panama could cause us in November," Scammon began, he was not worried about "idiotic kids" or "Zonians," but something larger. "Given the Castroite base among the students," the "politnik [*sic*]" in Panama could cause "trouble, crises, problems, and difficulties *ad infinitum ad nauseum*." Johnson's support "on the peace issue comes from the [fear of] the atomic question," Scammon continued, "and does not extend to getting pushed around by a small country about an area which every grade school history book features with an American flag, a snapshot of Teddy Roosevelt, and an image of gallant engineers overcoming the mosquito." Concessions to Panama, he warned, would give the Republicans their "first real solid muscled hit at the Administration." They could exploit a "ready-made 'wrap-us-in-the-flag' kind of situation." Scammon's warning circulated to Rusk and Vance, among others, while Johnson called it excellent and summoned the author for a private talk.[16]

Scammon's analysis was supported by a Gallup Poll indicating that of the 64 percent who knew about the Panama dispute, nearly half urged "firm policy," and only 9 percent favored concessions.[17] His politica antennae quivering, Johnson moved to silence opposition by taking bo sides of the question (a tactic he tried to repeat later on the Vietna issue). In February, for example, he said, "Our school children mad mistake in raising the United States flag without raising the Panaman flag," then quickly balanced this with, "but that does not warran r justify shooting our soldiers or invading the Zone."[18]

Johnson offered "to discuss all [*sic*] problems" with Panama. His ff was quickly called. After completing hurriedly arranged talks in d-January, Chiari announced that Washington was offering to reneg ate the 1903 treaty. LBJ heatedly denied this, claiming that only f her discussions had been agreed upon. The problem was apparently sed by the use of the Spanish *negociar* in the agreement; it mea both discuss and negotiate, thus satisfying the two sides at the talks but fus-ing everyone when it was publicly interpreted.

Although Johnson did not take kindly to Chiari's public pre re, it

16. Scammon to Ralph A. Dungan, Jan. 17, 1964, and Dungan to Scammon, Jan. 21, 1964, Central File, Panama, LBJ Papers.

17. George H. Gallup, *The Gallup Poll: Public Opinion, 1935–1971*, three vols. (New York, 1972), III, 1864.

18. *The Public Papers of the Presidents. Lyndon B. Johnson. 1963–1964*, two vols. (Washington, D.C., 1965), I, 288, 144.

was the United States President who broke the deadlock with an announcement in mid-March that sounded bland (and thus politically innocuous). He circumvented *negociar* by declaring he was willing to "review every issue" dividing the two nations. Chiari helped by privately promising Johnson that he would not demand a formal revision of the 1903 pact. Like LBJ, the Panamanian leader was trying to keep the delicate issue out of his country's upcoming elections. Chiari also had another reason. Johnson announced the United States would begin studies in Central America and Mexico for a new sea-level canal. Faced with the possible loss of their greatest economic resource, Panamanian negotiators were spurred by fear as much as by nationalism.

The canal issue did not affect either presidential campaign. Johnson effectively neutralized the question in the United States. The Panamanian race narrowed to Chiari's choice (and cousin), Marco Robles, and the quadrennial candidate, Arnulfo Arias. This was, however, a different Arias, for although he and Robles agreed on the need for a new Canal treaty, the former Panameñista firebrand had so cooled that he displayed charity toward the North American side of some economic questions. A few United States officials even hoped he would win. In 1964, therefore, the old Arias received nationalist backing and the new Arias won some United States support. But in the end he could not control the ballot boxes. As usual, the government controlled those, and the Panamanian axiom that "He who counts, elects" remained valid. With Chiari's public and private support, Robles won by a small margin.

The Idyllic, Rejected Treaty

A tough banker (whose apt nickname, so necessary for successful Panamanian politicians, was "the Rifle"), Robles displayed his moderation by spending a post-election vacation in New York City talking with leading businessmen, including David Rockefeller of the Chase Manhattan Bank. Robles then demonstrated his toughness by ordering the National Guard to stop student protests, an order which the Guard forcefully carried out twice in 1965 and once in 1966. The President rounded out his balancing act by announcing that Panama's sovereignty over the Zone must be recognized and the "in perpetuity" clause of the 1903 treaty removed.

Lyndon Johnson appreciated Robles' political skills. Re-elected in a smashing victory over Senator Barry Goldwater, the President announced on December 18 that he would seek "an entirely new treaty" with Panama to terminate the 1903 agreement, recognize Panamanian sovereignty, and allow the United States to operate and protect the Canal for a fixed time. It marked an historic turn in United States policy. (Not in the sense, however, that Daniel Flood alleged. To the unreconstructed Rooseveltian Rough Rider, LBJ's policy marked the triumph of the "Bolshevik Revolution of 1917 and the international communist conspiracy.") Johnson's timing was also a political masterstroke. Despite fulminations from a few such as Flood, the President received overwhelming support from the public, particularly from editorials in leading newspapers.

Part of Johnson's political success may have been due to the care with which he had the Central Intelligence Agency track down former President Eisenhower, then on a westbound train out of Chicago, to clear the policy with him, even down to the use of Eisenhower's name at the opening of the public announcement. LBJ also obtained Truman's public support. At the same time he showed Panama his high cards by downplaying the long-run importance of the present Canal. He announced the United States would start negotiations with four governments (Colombia, Nicaragua, Costa Rica, and Panama) for a sea-level route.[19]

A tough United States negotiating policy was outlined by Johnson's National Security Adviser, McGeorge Bundy, in a secret National Security Action Memorandum of December 28, 1964. Bundy observed that until the sea-level canal was built a new pact would have to govern the present waterway. Above all, that treaty must give the United States full power to protect and operate the Panama Canal "until it is replaced." The agreement would also "recognize Panama's sovereignty over the Canal and would provide for a termination date" for North American rights, but that date could only be after the sea-level canal opened. And even after the new canal began operations, the United States would retain a large military presence in Panama by negotiating a "new defense facilities agreement."[20]

Examining these "principles" a quarter century later, they appear idyllic. After 1970 the United States could not realistically hope for such

19. Lester D. Langley, "U.S.-Panamanian Relations since 1941," *Journal of Inter-American Studies,* XII (July 1970), 363; Philip Geyelin, *Lyndon B. Johnson and the World* (New York, 1966), p. 274.
20. "National Security Action Memorandum," Dec. 28, 1964, from Bundy; and "Memorandum for Mr. McGeorge Bundy," by Thomas C. Mann, Dec. 28., 1964; both in Executive File, Panama, LBJ Papers. The Eisenhower story is recounted in John A. McCone to Johnson, Dec. 17, 1964, Executive File, Panama, LBJ Papers.

concessions as control of the present Canal through the remainder of its life, or an indefinite military presence in Panama. The military chiefs in the Pentagon obtained all they could have wished. Bundy's paper did recognize the need to acknowledge Panamanian sovereignty in the Zone. This "principle" alone made the memorandum historic. Later another White House aide and State Department legal experts re-examined the question and agreed that officially the United States "has never claimed sovereignty in the Canal Zone" and "We have never had sovereignty."[21] But Bundy's "principles" granted Panama only the shell of sovereignty, while retaining control of the Panama Canal in Washington's hands. The NSC policy did not differ significantly from Theodore Roosevelt's approach when he dismissed the sovereignty issue as less important than ensuring United States control of the Canal.

That point ultimately occurred to the Panamanians. After eighteen months of talks the United States and Panama unveiled three treaty drafts in June 1967. One pact outlined arrangements for a possible sea-level canal. A second provided for the defense and neutrality of the present waterway, while the third set new ground rules for operating it. The United States explicitly recognized Panama's right to exercise sovereignty over the Canal, integrate the Zone into Panama, and receive a larger portion of the Canal's revenue. The entire Zone would revert to Panama in 1999. The Panamanians had long demanded those concessions. But in return they provided *quid pro quos*. The Zone would be operated by a commission comprised of five North Americans who could theoretically outvote four Panamanian members. A dual court system of one North American and one Panamanian would be established. United States military bases would remain until 2004 and their leases could be renewed.

Robles immediately came under fire in the National Assembly. The makeup of the Commission and the long-term bases were unacceptable to nearly all factions. The two leading candidates for the 1968 presidential election, David Samudio and the omnipresent Arnulfo Arias, condemned the treaty. Robles desperately sent an emissary to Washington for new concessions, but he returned empty-handed. Johnson would offer nothing more. His resolve was perhaps stiffened by a remark from General Robert W. Porter, commander of the U.S Southern Command stationed in the Zone. To abandon Panama in this "most critical period in the fight against Communism in Latin America," the General pro-

---

21. James R. Jones to W. Marvin Watson, Jan. 17, 1967, Executive File, Panama, LBJ Papers.

claimed," . . . would be contrary to the best interests of Panama, the United States, and the free world." For good measure Porter indicated that more, not fewer, bases were required, and that fears of an arms race in Latin America were only "a figment of the imagination."[22] Little flexibility remained in the United States position.

The Irony of the Alliance for Progress

Another confrontation over the Zone was developing. As in the 1930s and 1950s, it had to be understood in the context of the Panamanians' belief that only the power to tap the Canal's resources could save them from impending economic disaster.

The State Department and such powerful members of Congress as Leonore Sullivan had hoped the Alliance would strengthen the country's economy so the Zone would lose its interest to Panamanians. The strategy not only fizzled, but the results backfired. The failure grew in part from Johnson's growing disillusionment with the Alliance ("a thorough-going mess," one LBJ aide described it), his general disenchantment with Latin American officials ("The OAS," the President complained privately, "couldn't pour piss out of a boot if the instructions were written on the heel"[23]), a growing reluctance to work in the long shadow of the Kennedys and their pet ideas ("the touch football crowd isn't making the decision around here anymore," Johnson growled), and his intense preoccupation with Vietnam.

The Alliance's progress was questioned early. Between 1961 and the Panama riots of January 1964, seven constitutional governments in Latin America fell to military coups. Washington's good intentions in such areas as tax reform were deflated by highly publicized Latin American cynicism: "You know, Brazil's growth is based in part on *not* paying taxes," one South American told *Time* magazine. "If we paid, the government would spend it on foolishness like the army. . . . Taxation is an Anglo-Saxon fetish."[24] North Americans began to agree with the cynicism. The *Wall Street Journal* mourned the 1964 riots, then drew the conclusion: "This disgraceful business ought to be a sharp reminder to all the sentimentalists who believe we can uplift Latin America, and be loved for it, simply by handing out billions of dollars."[25]

22. Quoted in *Latin America*, I (Oct. 20, 1967), 206.
23. Goldman, *Tragedy of LBJ*, p. 89; Geyelin, *Johnson*, p. 254.
24. *Time*, Jan 31, 1964, p. 15.
25. *Wall Street Journal*, Jan. 13, 1964, p. 14.

Johnson was moving to that position. Applying with vigor the "muscle and common sense" approach of his chief Latin American affairs adviser, Thomas Mann,[26] LBJ landed 22,000 troops in Santo Domingo during May 1965 to destroy the prospect (already highly unlikely), that a Castro-type regime would come to power. Such use of force, contrary to United States assurances solemnly made when it signed the OAS charter of 1948, delivered a shattering blow to the staggering Alliance program. Johnson and Congress cut Alliance funds nearly 40 percent over the next two years. Vietnam was swallowing those resources, but LBJ and Mann also agreed that Latin America must depend on private, not governmental, monies. Private United States capital, however, was far from sufficient to reach Alliance goals.

Not all the blame could be laid at Washington's door. In Panama the ruling oligarchy was not known for unselfishness or a dedication to correcting glaring socio-economic inequities. Consequently, although Panama enjoyed a large influx of United States funds and one of the three highest growth rates in Latin America between 1961 and 1969 (a rate that doubled from the 1950s to an 8.1 percent annual average), the foundations of the economy remained weak. And although it boasted the highest per capita rate of economic growth during the 1960s of any Latin American nation, inequality and poverty also continued to grow.[27] The figures revealed deeply rooted economic and social crises.

Item. Per capita income in 1966 was $531, but 5 percent of the population received more than one-third the income. Half of the employed were farmers, and a large majority of farmers earned less than $100 annually. (Such inequity was not peculiar to Panama. United Nations figures showed that of the $100 per capita increase in Latin American income during the 1960s, only $2 reached the poorest 20 percent of the people.[28])

Item. While experts believed Panama should have been a net exporter of food, the country spent $12 million in 1968 to import staples. Lack of transportation in the interior, inequitable land holdings, and archaic agricultural methods were to blame, and so was the oligarchy's educational system. One scholar compared Panama's farming methods "with those existing in the time of the Pha-

26. Goldman, *Tragedy of LBJ*, p. 89.

27. Organization of American States, Inter-American Economic and Social Council, *Latin America's Development and the Alliance for Progress* (Washington, D.C., 1973), pp. 40, 334–335.

28. Commission on U.S.-Latin American Relations, *The United States and Latin America: Next Steps. A Second Report. . . .* (no place of publication, 1976), p. 22.

raohs,"[29] yet of the 6700 students in the National University, one-third studied Liberal Arts and one-fiftieth studied agriculture.

Item. Panama possessed over 2000 manufacturing firms, but only sixty employed 50 or more laborers, and these sixty—owned almost entirely by a few oligarchs and/or foreigners—accounted for 61 percent of the nation's manufactured products in value.

Item. The largest employers were the government (30,000 employees), the Canal Zone (13,000), and the United Fruit Company (11,000). The government provided the most lucrative, if inefficient, employment in the country, but mostly for those of oligarchical or skilled middle-class background who chose the right side in the presidential elections. Canal Zone employment had dropped steadily since 1945. The United Fruit Company had grown so large and powerful (providing the country's leading export by producing three pounds of bananas annually for every person in the United States) that the Panamanian government could not control it.

Item. Although the economic growth rate spiraled upward, unemployment reached 25 percent in 1966. The jobless congregated in the already congested slums of Panama City and Colon. The population meanwhile grew an incredible 3.3 percent annually nationwide, and over 4 percent in the urban areas. The picture was grim, and the oligarchy did little to brighten it other than blame the problems on United States control of the Canal Zone.

The oligarchy was careful not to condemn the North Americans for dominating the Panamanian economy itself. The elite was so closely integrated into—or dependent on—United States capital and markets that the oligarchs remained nabobs in an informal North American colony. Panamanians held 48 percent of the nation's investment in terms of value. United States citizens controlled 50 percent, including Panama's electric power and telephone services, oil refineries, and bananas, its leading export.[30] Many large Panamanian-held firms, such as dairy and food processing, depended on markets in the Zone or the United States. These companies certainly could not find sufficient markets in the impoverished cities or peasant-dominated provinces, even if the peasants could have been reached.

As the United Nations investigation of 1956 had prophesied, either

29. Larry L. Pippin, "Challenge in Panama," *Current History,* L (January 1966), 5.

30. Carl R. Jacobsen, "Basic Data on the Economy of the Republic of Panama," *Overseas Business Reports,* June 1968 (Washington, D.C., 1968), pp. 8–14; Xabier Gorostiaga, *Panama y la Zona del Canal* (Buenos Aires, 1975), pp. 52–58.

radical governmental intervention or an additional large amount of cash from the Canal was needed to pump-prime the economy. Neither was on the horizon. Tourists and markets associated with the Canal accounted for nearly one-third of Panama's gross national product, bridging almost single-handedly the huge gap between the country's large imports, such as food, and its exports. But in North American hands, the Canal's value to Panama remained limited. Despite a fifteenfold increase in traffic since 1914, the United States refused to raise the tolls, set when the passageway first opened, so Panama could receive a larger annuity. After the 1964 riots a number of Zonians who operated the Canal talked of early retirement. For a brief moment Panamanians hoped they might be trained for these jobs. The hope vanished as the Canal Company continued to recruit heavily in the United States for the higher-paying positions.

Out of choices, Chiari and Robles followed the usual line of least resistance and accelerated government spending. They wrote the budgets in red ink until creditors were reluctant to allow further borrowing. United States governmental loans helped, and the office that operated the Alliance for Progress, the Agency for International Development (AID), stepped in to take up some of the slack left by the exhausted Panamanian treasury.

AID worked closely with the "Plan Robles," pumping in over $65 million between 1964 and early 1968 to boost agricultural production and slow the rural-to-urban migration. The Alliance, however, demanded in return that an equitable tax system be created and enforced. Only a completely revamped system could close the gaping budget deficits. And only through an enforceable tax structure could the oligarchy be made more responsible—perhaps even saved from its own myopia.

It was a classic collision. United States officials, determined to promote evolution before revolution endangered their nation's interest in Panama, opposed a small oligarchy which wanted nothing to disturb the status quo. The scene was played out repeatedly in Latin America during the 1960s, but nowhere did United States prospects for success appear higher than in Panama, where Washington's power was overwhelming.

"Plan Robles" began auspiciously. Panamanians in the lowest income brackets traditionally paid a highly disproportionate share of the taxes, but now they received cuts. Larger incomes, particularly those in real estate, were taxed at higher rates. "It is not a new little tax law to patch up the already over-patched system." Robles warned. Alliance for Progress officials announced that the law was "one of the outstanding ones under the Alliance so far."[31] No one, however, anticipated what happened next, because apparently no one had thought through the effects a new tax law would have if it were actually enforced.

David Samudio was the Panamanian official responsible for carrying through the reforms. Samudio was a long-time bureaucrat and politician, a close friend of Robles, and the President's heir-apparent in the 1968 election. As expected in a man of his position, Samudio was sensitive to the delicacy of the situation. Washington wanted tax reform in return for its dollars; its dollars determined Panama's economic health; the economy's health would help determine Samudio's own political future; he therefore thought it wise to carry out large parts of the tax reform program. Samudio began to collect taxes from sugar refineries, an industry freed from taxes when established 35 years before, and whose millionaires continued to enjoy that freedom in the 1960s. He also focused on the booming, tax-immune cement industry.

Stunned by the actual imposition of taxes, oligarchs in sugar and cement joined with others in rebellion against the Robles-Samudio-Alliance program.[32] The President's Liberal Party coalition fragmented, but the effects of the reform did not stop there. The oligarchy itself further divided. Its headquarters, the Union Club in Panama City, had bounced back in the 1960s after enduring rough days during Remón's reign. Dedicated to the propositions of no more Remóns and no meaningful socio-economic change, the Club's members refused to remain united behind Robles. Some condescendingly pointed out that the President's own family was less a part of the oligarchy than merely related to it through the Chiari family's beneficence. Watching his political opposition self-destruct, Arnulfo Arias happily commented that Panama was "not yet a country but a tribal affair."[33]

As the fissures within the oligarchy threatened to engulf Robles, the President was left with few friends. The Panamanian leftists were politically impotent and unacceptable to Robles and Alliance officials. As the political situation became tense, the United States added the last straw—and several more for good measure. Congress reduced Alliance funds, and President Johnson announced in early 1968 another massive cut in developmental monies. United States banks simultaneously reduced foreign loans while the Inter-American Development Bank raised

31. Organization of American States, *Alliance for Progress Weekly Newsletter,* IV (Sept. 19, 1966), 3.

32. *Latin America,* II (March 29, 1968), 97–98.

33. *Wall Street Journal,* Oct. 18, 1968, p. 16.

its interest rates nearly 2 percent. Deserted by his political supporters in Panama City and, apparently, in Washington, Robles retained power only through the grace of the National Guard.

The Guard was not reluctant to demonstrate its authority. In 1966 students had rioted when one of their leaders, Juan Navos, was mysteriously murdered after his return from a trip to Moscow. The government never managed to find the murderer, but the Guard killed two students in smashing the riots. Two years later, Robles was threatened from the other direction. Working through the National Assembly, oligarchical leaders tried to impeach him on grounds that he was illegally using governmental monies to ensure Samudio's election. Condemning the impeachment proceedings as "a political pantomime," Robles refused to appear before the Assembly and instead appealed to the Guard. The army upheld the President, then paraded its power by raiding opposition party headquarters, arresting nearly 500 people, and keeping the Assembly from further mischief by prohibiting it from convening. The Guard commander, General Bolívar Vallarino, had one overriding aim: prevent Arnulfo Arias from gaining power. The Guard officers vividly remembered Arias's attempts in 1941 and 1950 to destroy their power by creating his own police force. That "coffee planter with the silver tongue," Vallarino declared, would not have a third chance.

But in the May 1968 election the oligarchy remained badly divided. Important members, including former President Chiari, joined Arias against Samudio. For two hectic weeks the National Election Board desperately tried to find enough votes for Samudio. Pro-Robles forces murdered an *Arnulfista* in an attack on a radio station, one student was killed attacking Samudio's headquarters, a National Guardsman was shot to death, and the Minister of Government and Justice's bodyguard was gunned down.[34] Samudio's supporters meanwhile grew discouraged. "We can do away with 25,000 [pro-Arias votes]," one remarked dejectedly, "but how can we get rid of 50,000?"[35] In the end they could not. Vallarino and the Guard announced they would support the duly-elected President. Why Vallarino switched became apparent when Arias assumed power.

Attempting to reform the oligarchical system, Robles and Samudio underminded it. The Alliance for Progress produced many unexpected and unwanted results during the 1960s, but none more ironic than the help it inadvertently gave in dividing an already tottering oligarchy and

34. Minor, "U.S.-Panamanian Relations: 1958–1973," pp. 214–215.
35. *Christian Science Monitor,* May 21, 1968, p. 2.

enabling Arnulfo Arias to become President once again. But a greater irony followed.

The Coup

Robles became incensed when the United States welcomed Arias's victory. Washington's view was shaped by two factors: its concern for stability and tranquility, rather than bloody haggling over election results; and its perception that Arias had turned pro-North American, particularly in matters relating to the Canal.

Robles responded bitterly with an anti-Yankee campaign in governmental newspapers and broadcasts, even accusing the Central Intelligence Agency of planting agents in the National Guard to push Arias into power. Some United States journalists, also blamed for aiding the CIA and Arias, received death threats. Robles went too far in mid-June, however. He decreed that Panamanian flagships could initiate trade with Cuba, China, and North Vietnam—Communist countries with whom United States trade was outlawed. Five days later the government blandly announced it was rescinding the decree "in view of [Panama's] existing international obligations and the incidence of various economic factors."[36] Robles had apparently been reminded that it was not the Communist bloc which controlled his country's economy.

With Washington's blessing, Arias became President on October 1, 1968. He immediately moved to neutralize the National Guard. After all, if its acquiescence allowed him to gain power, its opposition could dismiss him—for the third time. Arias worked out a deal with Vallarino. The Guard commander agreed to step down in return, apparently, for a post in the prestigious Washington Embassy. Arias then elevated trusted friends into command of the Guard while sending other officers into retirement or, as in the case of Colonel Omar Torrijos Herrera, to such foreign posts as El Salvador. The President meanwhile recruited a presidential guard which would be under his personal power.

On October 11, Torrijos and other threatened Guard officers staged a coup. Arias fled into the Canal Zone. The military junta accused the President of plotting a dictatorship and the inclusion of Nazis and Communists in his government. The accusation was window-dressing. The Guard acted because Arias was rapidly reducing its power. The thrice-deposed President searched desperately for help and was embarrassed

36. *Latin America,* II (June 7 and 28, 1968), 176, 208.

(as was the United States), when no Latin American nation offered asylum. He finally flew to Washington. While driving in from Dulles Airport he decided to conquer the Panamanian Embassy. After completing that operation Arias suddenly appeared before startled officials of the OAS to demand the ouster of the junta. Washington, however, can be a cold town to those who have fumbled away power. ("Power corrupts," a United States official once observed, "but being out of power corrupts absolutely.") The dejected Arias finally left for the warmer climes of Miami.

The State Department was nearly alone in its sorrow. Expressing shock that "a constitutionally elected chief of state" might be deposed in Latin America, Secretary of State Dean Rusk cut diplomatic relations with Panama.[37] Given the number of coups that convulsed Latin America during the 1960s (including at least one, in Brazil, which the United States encouraged), it is difficult to believe that State Department principles remained that virginal. More to the point, the coup caught Washington with its storm signals down. The top three United States officials in Panama and the Canal Zone, including Ambassador Charles W. Adair, Jr., were out of the country on October 11. Their advisers had assured them that Arias was firmly in control.[38]

The junta, however, moved quickly to win Washington's friendship. The Guard promised to restore all constitutional rights and hold free elections. Panamanians appeared to accept the new government. The State Department expected street demonstrations, particularly after Arias clandestinely used Canal Zone radio facilities to urge his supporters into the streets. United States Army units went on alert. But nothing happened.

During the November 3d Independence Day celebration, however, an old hatred re-emerged. As nearly a thousand faculty and students protested Guard rule, armed troops attacked. Many students fled into a hospital for safety. The Guard followed, using rifle butts and hauling more than 200 off to jail. Panama University closed down and student leaders were arrested.

Secretary of State Rusk coincidentally announced United States recognition of the junta. An era ended in Panama, an era which began in 1903. Yet the October events marked not a revolution but a coup. The junta finished what began in 1931 when United States military withdrawal made the Guard the keeper of the peace, in 1941 when Guard

---

37. *Department of State Bulletin,* LIX (Nov. 4, 1968), 470.
38. *Christian Science Monitor,* Oct. 15, 1968, p. 4.

commanders first overtly determined who would rule, and in the 1950s when Remón transformed the Guard into a tool of reform. The cycle was completed in 1968 when the oligarchy committed political suicide.

It was fitting that Arias provided a brief, chaotic epilogue. The Guard then moved into full control. It now confronted the old vexation of an economy both lopsided and colonialized. The nation's prized resource meanwhile remained not only foreign-controlled, but newly stained with North American and Panamanian blood.

6
Torrijos, Kissinger, and Carter

On October 10, 1968, Omar Torrijos was unknown outside the Panama National Guard. Forty-eight hours later he emerged as a member of the junta governing the country. In a year he personally controlled Panama. Soon no Panamanian, or visitor to Panama, could long escape the General's stare, for as a virtual dictator (albeit a benevolent one compared with some Latin American rulers), his picture hung on a wall in every bar, restaurant, hotel, airline terminal, and store in the country.

Most photos showed Torrijos in full field uniform with a large pistol slung carefully but ostentatiously on his side. The picture perfectly captured unalloyed *machismo,* directly appealing to Panamanian tradition while unsubtly warning potential political opponents. As a North American remarked after looking at the picture, Torrijos appeared to be typecast by Hollywood to play the role of a Latin American general. He strikingly contrasted with some Panamanian politicans of the pre-1968 era. Appearances count for much in politics, nowhere more than in Panama, and to most Panamanians Torrijos at least appeared to be a radical and welcome change.

Behind the pose was a highly complex man. Torrijos was born in 1929 at Santiago de Veraguas, 115 miles from Panama City. As the son of teachers, he came from the country's small but ultra-nationalistic, ambitious, and anti-foreign middle class, the class that first challenged the oligarchy effectively, if briefly, in 1931. He learned to appreciate romantic poetry and the work of García Marquez, but even his admirers would later disclaim that he was an intellectual. Novelist Graham Greene was nevertheless impressed that in interviews "sometimes a touch of poetry appears unexpectedly and unnoticed by himself when he speaks." Greene's example of Torrijos's "poetry"—"Intellectuals are like fine glass, crystal, which can be cracked by a sound. Panama is rock and earth"[1]—actually demonstrated that the General usually employed "poetry" when it was useful politically.

At seventeen he left Panama to attend a military academy in El Salvador, then by avoiding the political minefields of the National Guard he rose through the ranks. Courses in counterinsurgency warfare at the Canal Zone's School of the Americas helped the young officer distinguish himself in the early 1960s when he fought guerrilla movements in Panama's interior provinces.

Consolidating Power

Young Torrijos did not rise to the top immediately after the 1968 coup. The two senior Guard commanders headed the junta, which included five civilian members as well as military officers. After three months, the civilians accused the Guard of establishing a dictatorship and resigned. By that time it was clear that, with the aid of younger officers, Torrijos—the Guard's Commander-in-chief—and Colonel Boris Martínez—the Chief of Staff—controlled the government.

In March 1969 Martínez appeared on television, and with the General Staff at his side announced a radical agrarian reform program. He also declared that the Guard would not halt nationalist anti-Yankee demonstrations. Torrijos instantly moved against Martínez. Supported by oligarchical elements, and apparently with United States encouragement, he exiled the Chief of Staff to a comfortable post in Washington. (Martínez never reached Washington; he angrily joined his erstwhile enemy Arnulfo Arias in Miami.)

The Martínez episode revealed Torrijos's priorities. He was by no means another Castro. The Commander refused to antagonize the

1. Graham Greene, "The Country with Five Frontiers," *New York Review of Books*, Feb. 17, 1977, pp. 10–11; *New York Times*, March 20, 1973, p. 4.

United States and he did not want to encourage demonstrations. Martí-nez's summons to the streets could have triggered a repetition of the 1964 riots, pitting Guard against students and, if events got out of hand, demonstrating that the new government was unable to maintain order. Torrijos preferred to coopt rather than arrest students. His nationalist proclamations and reform program soon allied those longtime enemies, the Student Federation and the Guard. Rumors in Panama City sug-gested that the Central Intelligence Agency helped Torrijos depose Mar-tínez; in any case, the United States shortly thereafter gave $15 million for improving the capital city's water supply, the first grant issued since the coup. Torrijos celebrated by promoting himself to brigadier-general.

He celebrated too soon. In December 1969 the new General was attending horse races in Mexico City when a group of Guard colonels, led by Amado Sanjur, and rightwing oligarchs announced that Torrijos had been deposed. Supported by loyal Guard garrisons in David, and helped by Nicaraguan dictator Anastasio Somoza—who provided a pri-vate plane—Torrijos returned to Panama City, overthrew Sanjur, exiled the dissident colonels, and reclaimed his power. A State Department official later speculated that Torrijos actually invited the Sanjur coup in order to draw his conservative opponents into the open, where he could destroy them politically.

Maximum Chief and the Forty Thieves

The General shrewdly appointed a civilian, Demetrio Lakas, as provi-sional President. An engineer as well as politician, Lakas was highly regarded by some oligarchs and most North American businessmen. In reality, power lay in the upper echelons of the army, now an impressive praetorian guard of 6000 men, comprised mostly of blacks or, like Torrijos himself, middle-class mestizos. The Guard's elite groups, the Tigers and Pumas, were disciplined, well equipped, and intimidating. Since Remón built the Guard it had infiltrated most important facets of Panama's life. In the words of one observer, "Its intelligence is said to be omniscient, so that people think twice before telling anecdotes about it."[2] Torrijos consolidated his power by giving the Guard higher salaries. He also transformed the oligarchy's posh Union Club into a recreation center for Guard members and their families. (The old Union Club membership reinstalled itself in luxurious facilities on Paitilla Point,

2. Morris, "Terminal Case of American Perpetuity," p. 48.

where it again commanded a magnificent view of the Pacific, this time in a safer neighborhood of Panama City. The Union Club's reincarnation was an omen.)

Torrijos declared all political parties illegal. The Communists had been outlawed since 1950; other leftists were singularly ineffective. In late 1969, however, left-wing leader Floyd Britton was assassinated by unknown gunmen; urban guerrilla groups retaliated by forming the National Liberation Movement. After the Movement robbed a number of banks and casinos, the Guard trapped its leaders in 1970, killing two Cuban-trained members. A wave of repression accompanied this campaign.[3] Newspapers were either self-censored or shut-down. The government controlled radio stations, using its communications monopoly to urge that any "suspicious persons" and "important information" be reported instantly to the Guard. Estimates of political prisoners ran as high as 1600, and 200 reportedly remained in jail in mid-1971.[4]

In late 1968 the junta had promised open elections, but in 1971 the pretense was dropped. Torrijos publicly condemned the political processes developed by the oligarchs during the previous seventy years. "They allege that we are illegitimate because we are not born out of one of those things they call elections," the General proclaimed to a large Panama City rally. "This is precisely our greatest pride . . . not acquiring credentials of their kind, because we prefer the clean credentials of your support and not the one hundred credentials of their kind which are rolled in the mud."[5]

Torrijos refused to recognize the legitimacy of the oligarchy-ruled National Assembly. His feelings were best revealed when a close associate called it "Ali Baba and the Forty Thieves." That was probably a reference to the aftermath of the 1968 coup, when 24 of the 53 members of the Assembly joined Arias in fleeing the country.[6] The old Assembly was replaced by a new 505-member Assembly of Municipal Representatives. The delegates are elected at the local level in balloting controlled by the Guard. It meets once a year for one month to report on regional activities and vote on legislation. When the first Assembly convened in 1972 (in a Panama City gymnasium), its main order of business was to

3. Donald C. Hodges, *The Latin American Revolution* (New York, 1974), p. 222.
4. *Wall Street Journal*, June 17, 1971, p. 29.
5. Quoted in Steve C. Ropp, "Military Reformism in Panama: New Directions or Old Indications," *Carribean Studies*, XII (October 1972), p. 62; also Omar Torrijos Herrera, *Una Revolucion Diferente* (Panama City, 1972), pp. 81, 107.
6. *Latin America*, Oct. 18, 1968, p. 329, and Jan. 23, 1970, p. 31.

make Torrijos "Maximum Chief." Lakas continued in the subordinate role of President.

The Assembly also approved a new constitution to replace the 1946 document. It is required reading, especially between the lines, for an understanding of contemporary Panama. The constitution officially recognized the Guard as a governing body and flatly declared that "The Government alone may possess arms and implements of war." The "penalty of death, expatriation, or confiscation of property" was disallowed, but otherwise "public officials" enjoyed considerable discretion (to say the least), for they could "impose fines or arrest upon anyone who insults them or who is in contempt of their authority." That clause made mass roundups and arrests constitutional. Torrijos had now seized immense power. The days of oligarchical rule and legislative power were apparently over. An all-powerful executive, his authority resting on the National Guard, ruled Panama constitutionally.

The document allowed the Maximum Chief and his government to extend their reach into the far corners of Panamanian society. "The State" assumed the right to "oversee the rational distribution of land" and not allow "uncultivated, unproductive or idle areas." Although "engaging in economic activities is primarily the function of private persons," the supreme law directed "the State" to "guide, direct, regulate, replace or initiate such activities" as it thought the national economy required. "The State" also acquired the power to protect "marriage, motherhood, and the family," possessed "exclusive competence to organize and direct education," and, for good measure, was instructed to defend "the purity of the Spanish language."

The last proviso hinted that state power would be especially sensitive to North American presence. The constitution did not recognize a United States-controlled Canal Zone. It declared illegal the ceding of national territory to any foreign country; it provided that utility corporations and the Roman Catholic Church hierarchy be controlled by Panamanian citizens, and even set rigid restrictions on foreigners who planned to enter retail businesses.[7]

The old, open, laissez-faire Panamanian economy was to be transformed. The constitution indeed gave the government power to make radical changes throughout the system. Torrijos's far-flung authority raised the fundamental question of what he represented: a Castro-type departure or the surfacing of long-term trends?

7. Organization of American States, *Constitution of Panama 1972* (Washington D.C., 1974), especially pp. 5–7, 11–12, 15, 38–40, 43–44; for the weakness of Panama's public sector before the mid-1970s, Gorastiaga, *Panama y la Zona*, pp. 52–53.

In important respects the General seemed to belong to a 150-year tradition of the Latin American *caudillo* who assumed power when his nation began to free itself of the mother country. He usually emerged from army officer ranks, used arms to force civilians into line, and displayed the authoritarian attitudes of the military. The traditional *caudillo,* like Torrijos, often seized authority in a nation whose development had been stifled by excessive legalism, inefficient and corrupt civilian regimes, inequitable income distribution, deep racial antagonisms, and geographical obstacles which made the functioning of a truly national government highly difficult.[8] In such "stateless" societies (which Panama resembled), the weakness of the central government had allowed the rich to become richer and the poor to die young. *Caudillos* filled the political vacuum with military authority and built a popular base by promising the poor a better future. Torrijos thus resembled those numerous Latin American rulers who, far from being ideology-bound and left-wing, created personal, pragmatic, and authoritatian regimes with which the United States profitably cooperated.

Although Arnulfo Arias approximated the civilian version of the stereotype, a *caudillo* had never ruled Panama, but many aspects of *caudillismo* were common in Panamanian political life. Leadership on the Isthmus was traditionally based on personal, charismatic authority rather than on written rules or cohesive party systems. The President enchanted the masses if he conformed to "the virtuoso standard of masculine behavior" (as two students of Panama phrased it), appeared to be daring, and—at least since the 1930s—opposed United States domination.[9] Torrijos's style and some sources of his authority were therefore rooted in an appeal common to the Arias brothers, or even Porras of sixty years before.

But Torrijos also represented something different, a phenomenon perhaps best called a "new *caudillismo.*" For although his authority rested on the army and personal charisma, he had to deal with masses who were conditioned by new media, urbanization, anti-imperalism, and Fidel Castro's long shadow, problems that did not complicate the lives of the old *caudillos.* The new *caudillismo* therefore assumed populist aspects, as Torrijos perfectly exemplified when he condemned the Na-

8. General characteristics of *caudillismo* are taken from William H. Beezley, "Caudillismo: An Interpretive Note," *Journal of Inter-American Studies,* XI (July 1969), 345–352; Edwin Liewen, *Arms and Politics in Latin America* (New York, 1961), pp. 22–24; Eric R. Wolfe and Edward C. Hansen, *The Human Condition in Latin America* (New York, 1972), pp. 223–224.

9. Biesanz and Smith, "Panamanian Politics." pp. 389–393.

tional Assembly for selling out to the rich, and claiming that his power rested on mass support. His government's monopoly of the media ensured that the masses heard the proper message.

Resting power on the barrel of a gun, as had traditional *caudillos,* was one thing. But basing power on rifles, excitable middle-class university students, and masses suddenly experiencing the twentieth century was playing with fire. Particularly when a new *caudillo's* power ultimately depended on his ability to confer largesse, continually and in considerable amounts, upon those soldiers, students, and masses, his political base could erode quickly. Unless Torrijos could create new wealth internally, his future would depend on his ability to deal with ultimate power in Panama—the United States and its control of Canal revenues.

School of the Americas Radicalism

Close observers of Panama therefore understood that trying to pigeonhole Torrijos as a "Marxist" or a "reactionary" was useless exercise. His bases of power and his needs were too complicated for such simple categorization. And so was his program that began unfolding in 1969. He announced plans for massive structural reform in agriculture, including large-scale land distribution. Direct governmental interference in other areas of economic life aimed at stimulating both productivity and what was termed "social progress." The plans promised, in the words of a knowledgeable foreign observer, "a thorough-going revolutionary reform that would for the first time create a real nation out of Panama."[10] But to some it all too uncomfortably resembled Fidel Castro's Cuba in early 1959. Tremors were felt in Washington and oligarchical neighborhoods of Panama City. Panamanian businessmen pointedly suggested to North Americans that since they had allowed the General to assume power, they were responsible for deposing him.

The inspiration for Torrijos's reforms, however, was not Cuban. Nothing provided a better key to the General's politics than to understand that his program was inspired by that anti-Castro, counterinsurgency institution, the School of the Americas. Founded in 1949, the institution produced 34,000 graduates by the mid-1970s.[11] The

10. *Latin America,* Aug. 15, 1969, pp. 260–261; on the other hand, see the succinct statement by Torrijos in his *Una Revolucion Diferente,* p. 109.
11. The analysis of School of the Americas is based upon Ropp, "Military Reformism in Panama," pp. 45–57; Kahn, "Letter from Panama," p. 74; Joanne Omand in *Washington Post,* April 11, 1977, p. A16; Richard Gott in *ibid.,* April 16, 1977, p. A10:5–6; and author's interviews.

Panamanian Guard provided 3500, or the fourth highest number, of these graduates, ranking ahead of Brazil, Colombia, and Venezuela. Of the top 24 Guard officers in 1971, 19 attended the School. Torrijos was a proud graduate. As Maximum Chief he nevertheless demanded its removal since its presence violated United States pledges, made solemnly in the 1903 treaty, that any North American military installation would be for the sole purpose of protecting the Canal. The School of the Americas was for a considerably broader purpose of fighting insurgents throughout the hemisphere. Torrijos described it as "this great colonial encampment." On the other hand, his old school ties were such that he admitted Panama profited from the treaty violation, and he frequently visited the institution, taking students on tours of Panama in his helicopter.

The courses taught military officers to forget the old *caudillismo* and instead make their country immune to communism, not enrich their bankrolls. They learned that only military discipline could create the order needed for such development. Civilian politics were too compromising, chaotic, and corrupt. Through such courses as "Interrogation Techniques" and "Urban and Rural Counterinsurgency Concepts," the graduates learned to check both the greed of the right and the revolutionary ardor of the left so the state could benefit.

In the 1970s all of Central and South America was under military rule except Colombia, Venezuela, Costa Rica, and Mexico; nearly all the officers who assumed power were graduates of the School. As students who learned their lessons well, they demanded national discipline regardless of the effect on human rights. (The lessons were so well learned that many Latin American leaders were confused in 1977 when President Jimmy Carter began to emphasize human rights instead of fighting terrorists.)

As a new *caudillo,* Torrijos believed Panamanian development required the destruction of politicial parties, the National Assembly, freedom of the press, the rights of some private-property holders, and the jobs of perhaps 4000 useless, oligarchy-appointed bureaucrats. Some Panamanians expressed concern about such a tradeoff. A businessman worried in 1971, "For peace and prosperity we are giving up certain intangibles, like freedom of speech and other political rights. How soon we get to the point where the sacrifice of intangibles no longer is equal to the tangibles we have gained is the big question."[12]

Torrijos provided his own perspective in a remarkable letter to Sena-

12. *Wall Street Journal,* June 17, 1971, p. 25.

tor Edward Kennedy in 1970. After Castro, the General wrote, "there was a new orientation. We had more contact with people." "There was a preoccupation with social forces" in officer training. After encountering John F. Kennedy and the Alliance for Progress, Torrijos continued, the military became "well prepared professionals with good intentions, that speak, think, and live the language of development" which Kennedy inspired. Then came a revealing phrase: "[in studying Castro and Kennedy,] we came to the conclusion that there was a direct relationship between social justice and social violence."[13]

To achieve "social justice," Torrijos instituted two innovations that left a profound mark on his country. The first stressed massive governmental intervention in the economy. Multi-year developmental programs dated back to the 1960s, but they so depended on the private sector for leadership that the Chiari-Robles administrations remained out of many areas (such as public utilities), that in market-oriented Western Europe had long since been absorbed into the governmental sector. Panamanians were (and, as Torrijos would discover, continue to be) among the most dedicated of any Latins to private enterprise and laissez-faire capitalism. The relative absence of Spanish feudal traditions, and the fluidity resulting from four centuries of constant population movement across the Isthmus, encouraged individual enterprise.

The new *caudillo's* use of governmental power was consequently trailblazing and, to some, ominous. His regime sponsored urban housing projects and large apartment and office complexes in downtown Panama City. Fresh legislation increased personal and corporate taxes, especially on corporate dividends, to pay for the construction. For both political and economic reasons, Torrijos promulgated a labor law in 1972 that became the symbol of his "revolution." The old marketplace relationship between capital and labor was suddenly replaced by a code, enforced by a strong Ministry of Labor, that regulated job conditions, established minimum wages, protected domestic servants, and made collective bargaining compulsory. Political motives were obviously involved. Torrijos hoped to make a strong labor movement part of his political base, much as Juan Pefon used Argentinian labor a quarter-century earlier to establish virtual one-man rule and propel himself into international prominence.

In a second innovation, Torrijos placed top priority on rural rather than urban development. Of all Panamanian Presidents, only Harmodio

13. Quoted in Ropp, "Military Reformism in Panama," p. 54. Torrijos even referred to his version of the Alliance as an inspiration; *Una Revolucion Diferente*, p. 106.

Arias and the late, unlamented Remón had focused attention on the interior provinces, and the impact of their policies proved to be minute. The oligarchy otherwise pumped money and governmental favors into the cities where its own interests lay. Torrijos's new policies were shaped by a condescending dislike of the oligarchy, as well as his hope that the agrarian sectors, like the labor movement, would form an ethusiastic part of his political base. The Guard, moreover, recruited heavily from the countryside. Its men knew first-hand that most peasants earned less than $100 annually, and that their starchy diet created protein/calorie malnutrition in more than 60 percent of all children under five. Raised in the interior, Torrijos had fought guerrillas with whom he strongly identified. He disliked their terrorism, but, as he later reflected, it was understandable why they hoped to emulate Fidel Castro.

In early 1969 the government announced that within three years it would distribute 700,000 hectares of land among 61,300 families, so that ultimately average holdings would multiply nearly five times per family. The expropriated landowners received "agrarian bonds" paying one percent interest and repayable in 40 years. Farm schools were established; contrary to oligarchical educational policy, half the student's time was devoted to practical lessons of farming. Torrijos's most striking innovation was to establish 270 farm collectives of nearly 35,000 people. The collectives were democratically self-ruled, shared profits, and provided with equipment, technical assistance, capital, and over 300,000 hectares of land by the government. As one reporter observed, the collectives seemed "a cross between an Israeli *kibbutz* and a cooperative." On one successful collective, individual annual income grew from $400 in 1972 to $1400 four years later. Considering the new experiment ready-made for political organizing, Marxists tried to infiltrate some of the collectives. The Guard forcefully stopped such attempts.[14]

More serious was the opposition to Torrijos's plans from the Roman Catholic Church, which for centuries had worked among the peasants. Father Hector Gallego, for example, organized peasant cooperatives in Sante Fe Province, but under the direction of the Church, not the government. Of perhaps equal importance, Gallego's efforts to make his flock more self-sufficient hurt the interest of a local merchant who happened to be Torrijos's cousin. In 1971 government agents visited Gallego. Shortly thereafter he disappeared and has never been found.

14. Edward Schumacher in *Washington Post*, July 18, 1976, p. F3; the malnutrition suffered in the interior is analyzed in Looney, *Economic Development of Panama*, p. 39. A hopeful Marxist analysis of the collectives is in B. Gonzalez, "New Trends in Rural Panama," *World Marxist Review*, XVIII (June 1975), 124–129.

Archbishop Marcos McGrath of Panama City condemned the government and excommunicated anyone who might have participated in the abduction. McGrath was not to be trifled with. A tall, imposing figure who headed the only independent socio-political organization of any importance left in Panama, the Archbishop was well known for his ardent nationalism. Long before Torrijos appeared on the scene, McGrath worked to bring the Canal under Panamanian control. He enjoyed important political connections in the United States. Torrijos consequently dispatched President Lakas to explain his side of the story to the Vatican. But the Maximum Chief bent no further, threatening to retaliate by prohibiting missionaries from entering Panama. The General won the battle. Although Panama is overwhelmingly Roman Catholic, it has a long tradition of Church non-interference in state affairs. Panamanians tend to see the Church as unconcerned with their problems of poverty and disenfranchisement. McGrath has tried to change that image, but he could not rally support against Torrijos in the Gallego case.[15]

The General's two new departures—widespread use of governmental power and emphasis on rural development—were dramatically illustrated in his handling of the North American gift to radical Latin American nationalism, the United Fruit Company. By 1970 the company was no longer an easy target for Latin anti-imperialists. It was subsumed into United Brands Inc., and the company's Panamanian subsidiary was known as the Chiriqui Land Company (CLC). During the 1960s labor unrest plagued CLC, so much so that the company began selling off land to Panamaians, while keeping the rights to buy and distribute whatever they produced. CLC also sold or gave over 5000 hectares of land to the government for redistribution. Its banana business meanwhile flourished, accounting for two-thirds of Panama's total exports in the late 1960s. Then Torrijos entered the picture.

In 1973–74 an economic downturn combined with poor planning to create severe problems for the General's programs. In early 1974 he sought involuntary help from United Brands. Under his leadership, the seven leading Latin American banana exporting nations agreed to impose new taxes of 40¢ to $1 on each 42-pound crate of bananas. Torrijos immediately imposed the maximum amount on Panama's exports. The several companies affected bitterly protested and refused to pay the tax. Rumors circulated that they were plotting to overthrow the Honduran,

---

15. *Latin America*, Sept. 3, 1971, p. 281; J. Lloyd Mecham, *Church and State in Latin America*, (Chapel Hill, 1966), p. 339.

Panamanian, and Costa Rican governments. These rumors owed more to the memories of the 1920s than the realities of the 1970s. CLC, however did stop production. Several other nations cut back their exports. But the governmental ranks broke when Ecuador, the largest producer, and Nicaragua refused to impose the tax. They gathered in windfall profits by exporting large amounts of bananas. Torrijos was furious, threatening that if Panama lost the "banana war we shall throw our production into the Canal." In acts not unrelated to his anger, the General announced the uncovering of a plot to assassinate him during one of his trips to the interior, and in August 1974 mobs broke eighty windows of the U.S. Embassy.

Panama followed the toughest policy of any Central American producer, but in the end Torrijos was forced to compromise on a 45¢ tax. In 1976, however, the government expropriated CLC lands, leased 37,000 acres back so the company could maintain banana production, and required CLC to pay $2 million annually in rents, 50 percent tax on profits, plus the 45¢-a-crate export tax. (In the United States, meanwhile, customers wondered why they suddenly paid 25 to 50 percent more for bananas.) The remainder of the CLC land was to be given by the government to collectives. As for United Brands, the "banana war" helped expose questionable financial dealings within the company, dealings that apparently led its president to jump from the 42nd floor of the Pan American Building in New York City.[16]

From Revolution to Reality

The struggle against CLC revealed a glaring weakness in Torrijos's developmental program. He was forced to wage the "banana war" because funds were short. The problem was hardly new; it had threatened his plans from the beginning. During 1969 he stimulated the economy by pumping in $45 million of public investment, half from international banks. Another $50 million was borrowed from Swiss banks.[17] By 1972 debt service alone swallowed up a quarter of all governmental revenues. As credit sources were exhausted, economic growth shrunk from 8 per-

16. *Latin America*, Aug. 23, 1974, pp. 258, 260; *Wall Street Journal*, Jan. 9, 1976, p. 6; Thomas P. McCann, *An American Company: The Tragedy of United Fruit* (New York, 1976), pp. 215–219.
17. Minor, "U.S.-Panamanian Relations, 1958–1973," p. 225.

cent of the 1960s to under 4 percent in 1974. Along with other nations, moreover, Panama suffered from an inflation rate that shot up to 18 percent in 1973.

Panama's integration into the United States economy did not lessen the squeeze. Legally dependent on the dollar as the basis for their own currency, Panamanians had no choice but to buckle themselves up as United States inflation skyrocketed and the dollar value of their imports spiraled upward. They were consequently hit from two sides: North American goods cost more, and a less valuable dollar was used in their other international trade. Panama was so closely tied to the United States that it could control neither its currency nor, in many respects, its trade.[18]

The 1970 tax reforms proved insufficient for capital needs, but when new laws appeared in 1972 they imposed regressive rates on liquor, tobacco, cigarettes—taxes that especially hurt the lower classes. The law actually backfired, for it increased smuggling from the Zone to the point that although the measure doubled the tax on liquor, imported liquor revenues decreased. For Torrijos it was one more reason why Panama needed the Zone.

In formulating the 1972 tax program, Panamanian officials exhibited a necessary sensitivity to bankers in Panama City. Torrijos's dependence on them revealed the limits of his reform program. Only five foreign banks operated in the country in 1963, but 46 were there a decade later, and 74 by 1977. Bank assets tripled in the four years after 1967.

The turning point came with the 1970 banking law which made Panama the Switzerland of Latin America. Banks could be established with minimal requirements and funds whipped in and out of the country with no questions asked. The government helpfully imposed a lid on the interest rate paid domestic savings, but allowed other rates (for example, bank lending) to be determined by the vagaries of the marketplace. The 1970 law, combined with Panama's currency being interchangeable with the dollar, the country's excellent location, its foreign communications (which some bankers believed superior to London's), and its political stability made the Isthmus a banker's paradise. As the manager of a Dutch bank explained the operation, "We borrow in Europe, funnel money through Panama, and then lend it out to our

18. Harry Johnson, "Panama as a Regional Financial Center: A Preliminary Analysis of Development Contribution," *Economic Development and Cultural Change*, XXIV (January 1976), 286.

branches in South America. Because of Panama's laws, the profit we gain is tax-free."[19]

Only indirect benefits for Panamanians peeled off from the billions which traveled hurriedly through the country. Panama was at the banks' mercy, for it imposed no reserve requirements and consequently the institutions depended on policies made far from the Isthmus. If a parent bank weakened in Paris, or the London government forced a credit squeeze on British banks, the Torrijos government would be defenseless against the closing of Panamanian branches. One student of the system concluded that the 1970 law contributed little to the governmental tax revenues. "All things considered," his study ended, "the evidence does not lend much impressive quantitative support to the view that the growth of the financial sector is a powerful lever for promoting Panamanian economic development." But if a nationalist regime tried to control the nation's economy by cutting its ties to the dollar, the banks would close their doors and move elsewhere, while Panama's trade would be in chaos. The impact of the 1970 law on the internal economy is measurable: in 1960 local Panamanian banks controlled 70 percent of the deposits and 96 percent of loans in the country; in 1976 foreign banks controlled 91 percent of the deposits and 77 percent of the loans. The economy remained colonialized; only the forms were slightly altered.[20]

Torrijos's regime profited in one respect from the law: politically the measure placed the bankers squarely in the General's corner. The acid test occurred in 1973 when the economic downturn raised questions about the Maximum Chief's staying power. Stories circulated that Torrijos was about to share the fate of Chile's recently deposed president, Salvador Allende. At that point the Panamanian subsidiary of New York's First National City Bank created a banking consortium that loaned the regime $115 million to refinance the embarrassing national debt and maintain public investment rates.

The General soon returned the favor. At the bankers' request he rescinded his decree that threatened to impose restrictions on mortgage lending. Panamanian businessmen did not fare as well. When they planned a one-day strike to protest a three-year rent freeze and other discriminatory decrees, Torrijos proclaimed he would exile any pro-

19. *Wall Street Journal*, March 12, 1973, p. 6; Looney, *Economic Development of Panama*, pp. 96–97; Robin Pringle, "Panama, A Survey," *The Banker*, CXXV (October 1975), 1201; *Latin American Economic Report*, May 27, 1977, p. 78.
20. Johnson, "Panama as a Regional Financial Center," p. 284.

testor to Miami, "the valley of the fallen reactionaries of Latin America." There was no strike.[21]

His economic spokesman, Nicolas Barletta, had prophesied in early 1973 that the "excessive dominance of the Canal Zone would be broken" and "the country's dependence on the United States would be lessened."[22] The opposite occurred, and as Torrijos had to negotiate with the bankers, so he was forced to turn his attentions to the Canal.

History repeated itself not, as Karl Marx would have it, first as tragedy and then as farce, but repeated itself naturally and inevitably because Torrijos's Panama was ultimately as dependent on the Canal revenues for survival as was the Panama of Harmodio Arias, Remón, and Robles. Not only the country's greatest resource, the passageway was Panama's last hope.

Superficially the issue appeared unrelated to Torrijos's concern with the development of interior provinces. On one of his quick helicopter forays into the isolated interior, he supposedly asked a *campesino* what he thought about the Canal. *"Canal"* is Spanish for "channel," and since Panamanians are addicted to television channels two and four, the peasant replied, which *"canal—dos o cuatro?"*[23] The *campesino*'s immediate concerns were more closely tied to the waterway than he knew. Was cultivatable land needed for collectives or for orderly expansion of compacted Panama City and Colon? Then Panamanians noted that 51 percent of the Zone, or 250 square miles, was unused. (The United States employed 4 percent of the Zone for operating the Canal and 37 percent for military bases.) Was money needed in ever larger sums for developmental purposes? Panamanians observed that in 1969 the Canal's net income reached $15.6 million, but they received only one-seventh of the amount.

During his first four years in office Torrijos said little publicly about the Canal except in 1970 when, to no one's surprise, he declared the 1967 agreements dead and buried. In the autumn of that year he informed the Nixon administration that the Zone must be incorporated into Panama, a claim that led the *New York Times* to condemn Torrijos for bowing to undisciplined nationalism. Nixon, however, agreed to start discussions in 1971. Progress was agonizingly slow until 1973, when Torrijos, with economic problems closing around him, publicly demanded a radically new arrangement for the Zone. He caught United States foreign policy in the middle of a significant change.

21. *Latin America*, Oct. 26, Nov. 30, 1973, pp. 338–383.
22. Quoted in Looney, *Economic Development of Panama*, p. 5.
23. Kahn, "Letter from Panama," p. 69.

The Third Cold War

Since 1945 the United States has waged a long and often bloody Cold War. Three decades after its beginnings, however, the conflict appears to be not one but three different wars. The First, lasting from 1945 until the mid-1950s, pitted the United States against the Soviet Union in a world divided between the two superpowers. In the mid-1950s the Suez crisis, Eastern European revolts, and massive decolonization in Africa and Southeast Asia fragmented that "two-camp" world, ushering in an age of pluralism that provided the context for a major revision of United States-Panamanian relations.[24] After 1956 the United States dealt with many non-Soviet problems, and some of them, e.g., Vietnam and Castro, required close attention. Throughout the Second Cold War, North Americans continued to believe they possessed the military and economic power to solve or at least contain the problems on Washington's terms. Particularly in the economic arena, the United States appeared unchallengeable.

In the early 1970s a Third Cold War began. The Nixon administration continued to confront a host of problems relating to the ambitious, fragmented, developing nations of the southern hemispheres, but it no longer enjoyed overwhelming power to deal with them. The rapid decline of the dollar in 1970–71 and the success of the Arab oil embargo in 1973 revealed unexpected economic vulnerability. North Vietnam's triumph starkly displayed the limits of Washington's military and political power. The Third Cold War is consequently marked by highly complex problems and a growing inability of the United States to dictate solutions.

Richard Nixon understood this shifting balance of power. He hoped to gain time, and an honorable, perhaps triumphant, exit from Vietnam by playing off China against Russia in a delicate game of big power politics. Once the two Communist giants were sufficiently neutralized and the United States freed of the Vietnam morass, the logic of the Nixon policy ran, North Americans could deal with the developing nations to the south. Meanwhile Latin America would have to await developments in East-West relations.

Nixon accepted Johnson's approach to the Canal question. In the 1971–72 talks, the United States agreed to remove the "in perpetuity" clause and cede jurisdiction over the Canal to Panama at a definite date. The Panamanians would receive a large share of the revenues. Nixon,

24. See discussion in Chapter IV.

however, demanded United States control of the Canal for another fifty years, and, if a sea-level waterway was built on the site of the present Canal, for eighty years. Torrijos refused to allow Washington's control beyond 2003, a number which, for obvious historical reasons, began to have magical properties for Panamanians. Positions tightened, then the discussions halted.

Relations became critical, and in early 1973 *Newsweek* reported that two years before, the White House "plumbers" unit, now famous for the Watergate burglary and various other crimes, was assigned by unnamed top administration officials to kill Torrijos—because of his treaty demands—and other Panamanian officials who trafficked heroin into the United States. The "plumbers" were supposedly traveling through Mexico when the plans were cancelled.[25]

Other than the friendly bankers, Torrijos had little reason to show affection toward North Americans. United States relations with Panama, like those with many third world nations, were at their nadir in 1973 when Washington officials confronted a series of crises that symbolized the new Third Cold War: a growing realization that the Soviets were achieving military parity with the United States, the economic disasters slowly arising from the oil embargo, the final evacuation of Western troops from South Vietnam, and the withering effect Watergate exercised on those executive powers that directed Cold War strategies.[26]

The United States needed help, preferably from friends who would share their oil and raw materials at low prices. Latin America seemed an obvious candidate for a new partnership, but the Latins, to understate the case, were cool. Three years before, the Nixon administration not only refused to discuss long-term economic relationships, but declared virtual economic war by imposing a 10 percent surcharge on imports and attaching tough conditions on bilateral aid. In late 1973 the United States needed access to markets and raw materials in the south, and Secretary of State Henry Kissinger—who previously had pointedly ignored Latin America—moved to push aside political obstacles that impeded that access. Attempting to unclog diplomatic channels, Nixon and Kissinger asked for a "new dialogue." Few Latin Americans seemed anxious to respond. They were turning away from the United Stated to open relationships with Japan, Russia, Canada, and Western Europe. As Latins saw themselves as part of the southern third world rather than

25. *Newsweek,* June 18, 1973, p. 22.
26. Latin American policy is placed in this context in a speech by Assistant Secretary of State William D. Rogers in *Department of State Bulletin,* LXXIV (Jan. 5, 1976), 18.

a partner in the Western Hemisphere, the gap widened between South and North Americans.

Kissinger understood these changes. Noting that carrying on the "new dialogue" through regional diplomacy pitted the United States virtually alone against a Latin America that was acquiring a new identity, he switched to a divide-and-conquer bilateral diplomacy.[27] The United States would deal with one nation at a time. The limitations suddenly imposed upon North American power forced the employment of a rifle rather than the more prodigal shotgun approach. Even in Latin America.

The Seeds of a New Treaty . . .

In Panama, talks on the Canal issue were at a deadend. Many North Americans were pleased. In early 1973 the House Merchant Marine and Fisheries Committee, which exercised considerable power in Canal policy, announced that the United States must retain "undiluted sovereignty" in the Zone, then recommended that a special radio station be established to instruct Panamanians on the virtues of the status quo. A top State Department official dismissed stories that Torrijos might organize mass demonstrations against the Zone. If this occurred, the official believed, "it might show up the Panamanian authorities as being unable to control their own situation." (He did not dismiss the possibility, however, that spontaneous demonstrations could erupt.[28])

Torrijos shrewdly neutralized the mobs and appeased Panamanian nationalism by inducing the United Nations Security Council to hold a meeting in Panama instead of New York City. In the March 1973 meeting the General successfully focused world opinion on the Canal issue. Entering the Legislative Palace in Panama City, delegates could see on one side the city's steamy slums, on the other the Zone's air-conditioned bungalows and green fairways. (The did not see a restaurant formerly named "La Frontera," which bordered the Zone, for the government had "invited" the owner to change the name since it affronted "the sovereignty of Panama." Nor did the delegates see the nine-foot-high

---

27. Ben S. Stephansky, " 'New Dialogue' on Latin America: The Cost of Policy Neglect," in Ronald G. Hellman and H. Jon Rosenbaum, eds., *Latin America: The Search for a New International Role* (New York, 1975), pp. 153–157.

28. Stephen S. Rosenfeld, "The Panama Negotiations—a Close-Run Thing," *Foreign Affairs*, LIV (October 1975), 3–4; U.S. Congress, House, Subcommittee on Inter-American Affairs, Committee on Foreign Affairs, 93rd Cong., 1st Sess., *United States Relations with Panama* (Washington, D.C., 1973), p. 15.

fence in the Zone that had separated these two worlds; it was dismantled by U.S. officials when they learned of the meeting.)

The General did not intend to align himself with Russia or Cuba (he indeed assigned as the Spanish-speaking guide to the Soviet delegation a Hungarian who fought against the USSR during the 1956 uprising). Torrijos hoped instead to organize a broad international consensus against the United States. On March 21, thirteen of the Security Council's fifteen members supported a moderately phrased resolution that accepted Panama's view of the Canal problem. The fourteenth member, Great Britain, abstained. The fifteenth, the United States, killed the resolution by casting only its third veto since 1945. U.S. Ambassador John Scali explained that while his government wanted to continue negotiations, it refused to be "subjected to this kind of outside pressure." The resolution, moreover, ignored Washington's "legitimate interests."[29]

Torrijos made his point. Latin American support was particularly strong. President Carlos Andres Perez, of oil-rich Venezuela, later exemplified that support by asking, "How can the United States, which is a leader of democracy in the world, take a colonial's stance" on the Canal issue? Unless it was settled rapidly, he added, "Very bad relations will develop between the two Americas, North and South." Venezuela's emergence as the champion of Panama's case was significant. The Caracas government hoped to combine its surplus oil revenues with Panama's extensive banking facilities to create a launching pad for multinational corporations, under Latin American control, that could be used in the North-South dialogue on behalf of the poorer nations.[30] Kissinger's fear of a potent anti-Yankee bloc in Latin America was not misplaced. Relationships were further soured by Washington's aid to the Chilean army when it overthrew President Salvador Allende in 1973, and the 1974 publication of Philip Agee's *Inside the Company,* which detailed covert Central Intelligence Agency activities throughout Latin America. Traditional friendships began to chill.

Kissinger's alternatives were few. Plans for a sea-level canal, for example, provided Lyndon Johnson with leverage against Panama in 1967, but by 1974 the $3 to $4 billion cost virtually killed the project. New digging on a third lock system in the Canal itself would be more feasible. The leverage thus passed to Panama. Torrijos talked threateningly about the consequences if agreement was not soon reached. If a mob marched

29. Richard P. Stebbins and Elaine P. Adam, eds., *American Foreign Relations, 1973. A Documentary Record* (New York, 1976), pp. 134–139.

30. *Latin American Economic Report,* May 27, 1977, p. 78.

on the Zone, he announced, two alternatives would be available, "to smash it or lead it, and I'm not going to smash it."[31]

By 1974 the necessary conditions for fresh negotiations were in place. Washington's need for economic cooperation with Latin America, a growing anti-United States bloc among the southern nations, Torrijos's success in mobilizing world opinion, his desire (indeed his need), to cooperate with North American businessmen and bankers if the Canal question could be settled, the absence of the sealevel canal alternative—all of these developments finally resulted in an eight-point agreement between Kissinger and Panamanian Foreign Minister Juan Tack in February 1974. It marked a major step toward a final settlement.

The United States agreed to replace the 1903 treaty with a new agreement having a fixed termination date (instead of an "in perpetuity" clause). The Zone would disappear, and the area turned over to Panama in stages. The United States would retain specified rights in operating and defending the waterway during the life of the treaty, but Panama was to share in these functions and, at an undefined date, assume full responsibility for the Canal. In the interim, the Panamanians were promised a "just and equitable" (that is, greater) share of the revenues. These principles differed significantly from the Johnson demands of the mid-1960s. Washington retreated on nearly all the key points, starkly revealing the effects of the Third Cold War on United States foreign policy.

A United States negotiating team headed by Ellsworth Bunker began detailed discussions with the Panamanians. Bunker was nearly eighty years old, but his long international career in the sugar refining business, an almost equally long career as a top professional diplomat (who in his late 70s undertook the final negotiations with the North Vietnamese), and his fondness for Central American sun and risqué jokes made him a natural choice for the post.

. . . And the Frost of United States Politics: Snyder, Reagan, Ford

The Secretary of State soon found himself negotiating on two fronts. In March 1975 Bunker and the Panamanians deadlocked on three central issues: (1) The United States, under intense Pentagon pressure, demanded a 40- to 50-year lease, with possible renewal, for military bases

31. *Latin American Report*, II (November 1973), 6; *Wall Street Journal*, Aug. 21, 1975, p. 1.

to defend the Canal. Panama refused to allow any North American presence after 2003. (2) The two sides could not agree which, and how much, territory United States bases should occupy during the treaty's life. (3) No agreement could be reached on the specific duration of North American control over the Canal.

The first two items were the stickiest. Through the summer of 1975 an intense struggle ensued between the State Department and the Pentagon over the 50-year demand. The military won, and when talks resumed in Panama, Bunker renewed the offer of a 50-year lease with option to renew.[32] The talks again deadlocked.

Stymied on one front, Kissinger simultaneously faced an uprising on Capitol Hill. Even pro-treaty Congressmen complained that the State Department made no effort to keep them informed. News of the talks usually came from Panamanian sources. Congressmen who ardently wished to preserve the 1903 principles launched a public attack on Kissinger's policy.

In the Senate, Strom Thurmond (Rep.-S.C.) finally rounded up 38 signatures for a resolution declaring the United States must retain "sovereign rights" and full control in the Zone. Only 34 votes were needed to defeat a treaty, and Thurmond's signatories included chairmen and/or the ranking Republican members of a dozen important committees. The State Department was stunned; it had estimated that no more than 20 Senators would oppose a new treaty. On the Senate floor, Thurmond justified his resolution by arguing that the United States had purchased all the Canal lands "in fee simple." He attached a list showing that Washington paid $163,718,571 "for the land, rights, and titles to the Canal Company and the Canal Zone." His cosponsor, John McClellan (Dem.-Ark.), took another tack, arguing that since Panama "has seen 59 Presidents or different governments in the past 70 years," it was doubtful the country possessed the stability to operate and defend the Canal. McClellan added that the United States bore the burden of defending the Western Hemisphere. "We cannot do that by surrendering the sovereignty and control of the Panama Canal."[33]

In June the House of Representatives directly threatened the negotiations. The body was highly sensitive to the talks, partly because it possessed constitutional responsibility for passing on the sale or transfer of U.S. property in the Zone, partly because it was a hotbed of anti-treaty

32. Thomas M. Franck and Edward Weisband, "Panama Paralysis," *Foreign Policy*, no. 21 (Winter 1975–1976), 175–176.
33. James P. Lucier, "Another Vietnam?" *National Review*, Sept. 12, 1975, 989——990; *Congressional Record*, 93rd Cong., 2nd Sess., March 29, 1974. pp. S4729–S4734.

sentiment. A leading opponent of any new pact was Representative Gene Snyder (Rep.-Ky.) who proclaimed that "our sovereignty over the Canal Zone is as legitimate as our owning New York City." He was convinced that Torrijos formed one arm of a giant pincers movement controlled by Castro and the Quebec Liberation Front in Canada which aimed to snatch back the Canal in the South and the St. Lawrence Seaway in the north.[34] Snyder amended a State Department appropriation bill so no funds could be used for "negotiating the surrender or relinquishment of any U.S. rights" in the Zone. Without committee hearings or significant debate, it passed 246–164 on June 26, 1975.

The vote was widely interpreted as an indication that perhaps a majority of the House staunchly opposed significant concessions in a new treaty. A detailed analysis by Professor Joel Silbey of this and seven other House votes that followed made such an interpretation overly simplistic and revealed significant sources of pro-and anti-treaty feeling. Silbey found that the vote was the high-water mark of the anti-treaty contingent. Throughout the remainder of 1975 and into 1976, opponents of negotiations melted away until on June 18, 1976, they could round up only 12 votes to oppose a measure that took much of the sting out of the Snyder amendment. That ballot was also misleading, but Silbey could find only 121 Congressmen consistently supporting the extreme hardline position on negotiations, while a near majority 210 solidly and consistently voted in a way that could be interpreted as favoring Kissinger's efforts. The hard core opposition came mainly from Republicans and some Democrats representing southern, midwestern, and western districts. But the leadership, notably, was found in the near-majority favoring negotiations. Those most in favor of a new treaty were mainly Democrats and tended to come from outside the South. Gene Snyder and Daniel Flood received media attention because of their frothy attacks on Kissinger's policy, but neither seemed able to deliver significant numbers of votes from within their regional delegations or, in the case of Flood, from his own Pennsylvania group.

Silbey's analysis was preliminary and necessarily based on only eight roll-call votes, but it demonstrated that support for the Snyder-Flood position dwindled as Congressmen informed themselves on the issue (or, more likely, after they first immunized themselves from conservative attacks at home by voting for the Snyder amendment). The fall-off in the "anti" group was especially notable since it occurred during 1976 when

34. Stanley Karnow, "The Politics of Bluster and Ballyhoo," *Saturday Review,* July 24, 1976, p. 13.

Ronald Reagan used the Snyder-Flood approach to catapult himself into contention for the Republican presidential nomination. The analysis did not show, of course, the possible vote on an actual treaty. "Antis" would certainly number more than 12 and perhaps more than 140, but if the 1975–76 votes were indicative, the House contained a strong, near-majority pro-treaty core that solidly rested in the Democratic Party and the leadership of both parties.[35]

Kissinger's problem was less in the House than in the Senate, where he needed help quickly. He found it in Senators Hubert Humphrey (Dem.-Minn.) and Gale McGee (Dem.-Wyo.) In July 1975 Senator Harry Byrd (Ind.-Va.) prepared to introduce the Snyder amendment in the Senate. The Pentagon quietly but effectively tried to support Byrd's efforts. Humphrey and McGee nevertheless rounded up enough opposition votes so that Byrd decided not to push his proposal to a test on the floor. The two Senators' most effective argument, however—that the Senate should not interfere in the Executive's right to conduct negotiations—was hardly a ringing endorsement of Kissinger's policy. In September the Senate finally rejected Snyder's amendment by voice vote, and in conference with the House agreed only to warn the Secretary of State to protect the nation's "vital interests" in the Canal, not prohibit the negotiations. It had been a dangerous and ominous debate.

With his finger to the political wind, presidential elections only fourteen months away, and under severe Pentagon pressure, Kissinger committed a tactical blunder. Responding to a question from Governor George Wallace of Alabama, the Secretary of State declared in early September 1975, "The United States must maintain the right, unilater-

35. Silbey's analysis was based on eight roll-call votes that were brought together in a Guttman scalogram, a statistical device that orders legislative responses to an issue on a continuum from one extreme of opinion (in this case absolute intransigence against canal negotiations), to the other, successively marking off the groups of congressmen that fall in the various positions between these extremes. It has the virtue of including all votes in determining a legislator's position on an issue, rather than relying only on intuitively selected, and possibly unrepresentative, "important" votes. The eight votes scaled here concerned the Snyder amendment to a State Department appropriations bill. The votes are listed in the *Congressional Quarterly Almanac* for 1975 and 1976 (1975: pp. 808–809, 82-H, 126-H, 136-H; 1976 edition: pp. 241–242, 88-H.) The use of the scalogram in legislative analysis is explained and employed in Joel H. Silbey, *The Shrine of Party* (Pittsburgh, 1967). It should be noted that the Snyder amendment reappeared and was again voted on in the House during early 1977. It lost to a more mildly-worded substitute. The lines of division marked in the 1975–1976 voting had not changed. See *Congressional Quarterly Weekly Report,* May 7, 1977, pp. 882–884.

Unfortunately, Senate action on amendments comparable to Snyder's House amendments was by voice vote; individual responses could not be recorded and analyzed.

ally, to defend the Panama Canal for an indefinite future." Until this point he liked to argue that unless a new treaty was quickly completed, mobs would endanger United States interests on the Isthmus. He now made himself a prophet. His use of "indefinite" created a furor in Panama. No doubt on Torrijos's order, or at least with his permission, 600 students broke 85 windows in the U.S. Embassy and overturned cars parked around the building while the National Guard looked on. Without Kissinger's approval, Torrijos then released records of the three "conceptual accords" reached with Bunker. They showed that the United States had reneged on one of the eight Kissinger-Tack principles by insisting on indefinite control of the military bases.

At home and abroad the State Department's handling of the Canal issue was inept; indeed, dangerously so. And unlike the late 1930s, when President Roosevelt intervened to support the State Department against the military, President Nixon's appointed successor, Gerald R. Ford (former Republican Minority Leader in the House of Representatives), leaned toward the Pentagon view. While Ford wanted a treaty on the military's terms, Kissinger was willing to work for a more moderate agreement. The Secretary of State understood that military bases could not adequately protect the Canal against either sabotage or missiles. In the larger context he knew that settlement of the Panamanian question was a prerequisite to establishing the vitally needed economic partnership with Latin America.

As the 1976 presidential campaign progressed, negotiations continued in Panama, but on an inconsequential level. Torrijos realized that nothing could be accomplished for a year. Representative David Bowen (Rep.-Miss.) captured the feeling: "There is only one thing . . . that invariably makes [my constituents] cheer: 'I say that if we can keep the striped-pants boys out of it and leave the Canal to the Corps of Engineers, then things will work out fine.' "[36]

That insight was used by former California governor Ronald Reagan, who was fighting Ford for the Republican nomination. After setbacks in several primaries, Reagan listened to advisers who urged an uncompromising position on the Canal. He received a briefing on the issue from the exiled but ever-available Arnulfo Arias, who was searching for help in his campaign to bring down Torrijos. Calling Torrijos a "petty dictator," Reagan told enthusiastic Texas audiences that the Zone "is sovereign United States territory just the same as Alaska is and as the part of Texas that came out of the Gadsden Purchase and the states that were

36. Rosenfeld, "Panama Negoitations," pp. 11–12.

carved out of the Louisiana Purchase." The Zone "is ours and we intend to keep it."[37] Reagan suddenly began to win a string of primaries against an incumbent President. The Canal issue did not singlehandedly provide those successes (they occurred in states which were ideologically close to his domestic policies, and Ford's staff waged muddled, ineffective campaigns), but the waterway appeared to be an issue that catalyzed anti-Ford voters.

Reagan and his campaign staff indeed understood it was "a symbolic issue." "People sense in this issue some way, after Vietnam, and Watergate, and Angola, of reasserting the glory of the country," a top Reagan strategist believed. "People once more see a chance for Americans to stand up as Americans." The candidate himself thought the feelings aroused by Panama made "all the other issues possible."[38] It made little difference, as one high official of the Canal Zone privately remarked, that many North Americans were not sure of the Zone's location. Reagan appealed to the heart, not the head.

The challenger benefited politically, but his gains were limited, and the issue befogged, by Ford's tough position on the negotiations. The only difference between the two men seemed to be that Reagan wanted to keep the Canal without a new treaty and Ford planned to keep it through a new treaty. After Reagan won several primaries in April, Ford went so far as to repudiate publicly his own negotiator. Bunker had privately informed Congressmen that Ford, in writing, agreed to give up the Zone and the Canal after a long transition period. The President went on record "emphatically—that the United States will never [sic] give up its defense rights to the Panama Canal and will never give up its operational rights as far as Panama is concerned."[39] These words not only undercut key sections of the Kissinger-Tack principles, but reneged on the agreements already approved by Ford himself in the 1975 conceptual accords.

The President's image was further blurred to his political benefit when conservative Senator Barry Goldwater (Rep.-Ariz.) publicly agreed with Ford's approach and added, "I think Reagan would too if he knew more about it." The Senator thought the basic question was, "Are you willing to go to war over the Panama Canal?" When later asked how far he would actually go to retain the Canal, Reagan replied, "How far

37. Quoted in *Washington Post*, May 3, 1976, p. 11.
38. *Ibid.*, May 9, 1976, p. A6.
39. Captain Paul Ryan, USN (Ret.) "Canal Diplomacy and United States Interests," *U.S. Naval Institute Proceedings*, CIII (January 1977), 44, contains the Ford quotes.

would we go to stop someone from taking the state of Alaska?"[40] The former California governor, however, faced problems if he hoped to undercut Barry Goldwater from the right.

The Carter (and Kissinger) Consensus

Ford maneuvered himself into an untenable position that was too uncompromising to win over Torrijos, but too moderate to silence Reagan. He felt compelled to search out a consensus on the issue for domestic rather than diplomatic reasons, and the search continued after he secured the Republican nomination. In seeking that consensus, however, Ford was several steps behind his Democratic opponent. Jimmy Carter of Georgia searched out consensus with the alacrity of a choir director.

In a June speech to the New York Foreign Policy Association, Carter effectively worked both sides of the street. North Americans do not recall, he began, that Theodore Roosevelt's treaty "spelled out that Panama should have sovereignty over the Panama Canal Zone; that we should have control as though we had sovereignty." Then he crossed the road: "I would never give up full [sic] control of the Panama Canal as long as it had any contribution to make to our own national security." He recrossed: "I believe the Panamanians will respond well to open and continual negotiations and the sharing of sovereignty and control, recognizing their rights in that respect. I would certainly look with favor on the possible reduction in the number of bases . . . possibly a reduction in the number of military forces we have there."[41]

Resembling the fate of most foreign policy issues in election campaigns since the mid-nineteenth century, the Canal question played no important part in determining Carter's victory. The President-elect, however, placed it near the top of his diplomatic priorities. His Secretary of State, New York lawyer Cyrus Vance, believed a treaty based on the Kissinger-Tack principles was necessary in 1977. Vance's stout belief was notable, for the 1974 principles directly contradicted candidate Carter's avowal—as he said in the second televised debate with Ford—of "never" surrendering "complete control or practical control of the Panama Canal Zone." No doubt Vance's concern was sharpened by memories of his involvement as the Secretary of War who flew to Panama to stop the 1964 bloodshed and had to be protected from mob violence. Carter

40. *Washington Post*, May 3, 1976, p. 1.
41. *New York Times*, June 24, 1976, p. 22.

appointed Ellsworth Bunker and Sol Linowitz, a Washington lawyer and former U.S. Ambassador to the OAS, to lead the negotiating team. Linowitz fully agreed with Vance that the issue was a "high priority, urgent matter with a dangerous potential."

Linowitz advocated both a new, equitable treaty and a Latin American policy that harked back to the Good Neighbor approach. In reality he differed little from the post-1973 Kissinger policy toward the Americas. In 1968 Linowitz defined the United States role in Latin America as preventing conditions "in which despotism of the right can provide the foundation and impetus for a dictatorship of the left."[42] The ideal was apparently regimes which maintained order and whose center of political gravity was somewhere in the middle of the Latin American political spectrum. Torrijos was more complicated than that; his rule was not easily categorized along the "right-left" spectrum used by North American political analysts. But the General, despite censorship, exiling or jailing of political opponents, and refusal to hold general elections, maintained order and cooperated with the United States, even during such trying times as the 1976 campaign.

To Linowitz and Vance, as to Kissinger, Panama presented a small, if formidable, obstacle to be cleared on the way to the ultimate goal of developing a workable economic relationship with Latin America. President-elect Carter sounded the broad theme in an historic public hearing before the Senate Foreign Relations Committee when he announced, "The future, I think, of foreign policy might be changing," for there is a new "emphasis on economic matters."[43]

A month later a report appeared from the privately funded Commission on U.S.-Latin American Relations. Commission members included Linowitz as chairman, W. Michael Blumenthal, Carter's new Secretary of the Treasury, and Richard N. Gardner, ambassador-designate to Italy. The report repeated earlier Commission warnings that a fresh Latin American policy must "above all . . . be set in a consistent pattern of global economic policies" that would "make more stable and equitable the terms of exchange between the most industrialized" nations and those, "many of them in Latin America—which are rapidly expanding their participation in the world economy." The Commission saw clear sailing to realize "latent opportunities" in the Hemisphere, "except possibly in Panama." Otherwise, "no imminent threats to U.S. 'national secu-

---

42. Quoted in *Current History*, LVI (January 1969), p. 6.
43. U.S. Congress, Senate, Committee on Foreign Relations, 94th Cong., *President-Elect Jimmy Carter's Views Concerning Foreign Policy*, Nov. 23, 1976 (Washington, D.C., 1976), p. 8.

rity,' military or economic, are likely to be posed or perceived in the Americas."

Panama presented "the most urgent issue . . . in the Western Hemisphere." A failure at the Isthmus and the United States would indeed lose a prerequisite for meeting the complex challenges of the Third Cold War. If the Canal problem was solved, Latin America could again act as the laboratory for United States policies in the developing nations. As for the Canal specifically, it was "useful," but no longer "vital" to North Americans. The Commission further believed the United States did not need "perpetual control of the Canal nor exclusive jurisdiction" to protect nondiscriminatory access to the waterway: "The best protection of our interests in Panama is not outmoded [1903] Treaty language but rather Panama's own vital interest in preserving its greatest natural resource."[44]

Top Carter administration officials therefore viewed the Panama crisis as a key to their entire foreign policy. With a new treaty they could work out a *rapprochement,* at least on the economic level, with Latin America. That new relationship might serve as a doorbell to the remainder of the developing nations. And with those doors open, the North Americans would be better able to resolve the problems of the Third Cold War. The chances seemed bright, not least because of Torrijos's calculated policy shift in 1975–77.

Farewell to Reform

Like a reflex action, Panamanian governments traditionally pushed for a new treaty when their domestic economic programs hit dead ends. The Canal then appeared less as a waterway than a life raft. Torrijos's regime was no exception. The General stepped up pressure on the Canal in 1972–73 when the government's resources and the country's economy went into a parallel slide. The 8 percent annual growth rates of the 1960s declined to less than 2 percent in 1975. World inflation was to blame, but so were several home-grown problems. Heavy real estate speculation collapsed, leaving Panama City pockmarked with unfinished high-rise apartment and office buildings. Burdened with the highest external debt per capita of any Latin American government, Panama faced deep financial retrenchment after overspending during the pre-1972 boom. Rural areas suffered severely as world sugar prices plummeted.

44. Commission on United States-Latin American Relations, *The United States and Latin America: Next Steps* (No publisher, 1976), pp. 1–6.

Government corruption reappeared. During the early 1970s the Guard had cracked down on graft. By 1975 Guard officers themselves were accused of handling stolen goods in illegally established trading companies. Some officers apparently facilitated the stealing, especially from importers. Accusations of nepotism reached Torrijos himself: his brother became Ambassador to Spain where he allegedly invested the General's money in real estate, including a castle once owned by Cuban dictator Fulgencio Batista; more than 30 members of Torrijos's family prospered in high governmental positions, including such delectable posts as head of the national lottery and director of the government's casinos.[45]

The number of stories about corruption increased with the unemployment rate and prices of milk and bread. During the summer of 1976 the broadly painted slogans on walls in the National University area of Panama City infrequently demanded "Yankee Go Home," and instead roundly condemned the government for high prices and anti-student activities. The composition of the country's population compounded the economic downturn. Its 3.3 percent annual growth rated as one of the world's highest. Forty-four percent of the population was under age 15, and when that group began to bear children "the situation," one economist believed, would "become insupportable."[46]

Teenagers already threatened to flood a labor market in which one-quarter of the urban workers were unemployed. Despite the agricultural reforms, Panama City attracted rural laborers until its population spiraled from 200,000 to 500,000 in 15 years; most of the new arrivals piled up in the already horrendous slums. In 1976 per capita income of $800 ranked as the highest in Central America, but wealth was as maldistributed as during the pre-Torrijos years. Nor had the Maximum Chief solved the chronic unfavorable balance of trade. The balance even worsened. Panamanians developed expensive tastes for North American products. (On the street a visitor in the 1970s quickly noted these tastes even as he avoided the onrush of old, U.S.-manufactured cars. "Pana-Macs" are dispensed in large numbers beneath Golden Arches, and a bright sign in downtown Panama City proclaims, in Spanish, that the Colonel's chicken is so good "You'll Want To Lick Your Fingers.")

The intractable problems of the 1960s remained. Buffeted by the unfavorable economic winds, and with his reform program exhausted,

45. *New York Times*, Feb. 17, 1977, p. 2; Alan Riding, "Is America Giving Away the Panama Canal?" *Saturday Review*, July 24, 1976, p. 64; Martin C. Needler, "Omar Torrijos, the Panamanian Enigma," *Intellect*, CV (February 1977), 243.
46. Looney, *Economic Development of Panama*, p. 37.

Torrijos returned to the bankers for help. Citicorp (First National City Bank of New York) again formed a syndicate that gave a five-year, $45 million loan to bolster the governmental treasury. Continental Bank of Chicago led three banks in extending $17.5 million for sugar production.[47]

In 1975 Torrijos invited multinational corporations to bid for rights to develop the Cerro Colorado, possibly the richest undeveloped copper deposit in the world. Texasgulf won, gaining 20 percent equity interest. Panama retained the remainder. With no experience in large-scale mining, the Panamanians held the power to make policy decisions but gave Texasgulf authority to operate the mine during the five-year construction period and the first fifteen years of production. The pay-off promised to be worth the effort for Texasgulf. With at least one billion tons of copper ore in the mine, the multinational hoped to produce 180,000 tons annually by 1982, a year when analysts believed copper could be close to $1 per pound on the world market.[48]

Officials associated with left-wing politics lost their jobs. The new colonel in charge of land reform placed less emphasis on redistribution and more on discouraging political activities on the collectives. Labor, that other beneficiary of the early Torrijos programs, received similar treatment. The wide-ranging 1972 labor code was ignored as the government allowed the weakening of seniority rights, the dismissal of workers according to the company determination, the two-year freezing of labor contracts, and severe limitations on the right to strike. With little industry, no natural base existed for a strong labor movement. The Panamanian middle class feared the 1972 code would allow lower classes to threaten its privileges. Torrijos's alliance with labor was over, at least for a while.

Businessmen expressed delight with the General's policies, although some continued to protest against the regime's political repression. The National Council of Private Enterprise (CONEP) demanded more rights, especially freedom of the press. Torrijos immediately condemned such demands as "anti-Panamanian" since they could lead to what he called, in an interesting Orwellian phrase, "semi-information" that could "provoke social tempests."[49] The populist side of the new *caudillismo* required the media to remain in the Maximum Chief's hands.

47. *Wall Street Journal*, Sept. 9, 1975, p. 37; *Latin America*, March 28, 1975, pp. 101–102.
48. *New York Times*, June 15, 1976, p. 51; *Latin America*, May 27, 1977, p. 155.
49. *Latin American Report*, III (January 1975), 6.

Torrijos decided to quiet rising left-wing protest with a highly publicized junket to Cuba in early 1976. But his heart did not seem to be in it. Just several months before, he felt compelled to tell the Cuban Embassy staff in Panama (the second largest in the capital after the U.S. Embassy staff) to stop propagandizing governmental ministries and inciting Panamanian students. In Havana, Torrijos received what he wanted—a public endorsement of his cautious, patient Canal policy from Castro—then held his own press conference and left the country before he was supposed to join the Cuban leader in a public denunciation of United States foreign policy. When Cuban photographers maneuvered him into a picture whose background was a red sickle, Torrijos demanded that the film be destroyed.

Returning to Panama City, the General continued his balancing act by deporting ten businessmen who, the official explanation alleged, "received support from a U.S. presidential candidate" (obviously Ronald Reagan), in return for "anti-patriotic" statements on the Canal treaty. Torrijos took advantage of this opportunity to deport three outspoken Marxists along with the businessmen.

United States officials were visibly pleased. Torrijos, one State Department expert observed, was hardly "scullian," but he nevertheless got along beautifully with peasants and other rural Panamanians. The General was also trusted by the U.S. military and foreign bankers. The National Guard was disciplined and dependent on the United States for supplies. Its troops were not, in the words of one North American official, "the fat kind who beat up crowds." Like their Maximum Chief, they were "lean and mean." Best of all, in this official's view, members of the old, aristocratic oligarchy were making their peace with Torrijos— or he with them. The oligarchs still controlled important parts of the economy. "This is not an economic revolution, not a 1789 or 1917," he remarked with understatement.

A non-governmental expert on Panama, Professor Martin Needler, saw the same developments from a different perspective. He used the now familiar approach of comparing Panamanian and Cuban history. "It may not be farfetched," Needler wrote in early 1977, "to compare Torrijos with [Cuban dictator Fulgencio] Batista of the 1930s." Batista was also the "architect of a New Deal program partly out of populist sympathies, but mostly because it gave him a strong political base." The Cuban "ended up on the right wing as greed became his dominant motivation." Castro ultimately overthrew Batista. Needler saw in Torrijos's post-1968 political journey "the lineaments of a classic personalistic

Latin American dictatorship not interfering with the social and economic status quo."[50]

Certainly Torrijos responded in the classic manner during September 1976 when he confronted the most serious crisis of his years in power. A severe drought and world-wide inflation forced the government to decree higher prices for milk and rice. Repeating a tactic used by anti-Allende forces in Chile, protesting secondary school students and women banging empty pans swarmed into the street, symbolically on September 11, the third anniversary of Allende's overthrow and assassination. Riots broke out, looting began, and a new Trotskyist student organization moved to take control of the protests. National Guard troops, apparently alerted by CIA agents who infiltrated the student groups, attacked the protesters. Only after intermittent conflict that lasted ten days and resulted in the arrests of over 200 students was order restored.

The September riots opened a critical new chapter of the Torrijos era. Unlike every major outbreak since 1947, they were neither anti-Yankee nor directed against the Zone. One diplomat marveled, "In almost one week of riots here, there wasn't even a mention of 'Yankee go home.' " He believed the economic situation to be so serious that the students considered it more important than the Zone issue.

The role of the students was crucial. As we have seen, the Guard and students have been natural enemies since the mid-1930s, but Torrijos tried to win over the schools in order to focus their ardent nationalism against the United States. The Federation of Panamanian Students faithfully followed the Maximum Chief, but by 1976 the Federation lost ground to the Trotskyist and other left-wing groups. The traditional Guard-student hatreds resurfaced. Watching the police manhandle the students, one old man said, "They only want food for their families. I can't understand why the General is responding like this."[51]

The protesters discovered odd political bedfellows, for they were joined by North Americans from the Zone who, for their own reasons, wanted Torrijos to fall. The Guard arrested two civilian employees from the Zone, one U.S. Army private, and a Costa Rican worker from a U.S. military base, all of whom the Panamanians accused of leading looters or haranguing crowds. The government initially accused North Americans of fomenting the riots, but the U.S. Embassy protested the charges, and Torrijos dropped the accusation.

50. Needler, "Omar Torrijos," p. 243.
51. *Latin America,* Sept. 24, 1976, p. 290; *Washington Post,* Sept. 21, 1976, p. A16:4; the diplomat quoted in *New York Times,* Sept. 18, 1976, p. 26.

The General's problems were closer to home, and moving closer all the time. The National Guard was described by diplomats as "restive," with younger officers jealous of Torrijos; others complained of lags in promotions and benefits.[52] The chief danger threatened to come from Colonel Manuel Antonio Noriega, a tough, enigmatic figure who from a well-hidden bunker directed the Guard's intelligence and anti-insurgency operations. The State Department publicly discounted such threats. Officials noted that Noriega had long been staunchly pro-Torrijos, that the Maximum Chief enjoyed the personal loyalty of his other top officers, and that he had carefully built a command structure in which they reported directly to him, not to any intermediary. Only Torrijos was in a position to know all critical information. "He is numero uno," one Washington official said in early 1977, "and has it set up to remain that way."

But command structures, no matter how well conceived, have collapsed under pressure. As Guard discontent grew, civilian terrorist cells were discovered just before they set explosives in Panama City neighborhoods. The government linked the cells to right-wing Miami groups. Meanwhile the radical student organizations and anxious labor unions prepared for another confrontation with Torrijos.

But the fundamental danger to Torrijos, and indeed all Panamanians, was an economy that produced a zero growth rate in 1976. Exports slumped and the construction industry continued to stagnate. The home market was too small, the inflation rate too high, to attract needed investment. Half the total investment in 1976 was from public sources, financed primarily through foreign loans. As the debt grew, so did Torrijos's dependence on the banks. That dependence could only become greater if the government planned any kind of extensive development program. "The control factor is in the hands of the banks, not the Panamanian government," one expert wrote. An economist once observed that the Panamanian economy of the 1960s "reminds one of a ballgame in which only the stars are allowed to play. One cannot help but wonder how long the other contestants will be content to sit on the bench." That evaluation remained true in the mid-1970s. Only large Canal revenues could rescue the governmental debt and allow other contestants to play the game, and even those revenues could be insufficient.[53]

52. *Christian Science Monitor*, Sept. 22, 1976, p. 3.
53. *Latin American Economic Report*, April 22, 1977, p. 9; *ibid.*, Jan. 14, 1977, p. 5; Pringle, "Panama," pp. 1207–1210; Looney, *Economic Development of Panama*, p. 5.

The Gringo Victory: The Treaty of 1977

The rapidly deteriorating Panamanian economy and Torrijos's increasing dependence on outside private investors set the stage for the climactic negotiations of a new treaty during the summer of 1977. Leverage slowly but perceptibly moved into United States hands. The hesitant, interim government of Gerald Ford was replaced by a Carter administration determined to obtain a treaty—a treaty, moreover, that could be sold politically to the United States Senate.

Four major assumptions drove Carter's determination. First, a successful treaty would demonstrate his resolve to put North Americans on the side of change—not the status quo—in the rapidly changing, newly emerging world. The Soviets, who liked to pose as the friend of such change, would be outflanked. Thus the Canal issue would be "a litmus test," as Carter later labelled it in his memoirs, to show how he could understand and work with Third World interests. Second, as Carter's National Security Adviser, Zbigniew Brzezinski, later phrased it, "We saw the canal's strategic significance as having diminished while its potential as a source of conflict with the Panamanians had increased." Third, Torrijos seemed to be the best possible Panamanian with whom to deal. He had proven to be both reasonable and able to control his own people. Brzezinski recalled Carter's fear that any further delay could endanger the General's position, "and Panama without Torrijos most likely would have been an impossible negotiating partner." Finally, once the Canal issue was seen through these lenses, Carter had to succeed or he could say goodbye to much of his power in Washington. As columnist David Broder phrased it, "failure to persuade the Senate to approve the treaties would finish Carter, prematurely, as a significant factor in international affairs for the balance of his term."[54]

At its initial National Security Council meeting, the Carter administration agreed that Panama and the Middle East ranked as its most important foreign policy priorities. The NSC concluded that if violence erupted in Panama, it could spread throughout parts of Central America. Carter's first Presidential Review memorandum (PRM-1) analyzed the problem and outlined U.S. strategy. Secretary of State Cyrus Vance, Sol Linowitz, and Ellsworth Bunker told their Panamanian counterparts that the United States wanted two treaties—one dealing with joint opera-

---

54. George D. Moffett III, *The Limits of Victory* (Ithaca, N.Y., 1985) p. 174; Jimmy Carter, *Keeping Faith* (New York, 1982), p. 156; Zbigniew Brzezinski, *Power and Principle* (New York, 1983), pp. 123, 136.

tion of the Canal to the year 2000, and one detailing provisions under which the Canal would remain open and neutral after 2000. The United States had to have assured priority of access to the passageway and the right to defend it against external threats at all future times.[55]

Torrijos responded well—at first. He and Carter had common goals, although they were strikingly different personalities. As the U.S. Ambassador to Panama, William Jorden, put it, Carter was "deeply religious" and attended church faithfully. Torrijos "rarely bowed his knee" except at friends' funerals. Carter alienated most of Washington by banning hard liquor from the White House. Torrijos's "thrist for the hard stuff was legendary." Carter told *Playboy* he had "committed adultery in my heart many times," but had done nothing more. Torrijos was often not to be found in his own bed; his wife, Raquel, was described as "long-suffering."[56]

The Maximum Chief told Carter that all U.S. troops were to be out of the Zone by New Year's Day, 2000. Talks went well until May 2, 1977, when the Panamanians suddenly demanded $1 billion in a lump sum and $300 million annually until 2000 as compensation for past occupation, and also as payment for future expenses to maintain the Canal. The final deal, made after Carter warned the General there would be no better offer, gave Panama $10 million annually to maintain services in the Canal area; another $10 million out of Canal revenues to help out, if necessary, for extraordinary expenses; and 30¢ per ton on ships passing through the waterway.[57]

On August 11, 1977, thirteen years of intermittent crisis and intense negotiations were consummated with a new pact. Reporters were summoned to Panama City's luxurious Holiday Inn to hear the provisions of the two treaties. Four sections were most important.

First, when—or if—the pacts became law (that is, after U.S. Senate ratification and approval by a general Panamanian plebescite), Panama would immediately assume territorial jurisdiction over the Canal and receive part of the Zone's land. Panamanian legal jurisdiction would slowly replace North American authority over a three-year period. At the end of three years, the Zone would be intergrated into Panama. In reality, however, Washington would continue to operate and defend the Canal until December 31, 1999, for the United States would retain all lands and waters necessary for the passageway's operations and defense,

---

55. Carter, *Keeping Faith,* pp. 157–158; Brzezinski, *Power and Principle,* p. 51.
56. William J. Jorden, *Panama Odyssey* (Austin, Texas, 1984), pp. xii, and p. 449 *re* "long-suffering" Raquel.
57. Carter, *Keeping Faith,* pp. 157–158.

and would have the "primary" responsibility for defending it. During those decades a new nine-member United States governmental agency would operate the Canal. The North Americans would not only have a majority of five in the agency but would possess the power to appoint the four Panamanians from a list submitted by the Panama government. (Torrijos bitterly fought that appointment procedure before acquiescing to Washington's demand.) Throughout the 1980s and 1990s, Panamanian administrators and workers were to be slowly phased in to assume present North American responsibilities along the Canal, but until New Year's Day, 2000, the United States would operate and defend the water way much as it did before 1977.

Second, the United States citizens in the Zone who worked for the North American government and the new agency would retain many of the legal and procedural rights they enjoyed in the United States. Their jobs would have to relate directly to Canal operations, not to the commissaries, bowling alley, and stores, which Panamanians were to take over. The Zonians could remain in the governmental positions as long as they wished and would be replaced by Panamanians only when they quit or retired.

Third, in a key part of the second treaty, which was to govern the Canal after 2000, U.S. forces would have the permanent right to defend the Canal's neutrality (and until 2000, have the primary defense responsibilities). These provisions meant that the troops could be used to enforce Panama's guarantee that the United States would have— forever—nondiscriminatory access to the Canal for its merchant vessels and warships. This key provision marked Torrijos's major concession in the negotiations. Although Panamanian forces were to assume primary responsibility for defending the waterway after 2000, United States power could protect North American interests against outside threats.

Fourth, the United States obtained these sweeping concessions from Torrijos in part by paying for them—handsomely. In all, Panama was to receive, instead of the present $2.3 million annuity, $40 to $50 million each year until 2000, when it would control all revenues. In addition, the Carter administration promised to put together a separate package that would give Torrijos (or his successors) $295 million of economic loans and guarantees (not outright grants) over five years, and $50 million in military assistance during a ten-year period. Of course this package could tighten relations between the two countries, especially between the Pentagon and the National Guard.

Given previous Panamanian demands, the exposed North American position in the Zone, and limitations imposed on Washington's power by the Third Cold War, the treaty drafts represented a United States diplomatic triumph. Most important, the United States retained the right to intervene militarily to guarantee access to, and the neutrality of, the Canal. Since no time limits restricted the privilege, left-wing Panamanians condemned Torrijos for accepting another "perpetuity" clause that resembled the hated 1903 treaty provision. Even the fourth category, the economic settlement, gave Washington a kind of victory, for until the last days of negotiations Torrijos had demanded as much as $1 billion.

By New Year's Day, 2000, Panama would finally make the Canal its own, be free of North American military bases on the Isthmus over which it previously had no control, and receive a monetary infusion for its anemic economy. Despite these fundamental changes, the provisions incited intellectuals, left-wing Panamanian groups (especially Trotskyist students), and right-of-center business organizations to attack the agreements. The critics zeroed in on the long, two-decade transition period in which North American domination of the Canal would continue, the presence of United States military bases along the passageway until 2000, and—above all—Washington's right to use force after 2000. Panama's chief negotiator admitted the pacts were not all his government had hoped. It is "good for us in some basic aspects, bad in others, and," Romulo Escobar Bethancourt added candidly, "ugly in others." An alternative, he stressed, was violent confrontation, in which "the massacre of the best of our youth would bring more setbacks in the development of our own country."[58]

Constitutionally, Torrijos was in some danger, for he was legally bound to submit the treaties to a national referendum. With criticism growing, the General counterattacked. He quickly moved to consolidate ties with the moderate Panamanian Student Federation so the Trotskyist groups were isolated and vulnerable. Right-wing business criticism was dismissed as emanating from people sitting in comfortable "refrigerated offices" who wanted to send young men into a bloody conflict with U.S. troops. Many opponents were not even heard from; they lived in exile in Miami or Latin American cities. The extent of the General's political concern was perhaps best revealed a week before the new treaties were unveiled, when he quietly asked the leaders of five Latin American nations—including the highly respected nationalist regimes in Mexico and Venezuela—to help him sell the pacts to the Panamanian people. To ensure the success of the sales talk, the General maintained rigid censor-

58. *New York Times*, Aug. 13, 1977, p. 4.

ship within Panama. Only pro-treaty arguments could be heard on radio and television or read in the newspapers.

The referendum passed (although opponents, with some reason, believed a majority of votes actually opposed the pacts), and the Panamanians had finally taken the major step toward their long-sought authority over the Canal Zone, but under conditions that starkly revealed the extent of their continued dependence on North American power. For both political reasons (that is, to appease nationalist groups with which the National Guard alternately sympathized and fought in the streets) and economic needs which seemed limitless, Torrijos had demanded much—and accepted much less. The seventy-five-year treaty arrangements were ending, but the General and his fellow Panamanians were learning the difficulty of snapping seventy-five years of colonial ties.

7

Byrd, Baker, and Torrijos

As Bastidas and Balboa had discovered to their sorrow five centuries before, dealing with Isthmian affairs could be a bewildering experience. The historic debate in 1977 and 1978 over the two Canal treaties proved to be no exception. One of the most intensive propaganda campaigns in American history was waged, but relatively few North Americans changed their minds. The Senate devoted three months to exhaustive debate (the longest in nearly sixty years of the chamber's history), but at the end the two sides differed little from their composition at the start of the formal debates. President Carter captured headlines by his handling of the administration's case and his warning that success was essential for presidential authority in foreign policy, but the Senate leadership shaped and won the key final parts of the ratification process. Omar Torrijos remained discreetly silent during much of the time North Americans argued among themselves, but afterwards he dramatically announced that he had been ready to blow up the Canal's locks rather than enter into any new talks. Finally, after the treaties returning the Canal to Panama were ratified, Panamanian students promptly took to the streets in protest, and two were killed.

The debate thus contributed another strange chapter to U.S.–

Panamanian relations. But it also revealed the role (or non-role) of public opinion in foreign policy, the power of the Congress in an era of relative presidential weakness, and the effect of the Third Cold War on the making—and perceptions of—Washington's foreign policies.

Fighting for Public Support: Pro

The public struggle began in August 1977, when Carter urged Senate Majority Leader Robert Byrd (Dem.-W.Va.) to move rapidly on the treaties. Byrd bluntly replied that such a strategy would be "a total disaster" because public opinion overwhelmingly opposed the pacts. The Senator had the facts on his side. An early poll taken in June 1975 revealed that when Americans were asked who owned the Panama Canal, 44 percent admitted they did not know. Another 22 percent who guessed (Arabs, Israel, Cuba) were wrong. Two-thirds of those polled did not know who owned the waterway; 82 percent did not know the Canal was even an issue—but 66 percent said they wanted the United States not to give up the passageway. By May 1977 those wanting continued possession climbed to 78 percent; only 8 percent favored Panamanian control.[1] The *New York Times,* apparently through a typographical error, reported the 78 as 87 percent, and the odds seemed overwhelming. With good reasons, Byrd told Carter to launch a massive drive to reform opinion before the Senate acted on the treaties. Hamilton Jordan, Carter's White House Chief of Staff, who directed the campaign to approve the pacts, agreed in more down-home language: "Some of those bastards [in the Senate] don't have the spine not to vote their mail. If you change their mail, you change their mind."[2]

Carter had many other tough issues on his desk (a Middle East crisis, upcoming trips to Africa and Latin America, possible New York City bankruptcy, state visits by foreign leaders), but he launched what one observer called "the biggest diplomatic extravanganza Washington had seen in years." He invited the leader of every Latin American nation except Cuba to visit Washington for a week of parties, ceremonies, and talks that would climax with the signing of the two treaties by himself and Torrijos. Several top officials, notably the President of Mexico, did not appear, perhaps because they did not want to sit at the same table with the military dictators of Argentina, Chile, Brazil, and Paraguay.

1. Bernard Roshco, "The Polls: Polling on Panama—Sí; Don't Know; Hell, No," *Public Opinion Quarterly,* XLII (Winter 1978), 551–555.
2. Associated Press Dispatch, March 16, 1978; *New York Times,* Oct. 13, 1977, p. 67.

Many U.S. Senators refused to attend; some who did asked that they not be photographed. Carter's "Week of Panama," one White House aid noted, was nevertheless "right out of Cecil B. DeMille." Torrijos, moreover, publicly praised Carter by telling him that "some people don't live up to their ideals. You do. This has been an act of valor on your part."[3]

Also effective in quite another way was a meeting held in September by Brzezinski with congressional leaders. When asked by Senator Byrd how the United States would react if, after the year 2000, Panama suddenly announced that the Canal was being closed down "for repairs," Brzezinski replied: "In that case, according to the provisions of the Neutrality Treaty, we will move in and close down the Panamanian government for repairs." Brzezinski adds in his memoirs: "This brought the house down and I think assured a great deal of additional support."[4]

Equally helpful to Carter was the strong support expressed in congressional testimony by the Joint Chiefs of Staff and former Secretaries of State Henry Kissinger and Dean Rusk. The military leaders told both Carter and Congress that "a cooperative effort with a friendly Panama," not an "American garrison amid hostile surroundings," would best keep the Canal open. The commanding U.S. Army officer in the Canal Zone helped by estimating that he would need a force of at least 100,000 troops (not the present 5,000 to 10,000) to mount a reasonable defense of the Canal if the area turned hot.[5] Other groups joined Carter's cause, including the Sierra Club, the American Friends' Service Committee, and the Committee for Ratification of the Panama Canal Treaties headed by such establishment figures as Averell Harriman and John McCloy. The Harriman group raised hundreds of thousands of dollars, especially from such corporations as United Brands and Chase Manhattan Bank, which had large Latin American investments.

The role of the U.S. business community in easing the two pacts through the Senate is in dispute. Some scholars believe its contribution was quite small.[6] Shortly after the treaties were ratified, however, a White House official commented that business groups, especially the conservative National Association of Manufacturers (NAM), provided crucial support. The National Chamber of Commerce, on the other hand, early favored the pacts, but then polled its members (who, in contrast to NAM members, represented mostly small businesses) and turned increasingly

3. J. Michael Hogan, *The Panama Canal in American Politics* (Carbondale, Ill., 1986), p. 6; William J. Jorden, *Panama Odyssey* (Austin, Tex., 1984), p. 451.
4. Zbigniew Brzezinski, *Power and Principle* (New York, 1983), p. 136.
5. Jimmy Carter, *Keeping Faith* (New York, 1982), p. 155.
6. George D. Moffett III, *The Limits of Victory,* (Ithaca, 1985), pp. 150–156.

against ratification. The American Federation of Labor helped primarily by keeping disgruntled members in the Canal Zone fairly quiet. Highly influential were two other business groups. After the 1975 fight over the Snyder-Byrd amendment, Senator Gale McGee (Dem.-Wyo.), with the State Department's full support, asked representatives of more than two dozen multinational corporations to work for the new pacts. They formed the Business and Professional Committee for a New Panama Canal Treaty, complete with a half-million-dollar budget for propaganda and lobbying. The Council of the Americas, comprised of over 200 U.S. corporations with holdings in the southern nations, began buttonholing each senator individually to gather support for the treaties.

An unlikely volunteer in the fight was the American Institute of Merchant Marine (AIMM), made up of thirty-five companies that owned and operated over half the oceangoing ships in the U.S. merchant fleet. James J. Reynolds, president of AIMM, assailed Ronald Reagan's comparison of the Zone to the Louisiana Purchase as "sheer nonsense," and denied that the United States ever enjoyed sovereignty in the Zone. He demanded that the Canal be secure and—especially—that tolls for shipping be kept as low as possible. He concluded that the new pacts provided such assurances. If diplomacy broke down, Reynolds warned, rioting and sabotage could erupt. The results for "Canal users would be catastrophic."[7]

These business groups were joined by politically potent religious organizations. Roman Catholics were in the vanguard. They took their lead from Archbishop McGrath in Panama: "Morally, the justice of the Panamanian position is unquestionable. Historically [the Canal's] geographical location and configuration are Panama's principal natural resource." McGrath, similarly to Kissinger, Linowitz, and multinational corporation executives, viewed the issue in a larger framework. The Church, he believed, had to help solve the Canal question if it hoped to play a useful social role in advancing human rights throughout the hemisphere. The U.S. Catholic Conference and the National Council of Churches (made up of thirty-two denominations) also lobbied for the treaties. They were joined by individual Episcopal, Presbyterian, and Methodist groups who agreed with the USCC that "the moral imperative exists" to repudiate "the colonial politics of the nineteenth century."[8]

The Panamanian government, meanwhile, began a risky and expen-

7. *Panama Star and Herald*, July 25, 1976, p. 2.

8. *Time*, Feb. 20, 1978, p. 19; *National Catholic Reporter*, Aug. 28, 1977, p. 1; Religious News Service, "The Week in Religion," Sept. 16, 1977; Marcos G. McGrath, "Ariel or Caliban," *Foreign Affairs*, LII (Oct. 1973), esp. pp. 91–92.

sive propaganda effort in the United States. For nearly $200,000 it bought the services of a public relations firm headed by F. Clifton White (Barry Goldwater's top strategist in the 1964 presidential campaign) and other Washington insiders. The firm supposedly did not engage in lobbying on Capitol Hill, but focused on some 6,000 opinion-makers in the media and universities, who were sent thick, neatly arranged packs of pro-treaty material.[9]

The White House took a more direct approach: it invited opinion leaders from around the nation to meet personally with Carter. This experiment began when dubious editors from Kentucky were brought to Washington in the hope that after some presidential persuasion they would pressure their state's senators to vote for the pacts. (In the end, one senator did and the other did not.) Senators quickly saw such visits as a means of shifting public pressure from themselves to Carter. They besieged the White House with requests to invite folks from back home. He finally talked to more than 1,700 people in these sessions. Carter also sent officials across the country to make speeches to virtually any group that extended an invitation. This became known in the State Department as "The PITS"—Panama Information Track Score. By late February 1978, as the Senate debated the issue, The PITS showed that officials had given more than 800 speeches and interviews on the treaties.[10]

Carter of course personally courted senators. At the start he tried to counter the public opposition by asking that the lawmakers not act or say anything until they had read the treaties. As the President recalled, "Apparently it worked with most of them except a few nuts like Strom Thurmond [Rep.-S.C.] and Jesse Helms [Rep.-N.C.]"[11] The President especially benefited when senators traveled to Panama to see for themselves. Some forty-five visited Torrijos, who turned out to be a superb and sensitive political host. Senator Spark Matsunaga (Dem.-Ha.) testified to one result of the first-hand witnessing: "When I flew over the Canal, I almost wished I was the commander of a company of infantry with the mission of putting it out of order. Why, there'd be nothing to it." After mining locks, "the ships would be like sitting ducks—I could knock 'em off with bazookas."[12] Such testimony supported the Joint Chiefs' case for the pacts.

Carter also gained ground (or, at least, did not lose it) by what he did not say. In his Inaugural and other major foreign policy speeches, he

9. *Washington Post,* March 24, 1977, p. A12.
10. *Washington Post,* Feb. 26, 1978, p. 4.
11. Carter, *Keeping Faith,* pp. 159, 162.
12. Moffett, *Limits of Victory,* p. 86.

made human rights a cornerstone of his diplomacy. But when opponents of the treaties raised human rights violations in Panama (such as the 1971 disappearance of Father Hector Gallego—see p. 134), Carter downplayed and/or denied the charges. State Department official Pat Derian was in charge of fighting for human rights, but when she tried to do so in Panama—even after the treaties were ratified—she was stopped by the White House, especially Hamilton Jordan. "Hamilton always said that Torrijos was his favorite dictator," Derian recalled. "When you're in a hurry it's always easier to deal with dictators."[13]

The Carter advisers also played down evidence that Torrijos, or at least individuals close to him, were deeply involved in drug trafficking. During the Senate debate in February 1978, Senators Dole and Helms declared that Torrijos and his family were active in the trafficking. At the time and later Carter said, "None of these charges was true," and was pleased that after the Senate investigated them in secret session the issue was largely dropped.[14] But later stories indicated that perhaps not all the evidence was considered. One official who had access to intelligence information recalled, "we had drugs—and Noriega—all over the place." General Manuel Antonio Noriega was Torrijos's supposed second-in-command, but his control of Panamanian intelligence, and his lack of scruple in using what he knew, had placed many others—including Torrijos—under his influence. Both the drugs and Noriega's power and involvement in the drug trade were nevertheless downplayed. Once that evidence was ignored and the treaties were ratified, the U.S. official later declared, "the Panamanians got the word that the United States was open for business" for drug traffickers.[15] In January 1980, the U.S. Attorney's office in Miami believed it had enough evidence to indict Noriega and other Panamanians for illegal arms sales, but the State Department apparently stopped the indictment in its tracks.[16] As for Torrijos himself, a former U.S. Ambassador to Panama recalled driving around Panama City with Torrijos earlier in a panel truck. "Omar was really bombed, with a bottle of Chivas Regal between his legs. He turned to me and said, 'What bothers me the most is that [Torrijos's brother] Monchi is only shipping five kilos [of marijuana] a

13. Larry Rohter, "America's Blind Eye," *New York Times Magazine*, May 29, 1988, p. 27; Steve C. Ropp, "Negotiating the 1978 Panama Canal treaties: Contending Theoretical Perspectives," in John D. Martz, ed., *United States Policy in Latin America: A Quarter Century of Crisis and Challenge, 1961–1986* (Lincoln Neb., 1988), p. 196.

14. Carter, *Keeping Faith*, p. 67.

15. *New York Times*, May 4, 1988, p. A27.

16. Rohter, "America's Blind Eye," p. 27.

week. Why make a big deal of that?' "[17] Few people did in 1977–80. The United States too badly needed Panamanian cooperation.

The Fight for Public Support: Con

It was, as Richard Nixon liked to phrase it, "political hardball," and Carter had to square off against strong opponents. Opposition to the pacts was widespread in Washington as well as in the country at large. The Pentagon officially endorsed the treaties, but many military officers were angry. Those associated with the School of the Americas, for example, had been fighting rearguard actions for years, particularly after some of the School's Latin American graduates returned home to torture and jail political opponents. Led by Michael Harrington (Dem.-Mass.), the House of Representatives outlawed urban counterinsurgency courses at the School. Staging a tactical retreat, the School abolished the courses, then continued teaching similar subjects under new names—a substitution made easier since the School lay deep in the Zone, far from Capitol Hill. The treaties allowed the School to remain at least five years, but then it might have to move to Florida, where costs and Congress's oversight would be much greater.[18]

Other officers, and their supporters in Congress, disliked the treaties' requirement that the U.S. Southern Command be moved from the Canal Zone. Such a move could cramp a lifestyle on a base that served as a rehabilitation center for some officers who had served elsewhere. As the *Wall Street Journal* reported on January 10, 1974, the Southern Command had only 10,500 military people, but "no fewer than 10 generals . . . plus two admirals and four separate headquarters." The naval unit, "to its embarrassment, doesn't have a single warship here. Its 'fleet' consists of two 45-foot fishing boats used by the brass." A special Defense Department panel in 1970 had recommended that the Southern Command be abolished, but President Nixon sided with the Joint Chiefs, and the post survived. Ironically, as the debate intensified in Washington, the Southern Command became more important in Panama. Insurgencies in El Salvador, Guatemala, and Nicaragua were posing challenges to U.S. interests in the region. But for once, timing favored Carter: Central America's revolutionary unrest did not boil over until after the treaties were ratified.

Some military strategists argued that the Canal had to be under full

17. *Ibid.*, p. 26.
18. *Washington Post*, April 16, 1977, p. A10.

U.S. control because otherwise taxpayers would have to spend massively for a larger two-ocean navy—a huge fleet not then necessary because the Canal allowed rapid passage between oceans. This argument carried some weight, even though the fleet's thirteen aircraft carriers were too large to use the waterway. One former naval officer took a different tack: the United States had justification for acting like the Soviets toward small nations, and Panama would have to submit:

> Panama's lot can be roughly equated with that of Finland, Sweden, Vietnam [sic], Cambodia, and other small nations. It is linked inexorably to that of a major nation, and whether that major nation is a "good" democracy or a "bad" totalitarian state is beside the point. . . . Finlanders, for example, have accepted the truth of impaired sovereignty with resignation, while Panamanians probably do not recognize the sense in which their situation can be compared with Finland's.[19]

The 10,000 U.S. civilians in the Zone were not quiet. About 4,000 worked in the Zone (the remainder were dependents). Senator Alan Cranston (Dem.-Calif.) claimed that only 1,300 actually operated the Canal: the other 2,700 worked in schools, movie theatres, golf courses, and commissaries, work that Panamanians could perform as well. The elite 1,300 employees were vital, especially the 200 pilots, whose incomparable skills were not soon replaceable. Despite promises made to Panama since the 1950s, in 1976 only two Panamanians belonged to the select group of pilots. The 1977 treaties protected the 1,300 Canal operators, but not the other 2,700 positions, which would be opened to Panamanians, who already accounted for 73 percent of the Canal Company's total work force. They occupied, however, only 10 percent of the jobs in the eight highest-paying levels. The question of the national origin of the labor force, moreover, was complicated because many Panamanian employees in the Zone were descendants of blacks brought from West Indian islands as laborers during the construction of the Canal. This group had long been a convenient source of English-speaking service workers for the United States in Canal operation and military bases, but they were resented by some Hispanic and black Panamanians who felt the descendants of West Indians had preferential access to jobs at Zone pay scales much higher than those prevailing in Panama.[20]

19. Captain Paul Ryan, USN (Ret.), "Canal Diplomacy and U.S. Interests," *U.S. Naval Institute Proceedings*, CIII (Jan. 1977), p. 52.
20. Robert G. Cox, "Choices for Partnership or Bloodshed in Panama," in Kalman H. Silvert, ed., *The Americas in a Changing World* (New York, 1975), p. 146; Alan G. Riding, "Is America giving Away the Canal?" *Saturday Review*, July 24, 1976; Michael L. Conniff, *Black Labor on a White Canal: Panama, 1904–1981* (Pittsburgh, 1985), pp. 156–179.

As treaty talks accelerated, Zonians felt defenseless. In 1976 some 290, or twice as many as in 1975, quit the Canal to look for jobs back in the United States. The number included fourteen pilots. Some who had committed youthful indiscretions vividly remembered nights in Panamanians jails, knew the history of Zone-Panama relationships, and did not look forward to dealing with Panamanian police. As one North American remarked, "If there is a change in the canal, and I have to work for a Panamanian, I don't want to bear the burden of what Joe Redneck did to his dad sometime long ago."[21] In March 1976, the pilots and 500 other elite personnel protested by walking off the job. As ships halted, Panamanian workers—under Torrijos's orders—remained on the job. Under intense pressure the pilots returned to work. The protest was understandable but had not turned out as well as the Zonians had hoped.[22] In April 1977, the Zonians mounted a massive, but unsuccessful, lobbying effort in Congress. Perhaps their frustration was best demonstrated by the Zonian who took paintbrush in hand and, on a Panama City wall that bore such student slogans as "YANKEE GO HOME," wrote in bold strokes, "KISS MY AMERICAN ASS."

Frustration grew even as other groups joined the protests. Most vocal were conservative organizations: the Committee on Latin American Policy (part of the John Birch Society), the Liberty Lobby, the National States Rights Party. An active lobbyist was Phillip Harman, a fifty-five-year-old southern Californian who sent out reams of anti-treaty literature. Harman apparently interested Ronald Reagan in the issue and arranged the original meeting between the Republican candidate and Arnulfo Arias in late 1975.[23] An especially effective opponent was Richard Viguerie, a master of direct-mail techniques that used new computerized technology. He had begun by raising money for the 1964 Goldwater presidential campaign and again for pro-segregationist Alabama Governor George C. Wallace in the 1968 presidential race. By 1977 Viguerie's computers could riffle through the addresses of thirty million Americans to find support. "Our strength is in Peoria and Oshkosh," Viguerie believed, "and that's where we're going."[24]

The Conservative Caucus sent out two million letters and raised

---

21. *New York Times,* May 8, 1976, p. 6.
22. *Washington Post,* March 25, 1976, p. A18.
23. Richard Hudson, "Storm Over the Canal," *New York Times Magazine,* May 16, 1976, p. 22.
24. Hogan, *The Panama Canal in American Politics,* pp. 120–128; William J. Lanoutte, "The Panama Canal Treaties—Playing in Peoria and the Senate," *National Journal,* Oct. 8, 1977, p. 1560.

nearly $1 million to fight the pacts. But the conservative opponents had a major problem: several of their best-known voices spoke up for the treaties. William Buckley, known for his syndicated columns and television programs, returned from a visit to Panama and announced support for both Torrijos and the treaties. After working out defense procedures, security for the Zonians, and fair tolls, he declared, the United States should "get out—while the initiative is still clearly our own. That is the way great nations should act."[25] In a nationally televised debate with Ronald Reagan, Buckley scored with such arguments. Reagan also came under attack from his Hollywood friend, John Wayne. A personal friend of Torrijos's and a lover of deep-sea fishing in Panamanian waters, Wayne wrote an open letter to Reagan noting that "it is quite embarrassing to General Torrijos to be called a 'tinhorn' dictator. . . . This is more the style of a liberal punk who doesn't have to answer for his words." When Reagan continued to attack the treaties, Wayne wrote that he was going to the Republican National Committee and "show you point by God damn point in the Treaty where you are misinforming the people."[26] Buckley and Wayne seemed to agree with the business executive who noted that, if (as Torrijos planned) "you're building an international banking and tourist center, you don't want your downtown burning up."[27]

The country was listening to the debate, but how many minds Carter was changing remained unclear. His televised "fireside chat" of February 1, 1978, that defended the treaties received good ratings but mixed reviews. He had probably made his most significant move to check the opposition four months earlier. In October 1977, the White House had concluded the Senate would kill the treaties unless the United States received unequivocal right to defend the Canal after the year 2000. After conferring on the telephone, Carter and Torrijos agreed on a Joint Statement of Understanding:

> The correct interpretation [of the principle of the United States' right to intervene] is that each of the two countries shall, in accordance with their respective constitutional processes, defend the Canal against any threat to the regime of neutrality, and consequently shall have the right to act

25. William F. Buckley, "On the Right," *National Review,* Nov. 12, and 26, 1976, pp. 1253, 1306; Jorden, *Panama Odyssey,* pp. 458–459.

26. Garry Wills, *Reagan's America* (New York, 1988), p. 397.

27. *Wall Street Journal,* Aug. 21, 1975, p. 19; *U.S. News and World Report,* May 24, 1976, p. 29; Penny Lernoux, "American Imperialists," *The Nation,* April 3, 1976, p. 393.

against any aggression or threat directed against the Canal or against peaceful transit of vessels through the Canal. This does not mean, nor shall it be interpreted as, a right of intervention of the United States in the internal affairs of Panama.

The last sentence aimed at quieting Torrijos. The rest of the Statement aimed at appealing to senators, who could now claim they would vote for the treaties because they had forced Carter to ensure the U.S. right of intervention to protect the Canal. In January 1978, the Joint Statement was incorporated into the treaty itself.[28]

Suddenly the media noted that public opinion seemed to be swinging around to Carter's side. The Joint Statement seemed to have done it. In January, "NBC Nightly News" noted that most Americans opposed the pacts, but nearly two-thirds of those polled approved ratification if the United States had the right to intervene in emergencies. *Time* also recorded such a turn. The Joint Statement supposedly ensured such a right of intervention. Public opinion no longer seemed an obstacle to quick approval in the Senate. Just how much that opinion really changed has been, and will probably always be, a matter of debate. By April 1978, after the Senate did ratify the pacts, only 37 percent of the public approved the treaties—even with the Joint Statement. Five months later an "NBC News" poll showed that 56 percent of Americans opposed the treaties, which were now the law of the land. It seems that between the time of the signing in September 1977 and the months after the Senate ratification in April 1978, the opinions of North Americans actually changed little. In the words of an excellent study of this opinion, the trend "could have been graphed with a straight horizontal line."[29]

But the overall trend also proved largely irrelevant. On the eve of the Senate debate the national media solemnly announced that with the right of the United States to use force in Panama, the treaties were acceptable to most North Americans. The Carter administration trumpeted news of the turnaround throughout the land. As the music swelled, senators met to cut the deals that would actually get the treaties passed.

28. Moffett, *Limits of Victory*, pp. 90–92.
29. Roshco, "The Polls," p. 562; Hogan, *The Panama Canal in American Politics*, pp. 205–206; Walter LaFeber, "Covering the Canal; Or, How the Press Missed the Boat," *More, The Media Magazine*, VIII (June 1978), 26–31—argues at more length the ineffectiveness of public opinion; Moffett, *Limits of Victory*, pp. 124–126—argues against the interpretation in *More*.

The Senate: Byrd and Baker as Dealmakers

The two key dealmakers were Majority Leader Robert Byrd and Minority Leader Howard Baker (Rep.-Tenn.). Carter was not assured of their help. Byrd and the President were not warm friends, and Senator Byrd was a cautious conservative who would not call for a treaty vote until he believed he had the needed sixty-seven votes. State Department lobbying and his own extensive studying convinced Byrd that the pacts were necessary for U.S. security. He soon invited the two top State Department lobbyists, Douglas J. Bennet and Robert Beckel, to brief fence-sitting senators in meetings, which he hosted. Byrd, one Senate staff member recalled, was pivotal for four reasons. As Majority Leader he held the political plums that could be dispensed to cooperative Democrats. Moreover, he set a personal example as a former doubter who had moved to support the treaties, despite strong anti-pact sentiment in West Virginia. In the debate itself, the Majority Leader controlled the Senate floor. "As long as Byrd was there," one Senate staffer remarked, "nothing [of the opposition's] was going to sneak through." Finally, it had been Byrd, along with Baker, who had persuaded Carter to call Torrijos and work out the Joint Statement.

Baker's political pilgrimage to the pro-treaty group was even tougher than Byrd's. Facing a reelection campaign in 1978 and reaching for his party's presidential nomination in 1980, the Tennessean repeatedly heard from Republican leaders that open support for the treaties could doom all these hopes. His own party, moreover, was bitterly divided over the pacts. The anti-treaty forces believed they could make Baker squirm "like a worm on a hot brick." The American Conservative Union ran full-page newspaper ads in Tennessee announcing that "SENATOR BAKER ALONE CAN SAVE THE PANAMA CANAL," targeted Tennessee for its traveling "truth squads" of speakers, and flew a banner over a crowd of 84,000 (including Baker) at a Tennessee–Memphis State football game that urged fans to write the senator. Baker's office received more than 60,000 pieces of mail about the treaties, and nearly all were in opposition.[30]

Baker nevertheless decided in December 1977 to support Carter. He believed the right-wing opposition was receding, especially after the Carter-Torrijos Joint Statement. Baker's own private poll showed that

30. Much of the information on Baker is drawn from Lisa Kremer's unpublished paper, "Senator Baker and the Latin American Ditch," May 1978; and Robert Kaiser's analysis in the *Washington Post*, March 19, 1978, p. A8.

60 percent of Tennesseans surveyed actually favored a treaty that protected U.S. security. (That result, and similar polls, led many senators to discount heavily the organized mail campaign waged by anti-treaty groups.) But the Minority Leader took his major, and rather incredible, step toward supporting the treaties in January 1978. He led a Senate delegation to Panama and convinced Torrijos that because the legal significance of the Joint Statement was unclear (indeed, Panamanian officials had dismissed it as legally meaningless), it should be incorporated into the Neutrality Treaty. Baker's achievement was stunning. The senator of the minority party had acted overseas as if he were Secretary of State. Carter allowed Baker to pull off the trick. The President had little alternative if he hoped to have the pacts ratified.

The beleaguered Torrijos also bent. In the previous October he had submitted the unamended treaties to a national plebescite as Panama's constitution provided. Under U.S. Senate pressure, the General allowed political debate for the first time in eight years. Political parties reappeared. His opponents, led by left-wing university students and some businessmen, seized the chance to attack Torrijos's regime instead of merely attacking the treaties. They especially zeroed in on provisions legalizing both U.S. military presence in the area and the Pentagon's cooperation with the National Guard. Such cooperation, many charged, meant U.S. domination of the Guard and hence—since the Guard ruled the country—of them. One survey revealed that some Panamanians simply assumed that "the treaty is a trap of the Gringos."[31]

When the Carter-Torrijos Joint Statement was announced nine days before the scheduled plebiscite, it nearly destroyed Torrijos's chances. He had hoped for 80 percent approval. He received 67 percent, despite putting his personal prestige on the line and heavy government hands on the vote counting. "Another month of debate and the treaties would have been rejected," one foreign expert later remarked in Panama City.[32] After Baker persuaded the General in January, 1978, to insert the Joint Statement in the pact itself, Torrijos refused to submit the documents to a second plebiscite. He argued that Panamanians had known about the Joint Statement before they cast their earlier vote. His explanation appeased few opponents. In mid-February of 1978, as the Senate debate began, leaders from the four major Panamanian parties met in Miami (where several, including Arnulfo Arias, had learned to tolerate

31. An excellent summary of Panamanian attitudes in October 1977 is in J. P. Morray, editor and translator, *The View from Panama* (Monmouth, Ore., 1978), especially the Villalobas and Porcell articles.
32. *New York Times*, Feb. 12, 1978, p.8.

exile), to announce their opposition to Torrijos and their reservations about the pacts. Baker's use of the Joint Statement might have helped save his political career, but it did little for Torrijos's.

The Senate: The Debate and DeConcini

For six weeks in February and March of 1978, the Senate debate droned on over the Neutrality Treaty (which stipulated how the Canal would be protected after 2000 when the Panamanians assumed control). The discussion thoroughly aired the treaty's provisions, but produced no memorable speech-making. Senate debates were broadcast for the first time when the National Public Radio, comprising 213 stations, carried the arguments to as many as fourteen million listeners. Unfortunately for Torrijos, the radio carried the debate to Panama as well. Words spoken for North American ears incensed many Panamanian listeners. Some senators accused Torrijos and his countrymen of being corrupt and inefficient. Byrd later admitted the speeches created "ill will" and "could very well have precipitated some disorder" in Panama.[33]

The Senate leadership's objective, however, was not memorable speech-making, but ending the debate as soon as members had made a record for the folks back home. Byrd and Baker seemed to have the necessary sixty-seven votes in hand at the start of the sessions. This became evident on February 22 when, in the first major test involving a procedural point, the pro-treaty forces won, 67–30. Three senators shifted positions on the final treaty vote, but the two-thirds margin held. Byrd and Baker had several votes in reserve if further defections had occurred.

The leadership's problem was to hold the sixty-seven votes and not allow a new issue to undercut support or permit a political error to alienate key senators. Challenges on issues were swiftly handled by a chain of command that began on the Senate floor and ended across town in the State Department or the Pentagon. When a substantive point arose, a staff member, who was always present on the floor to assist Byrd or the floor leader for the treaties (Frank Church, [Dem.-Id.]), rushed into an office just off the chamber that was controlled by Vice President Walter Mondale. The officer contacted the State Department and Pentagon experts, who quickly sent information to kill opponents' charges. These task forces across town telefaxed the information back to the Senate office, and staffers took the material onto the floor for use in debate.

"The State and Defense teams were superb," one Senate staff member later remarked. "On the other hand," he added, "the White House lobbyists didn't know what they were doing. They were going through on-the-job training." That opinion can be somewhat discounted, but it reveals a characteristic of the debate: growing problems between the Senate and the White House. At first, the two branches had worked well together. When Senator Robert Dole (Rep.-Kan.) damned the treaties with the charge that Torrijos was involved in drug traffic, the White House provided detailed evidence to counter the charges. Republican Jacob Javits of New York expressed a general feeling: "We don't have to prove that Torrijos is an angel. I don't think he is. . . . What is important is whether the treaties [are in the U.S. interest] . . . and I think they are."[34]

Carter also handled some individual senators well. Richard Stone (Dem.-Fla.) had earlier condemned Torrijos and opposed the pacts, but changed his mind partly because of Florida's close ties with Latin America, especially in the economic area. When Stone therefore asked Carter to neutralize the rising emotionalism by pledging opposition to any Soviet efforts to establish further bases in the hemisphere, the President wheeled out the 155-year-old Monroe Doctrine and promised to maintain U.S. outposts in the Caribbean. Stone publicly switched to support the treaties.[35]

As the vote neared on the Neutrality Treaty, however, the White House lost some of its touch. On March 14, just two days before the scheduled vote, the *New York Times* reported that Carter was bargaining for the support of key senators by sponsoring bills for farm subsidies and copper purchases he had earlier condemned as inflationary. One high administration official was quoted as saying, "I hope the Panamanians will get as much out of these treaties as some United States senators." Legislators who were risking their political lives by supporting the pacts from the start were furious. Robert Packwood (Rep.-Ore.) warned that Carter should not act as "master of ceremonies at 'Let's Make a Deal.' " Angry at the White House stories, Senator Byrd tried to counter them by commenting that senators "would spit in your face" if offered "deals in return for

---

34. *Time,* Feb. 20, 1978, p. 19.
35. Tom Fiedler's column in *Miami Herald,* Feb. 7, 1978, p. 24.

votes." He carefully refrained from saying whether any "deals" had been offered.[36]

The crucial, almost fatal, mistake occurred twenty-four hours before the vote, when Carter negotiated with Senator Dennis DeConcini, a forty-year-old freshman Democrat from Arizona. In that state the copper industry was depressed, but hatred for the treaties prospered. For the national interest and his party's president, the conservative DeConcini wanted to support the pacts. But his brother Dino was running for state attorney general in Arizona, and one poll revealed that 84 percent of the state opposed the Canal pacts. In December, moreover, DeConcini had taken his family to Panama. Torrijos, whose mother had recently died, lavished attention on DeConcinci's mother and talked about his own until he began to cry. But when the senator asked whether the Neutrality Treaty allowed the United States to protect the Canal after 2000 if it were closed due to internal threats such as revolution or labor strikes, Torrijos bluntly said no. Panamanians later recalled DeConcini as "a nice guy, somewhat naïve," who "kept checking with his mother" while "his wife asked more penetrating questions than the man himself."[37]

The Panamanians had badly underestimated their guest. Back in Washington, DeConcini told Carter he could vote for the Neutrality Treaty only if it contained a "condition." (A condition, unlike an amendment, is not legally binding on both parties to a treaty, but provides one party's understanding of what a provision means.) DeConcini's condition stipulated that, if the Canal were closed for any reason after 2000, the United States or Panama could take unilateral action "including the use of military force *in Panama* to reopen the Canal." (Italics added.) The language contradicted other provisions in which the United States promised not to intervene in Panama's internal affairs, the most sensitive of all points to Panamanians. DeConcini warned that only with this condition could he and as many as four other senators vote for ratification. At a last-minute talk with the Senator, Carter asked Deputy Secretary of State Warren Christopher whether Panama could accept the condition. Torrijos would swallow hard, Christopher replied, but would accept it.

Carter then sent the condition to Capitol Hill with his blessing. Senate experts were confused. Some believed it was only a restated Joint Statement. Other staffers, however, doubted Torrijos would accept the condition. Senator Edward Kennedy (Dem.-Mass.)—who, polls revealed,

36. *New York Times,* March 14, 1978, p. 1; *Washington Post,* March 15, 1978, p. A11; Associated Press Dispatch, March 19, 1978.
37. *Washington Post,* April 28, 1978, p. A16.

was ahead of Carter in the race for the 1980 Democratic presidential nomination—blasted the new provisions: "We are asking Panama to accept an amendment [*sic*] which has the ring of military intervention— not just during this century, but for all time."[38] News spread that Torrijos so strongly objected that he would denounce the condition on television and perhaps kill the treaties. Carter called the General and talked him out of that plan. Despite its knowledge of the Maximum Chief's bitterness, the Senate passed the DeConcini condition, 75–23. Several of the leading anti-treaty legislators voted in favor, and a dozen liberal, pro-pact senators opposed. The Senate then ratified the entire amended Neutrality Treaty, 68–32.

White House officials later argued that DeConcini's demand had to be met or the necessary sixty-seven votes could not have been tallied. A deeply involved Senate staffer admitted he did not know what the vote count would be until it was finally announced. Another official close to the fight believed that Byrd had two other votes in his pocket that could have been used if DeConcini and another senator had turned against the treaty. But as one Senate staff member emphasized, the crisis could have been averted by forcing DeConcini to water down his language. Carter had less leverage to do this than did the Senate leadership. If, this staffer argued, the Arizona senator had dealt with the leadership, they would have changed the wording and told him to take it or leave it. If DeConcini had fought back, he would have been reminded that he was ninety-seventh on the seniority list of one hundred senators, and if he refused to go along: "You'll never get another bill passed as long as you're here."

During the next four weeks the Senate debated the second treaty, which stipulated how the Canal would be governed until 2000. Carter and the Senate leaders desperately sought wording acceptable to both the determined freshman Senator and the embittered Maximum Chief once again.

The Senate: A Single Thread

Torrijos was in trouble. In mid-February the largest rally in Colon since 1968 protested not the treaties, but his domestic policies. After the Neutrality Treaty passed with the DeConcini condition, Torrijos told aides, "This is not a day for celebration. There is nothing to celebrate."

38. *Congressional Record,* CLXXIV (March 16, 1978), S3824.

A poll of 150 Panamanian businessmen, who were usually staunchly pro-U.S., showed 118 opposed to the amended treaty. A Panamanian who was a controlling stockholder in one of the nation's largest breweries and also owned the Coca-Cola concession originally supported the pacts, but turned against them after the Senate insisted on specifying "how, when and where the [United States] troops would come and rape us." A Panamanian lawyer labelled it "the DeConcini corollary to the Brezhnev doctrine. It says the U.S. can treat Panama the way the Russians treat the Hungarians and Czechs." Students began to move into the streets. On April 7, they burned an effigy of Carter. Six days later, youths destroyed a flag in front of Washington's embassy. Only National Guard forces prevented them from pulling down the embassy flag.[39] The anti-Yankee feelings could easily have turned against Torrijos.

On April 6 the General sent letters to 115 heads of state, implying that Panama would reject the treaties if the DeConcini condition remained.[40] Deeply angered, Carter asked Hamilton Jordan to call Torrijos and demand a statement declaring that the General had not decided to reject the pacts. Torrijos again gave in and issued the statement, but the tension and bitterness grew. Howard Baker lectured "our friends in Panama" that "just a twitch of an eyelid, just the slightest provocation . . . and the whole thing could go down the tube." In six states—Wisconsin, Louisiana, Missouri, Montana, DeConcini's Arizona, and Baker's Tennessee—anti-treaty groups organized campaigns to recall senators who had voted for ratification. The groups' chances for success were minute due to lack of time and the well-rooted precedent that only the Senate removes its own members. But the signs were ominous and threatened to force several wavering senators to switch sides and thus kill the second treaty.

On April 9, 1978, an embattled Carter described the chances of passing the second treaty as "hanging by a thread." The *Cincinnati Enquirer* caught the general feeling when it headlined the comment with, "Canal Issue Has Carter on Brink of Calamity." Senator Byrd again took the lead. Two Senate staffers had conducted vote counts and agreed that no one had yet changed from the alignment on the first treaty ballot. Byrd hoped that everyone would now "cool it" and not overreact to Torrijos's attempt to placate angry Panamanians. Carter quietly lobbied hard to keep three votes from switching.

---

39. *New York Times*, March 18, 1978, p. 7; Associated Press Dispatches of April 9, 15, 7, 13, 1978; *Washington Post*, April 12, 1978, p. A28; *Time*, April 28, 1978, p. 27.
40. Torrijos's letter and important related documents are in the *Congressional Record*, CLXXIV (April 7, 1978), S4999–S5001.

One was Howard Cannon (Dem.-Nev.), who heard that his constituents opposed the pacts by twenty to one. The President kept him in the fold with personal pleas, as well as through direct calls to Mormon leaders in Nevada and to a leading Nevada newspaper editor whom Carter urged to treat Cannon gently. A second fence-sitter was James Abourezk (Dem.-S.D.), who threatened to vote against the Senate leadership because he disliked its holding closed meetings from which he was barred. Abourezk also wanted the President to stand firm on the sale of F-15 fighter planes to Saudi Arabia despite Israel's objections. Carter had no control over the meetings, but he asked the leadership to treat Abourezk more kindly, and, as the President recorded it, persuaded "mutual friends in Saudi Arabia" to call Abourezk (who is Lebanese) to persuade him to vote yes. A third was Senator S. J. Hayakawa, a scholarly, erratic California educator who threatened to switch until Carter promised to talk with him more regularly about African affairs (a subject in which Hayakawa had little known competence), and to read one of the senator's books on semantics. "It may not have been bedtime reading, but I needed his vote," Carter recalled. Hayakawa finally voted for the treaty.[41]

That left DeConcini, who again asked that his condition be attached to the second treaty. Senators Byrd, Church, Cranston, and Paul Sarbanes (Dem.-Md.) now took over. On Sunday, April 16, two days before the scheduled vote on the second treaty, they met with Gabriel Lewis, Panama's Ambassador to the United States; William Rogers, former U.S. Assistant Secretary of State for Latin America, who had become a private intermediary between Torrijos and the State Department; and Deputy Secretary of State Christopher. The Panamanian Ambassador set the tone early with his remark, "We're sick and tired of DeConcini." The group started with a compromise draft offered by DeConcini, who was (notably) excluded from the session. The draft was then reworded to Lewis's and the senators' satisfaction. Attached to the second treaty, the provision modified the DeConcini condition by stating that any United States action in Panama shall not be interpreted as indicating any right of intervention, nor have as its purpose "interference with [Panama's] political independence or sovereign integrity."[42]

That same day a story appeared in the *Washington Post* that raised a fundamental question about the original condition—and, indeed, about the demand of many North Americans that the United States reserve the

41. Carter, *Keeping Faith*, pp. 175–177.
42. Cyrus Vance, *Hard Choices* (New York, 1983), chap. 8; Jorden, *Panama Odyssey,* pp. 488–495.

right to intervene militarily in the Canal area. Reporter Marlise Simons asked officials in the Zone whether the U.S. Army could operate the waterway in such an emergency. A spokesman replied that because of the long training required, "It would be ridiculous to say [we] could just take over canal operations." One pilot believed, "This place would turn into a ships' graveyard if the military just took over." He estimated that at least three years of practice would be required before outside pilots could guide large ships safely through. As for the Zonian pilots' helping in an emergency, one said flatly, "I wouldn't return to bail out the government."[43] The right of U.S. military intervention had seemed a good idea to many in Washington, but few apparently had thought of what the military would be able to do after it intervened.

On April 18 the Senate accepted the modification of the DeConcini reservation by a vote of 73–27, then ratified the treaty by 68–32. Every senator voted as he or she did on the first treaty a month before. Carter immediately appeared on national television to underline the policy assumption that had driven him to work so hard for the pacts: "These treaties can mark the beginning of a new era in our relations not only with Panama but with all the rest of the world. They symbolize our determination to deal with the developing nations of the world . . . on the basis of mutual respect and partnership."

The Senate leadership group succeeded in guiding the treaties through the Senate while defeating seventy-seven amendments intended to emasculate or kill the agreements. Another pro-treaty hero was Democrat Ernest Hollings from South Carolina, a state in which anti-treaty sentiment was regularly whipped up by its powerful senior senator, Strom Thurmond. Hollings educated himself on the issue, supported the pacts from the start, and personally wrote newsletters to his constituents that included some of the best reasoned and researched material available to the pro-pact forces. On the day of the vote, Hollings spent hours with several wavering colleagues to keep them aboard. Less of a hero to some senators was Carter. They had desperately hoped he could deflect public opinion pressure from Capitol Hill, but he had not done so to their satisfaction. Perhaps that was an impossible job anyway. But the President's inability in March to force DeConcini to modify his language had led to the debate's major crisis. As exhausted senators filed off the floor after the final vote, a Senate staffer recalled that he heard one mutter that Carter "couldn't sell [prostitutes] on a troop train."

43. *Washington Post*, April 16, 1978, p. A22; Jorden, *Panama Odyssey*, p. 622.

To Panama—and Beyond

But the President had demonstrated real powers of persuasion in negotiating the treaties and then gaining the Senate leadership's agreement to push them through. He also displayed personal courage in traveling to Panama in June 1978 for a formal signing ceremony. The trip won Carter little popularity at home, and one had to marvel at his decision to go into the Canal Zone and personally explain to bitter Zonians why the treaties were in the national interest, if not in their own. The Zonians responded with frustration, but also a kind of black humor that was illustrated by a parody of the Lord's Prayer that they circulated hand-to-hand:

> Give us this day our enabling legislation
> And forgive us our manicured lawns
> As we forgive those who take them from us.
> Lead us not into the *Cárcel Modelo* [Model Jail]
> And deliver us from the *Guardia*.[44]

Nor were Torrijos and the Panamanians overjoyed. The General did proclaim Carter's visit "the Day of Liberation," but his enthusiasm was restrained. The broadcasting of the Senate's insults to Panama, the imposition of the DeConcini condition, an unshakable economic depression that did not magically lift with the ratification of the treaties, intense U.S. pressure to ease his political controls, the apppearance of a growing opposition movement that fed on the treaty debate—all combined to dampen Torrijos's moment of triumph. On national television, he blurted out, "Never has a country been subjected to so much disrespect as Panama." British novelist Graham Greene, who had become a friend of Torrijos's, wondered whether the General had actually hoped to have the Senate reject the treaties: "He would be left then with the simple solution of violence which had often been in his mind, with desire and apprehension balanced as in a sexual encounter."[45]

That delicate balance was nearly broken just twenty-four hours after the Senate vote in April, when Torrijos shocked North Americans by declaring that if the treaties had been rejected he would have sabotaged the Canal rather than enter into new talks. Howard Baker expressed anger, and a Panamanian political opponent thought that Torrijos "must be on drugs." The growing tension and frustration, however, made the

---

44. Herbert and Mary Knapp, *Red. White, and Blue Paradise: The American Canal Zone in Panama* (San Diego, Calif., 1984), p. 259.
45. Graham Greene, *Getting to Know the General* (New York, 1984), pp. 139–150.

General's outburst understandable. After all, a Western diplomat in
Panama City observed, Torrijos "spent months bowing and kissing the
hands of visiting American senators, swallowing abuse. And all along
he's had to keep his mouth shut for fear of losing points."[46]

Nor did Torrijos enjoy the turns of Panamanian politics. In the late
spring of 1978 he allowed exiled politicians to return. Some immediately
attacked the amended treaties; many went after Torrijos himself. "It's
like the hunting season opened," one Panamanian official complained.[47]
In June the most renowned of all the political huntsmen returned.
Seventy-five-year-old Arnulfo Arias stepped off a private plane from
Miami to be welcomed by 100,000 people. The political fires heated up.
Anti-treaty radical student groups moved into the streets to protest
Carter's visit. They were met by armed pro-Torrijos students led by the
Federation of Panamanian Students. Two of the protesters were killed.
Only then did the National Guard clear the streets, close the university,
and ensure quiet during the President's stay. But economic infection
continued to weaken the country's stability. The nation's only hope was
a long period of quiet in which it could use the new revenues from the
Canal, along with foreign investments, for much overdue development
projects that would stop the rural-to-urban migration and somehow
make conditions in the packed slums of Panama City and Colon more
civilized. The quiet was not to be found in 1979.

Implementing the Treaty: A Turn of the Screw

Diehard opponents of the pacts in the U.S. House of Representatives
tried throughout the debate to argue that the House as well as the
Senate had to pass on the two treaties. Whenever U.S. property was
being transferred, they declared, the House had to pass appropriate
legislation. These opponents were beaten back during the debate (in
large part because the senators, regardless of whether they favored or
opposed the pacts, did not want to share their power with the House).
But everyone knew that the House did have to act on implementing
legislation that would determine the details of how the Canal would be
turned over to Panama in the 1980s and 1990s.

The House debate in early 1979 on this lesiglation was explosive, and
Carter again had to lobby hard to save the treaties from being picked

46. *Washington Post,* April 20, 1978, p. A3.
47. *Ibid.*

apart until they were in shreds. He faced not only House opponents but angry Zonians who were determined to protect their jobs and pensions. As two Zonian authors angrily said, they had to become "a group of one-dimensional 'economic men and women.' "[48] A massive lobbying effort to protect their pensions and early retirement terms did indeed pay off.

But they and other opponents of the pacts were ironically helped by Torrijos himself. In early 1979 the Sandinista revolutionaries in Nicaragua accelerated their eighteen-year war to destroy the pro-U.S. dictatorship of Anastasio Somoza. Torrijos cared little for Somoza, not least because Somoza had tried to sell U.S. financiers on the idea of building a competing sea-level canal in Nicaragua—which, he argued, would be more stable and cooperative than Panama had proved to be. Since 1975 Torrijos had turned his country into a rear base for the Sandinistas. U.S. officials complained, but they never publicly identified the "smoking gun" directly linking the General to the revolutionaries. Some have doubted whether the State Department and National Security Council looked that hard. Such a "smoking gun" could have shot down the Panama Canal treaties. Even as the White House warned Torrijos about his activities, he formed a semi-secret military unit under the leadership of Hugo Spadafora, who had worked with guerrilla armies in Africa. During the autumn of 1978, Spadafora led sixty-five Panamanians into Nicaragua to help supply and fight along with the Sandinistas. Perhaps some pragmatic U.S. officials looked away in the hope that Torrijos would work with the more moderate wing of the revolution and help keep it under control. If so, the value of such pragmatism escaped treaty opponents in Washington. On June 20, 1979, the House held a secret session (its first since 1830) to discuss Torrijos's gun-running. But not enough convincing evidence came to light.[49]

Led by conservative opponents such as John Murphy (Dem.-N.Y., and a close friend of Somoza), Robert Bauman (Rep.-Md.), and George Hansen (Rep.-Id.), the House nevertheless turned the screw on Panama. The first turn came when the chamber declared that Congress, not the Panama Canal Commission established by the treaties, would control funds needed to operate the Canal until 2000. Bauman said directly that he wanted Congress, not the joint U.S.-Panamanian group, to control "operation of the canal." The second turn came when the U.S. Secretary of Defense was given power over the North American mem-

48. Knapp and Knapp, *Red, White, and Blue Paradise*, pp. 257–263.
49. Steve Ropp, *Panamanian Politics: From Guarded Nation to National Guard* (New York, 1982), pp. 127, 129; Rohter, "America's Blind Eye," pp. 26–27.

bers of the Panama Canal Commission, which was responsible for overseeing the waterway's operations. The commissioners were not to be independent and above politics. Panamanians objected that they were being pushed out of power, and also that, with Congress controlling funds, any long-term plans for maintaining and expanding the Canal would be impossible. These protests were largely ignored. The Senate watered down the legislation, but the House-Senate conference retained these two points. The House accepted the legislation on September 26, 1979, by a vote of 232–188. Some former opponents of the measure now voted for it because of the timing: if the implementing legislation was not passed, the treaties were automatically to go into operation anyway just five days later, on October 1, 1979.[50]

It had not turned out as Torrijos had planned. Panama would presumably receive the Canal in 2000, but the United States retained the right to return whenever it believed its national interest required intervention. Until 2000, North Americans would actually rule the area. And though Panama supposedly was to take over the post offices, schools, and other facilities in the Zone during the 1980s, many of these institutions were simply placed under U.S. military jurisdiction, where they continued to operate largely as before.[51]

Not even the General's enterprise in Nicaragua turned out as he had hoped. When the Sandinistas triumphed in July 1979, Torrijos believed, until his death in 1981, that "the process of change [in Central America] is irreversible, although there might be some transitory setbacks. " After Ronald Reagan won the presidency in 1980, the General declared that Reagan could not, despite his hatred for the Sandinistas, roll back time and restore Somoza to his bunker in Managua.[52] But by the end of 1979, hard-line Sandinista leaders had succeeded in breaking off plans with Torrijos for training police and military. The revolutionaries feared that he might become a funnel for U.S. influence. They replaced Panamanian advisers with Cubans.[53]

Carter and Torrijos had laid their political careers on the line to obtain the two treaties. They had obtained the treaties but were losing their political careers. U.S.-Panamanian relations were indeed at a high point in 1980 ("The canal is one of the happy stories in the vale of tears of

50. G. Harvey Summ and Tom Kelly, eds., *The Good Neighbors* (Athens, Ohio, 1988), pp. 104–109; Jorden, *Panama Odyssey,* pp. 663–681.

51. Ropp, *Panamanian Politics,* p. 105.

52. Omar Torrijos, *Imagen y Voz* (Panamá, 1985), pp. 200, 215.

53. Ropp, *Panamanian Politics,* pp. 129–130; Jorden, *Panama Odyssey,* pp. 673–674.

Central America," one U.S. official declared[54]), and cooperation was close. Torrijos even went along with Carter's boycott of the Olympics after the Soviets invaded Afghanistan in December 1979–80. The General also took in the deposed Shah of Iran at Carter's pleading after other supposed allies refused. (The Shah allegedly helped by paying Torrijos $12 million.) But none of this finally saved either Carter's or Torrijos's policies. The United States President had won a great victory in obtaining ratification, but that victory did not translate into an enhanced reputation, new political power, or more triumphs. In 1978–1980 he and his policies instead suffered a series of devastating setbacks in Nicaragua and Afghanistan, with a major arms control plan worked out with the Soviets, and from a run-up in oil prices (and inflation) because of the Arab oil cartel's success.[55]

As for Torrijos, he faced the problem of guiding a dependent Panamanian economy, as well as the Canal lifeline that remained under actual U.S. control, into a new era—an era when, for the first time in Panama's history, its relations with the United States had to depend on partnership and consensus between sovereign equals. In the 1980s, however, the partnership not only dissolved, but—in a final irony—within a decade after the treaties became law, U.S.-Panamanian relations were mired in one of their lowest points in history.

54. *Washington Post,* Oct. 2, 1980, p. A33.
55. A good discussion of this point is in Gaddis Smith, *Morality, Reason, and Power: American Diplomacy in the Carter Years* (New York, 1986), p. 115; also Vance's memoirs, *Hard Choices,* chap. 8; Moffett, *Limits of Victory,* pp. 9–12, 107–111, 204; Hogan, *The Panama Canal in American Politics,* pp. 216–217; and, especially for Panama, Ropp's fine analysis in *Panamanian Politics,* pp. 122–123.

8

Noriega,
Reagan,
and Abrams

Omar Torrijos assumed that the two great objectives of his 1968 "revolution" had been completed in a single decade: "First the recovery of the Canal and, second, changing a caricature of a country [una caricatura de país] into a nation."[1] He assumed too much. As noted at the end of the last chapter, the Canal had by no means been "recovered" by Panama. More immediately, an economic crisis (or, more accurately, economic crises) struck Panama—crises that made the nation more dependent on foreigners, increasingly polarized Panamanians, and helped cause a series of political shocks that shook the country and its relationship with the United States. Something had gone tragically wrong with Torrijos's and Carter's hope that the treaties would mark a historical break and usher in better times. An accurate phrase to explain the 1980s would be "the burdens of the past," or perhaps "the falseness of time."

The "Gravest Economic and Social Problem"

Some early signs were promising. Canal traffic increased at a rate of 8.5 percent between 1977 and 1981, Panama's gross domestic product

1. Omar Torrijos, *Imagen y Voz* (Panama, 1985), p. 192.

(GDP) grew at nearly a 5-percent rate by 1981–82, life expectancy rose from sixty-six years in the early 1970s to seventy-one years by the 1980s, and literacy jumped from 79 percent in 1971 to 88 percent a decade later. In 1982, however, ominous signs appeared, and by 1984 both gross national product and per capita income plummeted.[2] The 2.2 million Panamanians were divided roughly between urban and rural sectors in equal numbers, and both sectors suffered devastating blows. By the mid-1980s, one knowledgeable Panamanian warned that the unemployment rate, conservatively estimated at 19 percent (and reaching 40 percent in some regions), "is, without doubt, the gravest economic and social problem that the Republic faces."[3] This warning appeared as North Americans were thinking that drug traffickers and Central American wars were the worst problems for the region.

Torrijos had tried to rebuild his nation's economy on two cornerstones: first, an increased state investment to build infrastructure and basic industry; and second, an international service sector that revolved around the Canal and the powerful multinational banking complex in Panama City. After 1982, both cornerstones began to crumble. The state had borrowed heavily to finance its projects; so heavily that a 1968 external debt of $113.8 million had ballooned by the mid-1980s to over $4 billion, the largest per capita debt in the hemisphere. By 1987, debt payments ate up half of Panama's national budget. Construction projects stopped as the government had to cut spending. Agriculture suffered, despite an infusion of some new land as the United States turned over about 65 percent of the territory it had controlled. The land was mishandled by Panama, and little development resulted. GDP growth approached 3 percent again by 1987, but it did not help most Panamanians. Workers in the industrial sector actually continued to lose real income.[4]

The other cornerstone, the Canal and banks, had been considered less a cornerstone than money machines. Growing at a 7.7 percent annual rate between 1978 and 1982, this international service sector generated

2. United Nations Economic Commission for Latin America and the Caribbean, *Economic Survey of Latin America and the Caribbean, Volume I* (Santiago, Chile, 1986), p. 473; The Economist Intelligence Unit, *Country Profile: Nicaragua, Costa Rica, Panama, 1987–1988* (London, 1987), p. 45; Ricardo Arias Calderón, "Panama: Disaster or Democracy?" *Foreign Affairs*, LXVI (Winter 1987/88), pp. 336–337.

3. José E. Torres A., "Las causas de la crisis actual de la Economía Panameña," *Tareas*, No. 65 (Enero–Mayo 1987), pp. 5, 19.

4. *U.S. News and World Report*, Nov. 1, 1985, p. 31; *Central America Report*, Feb. 20, 1987, pp. 51–52.

an amazing 78 percent of the nation's total growth. But the Canal's cargo traffic dropped 22 percent in 1983, mostly because the new Trans Isthmian Oil Pipeline took the lucrative business of shipping 600,000 barrels of Alaskan oil each day to the U.S. East Coast. Built by U.S. corporations and Panama's government in 1981 and 1982, it produced rich tolls, but less employment than had the Canal traffic. By the mid-1980s, moreover, it was about to be outflanked by a new pipeline opened between California and Texas.[5]

On the other hand, the number of Panamanian workers in the Canal increased 13 percent, to 7,000, between 1979 and 1987. The number of U.S. employees meanwhile sank 43 percent. The work force handled fewer ships, however: traffic fell from 14,000 vessels and 186 million tons in 1982 to 11,384 vessels and 146 million tons in 1984. Cargo tonnage rose in 1987, but this was too little, too late. Tolls had to be raised, but even the new revenue could not give enough help to the embattled economy.[6] Nor could the famous banking center. Its $49 billion of assets held by 124 banks in 1982 dropped to $39 billion two years later. As political crises erupted between Washington and Panama City in 1987, the figures plummeted to $20 billion held by 120 banks.[7]

The economy had been struck from different directions. It suffered as its major markets in the United States and Latin America endured economic depression and their own growing debt burden. Amid these problems, Panamanians seemed unable to help themselves. Their own domestic market was small, their 69¢ (hourly) minimum wage too low to have much mass buying power. Nor were they able to find rich regional markets as much of Central America dissolved in bloody conflict. Government policies that seemed to place quotas and tariffs on goods at a whim made trade unpredictable, especially when the whims seemed at times to be inspired by large-scale corruption. By 1987, Panamanian businessman Eduardo Vallarino could observe that the principles for

5. World Bank, *Panama, Structural Change and Growth Prospects* (Washington, 1985), pp. 105–106; *Wall Street Journal*, March 18, 1981, p. 40; Economist Intelligence Unit, *Country Profile*, pp. 45–47.

6. Steve C. Ropp, "Panama's Struggle for Democracy," *Current History*, LXXXVI (December 1987), p. 422; United Nations, *Economic Survey*, p. 480; *Central America Report*, Sept. 11, 1987, p. 278.

7. Two important overview articles on this and other parts of the economy are Charlotte Elton, "Serving Foreigners," *NACLA Report on the Americas*, XXII (July/Aug. 1988), esp. pp. 27–28; and Steve C. Ropp, "General Noriega's Panama," *Current History*, LXXXV (Dec. 1986), esp. p. 423.

doing business in such a corrupt system are "not covered by any of the courses taught in well-known Ivy League business schools." It was, he concluded, "a never-ending nightmare."[8]

In the Canal Zone, the railroad became unsafe, streets became pot-holed, airport runways became grass-covered. Ships were damaged in port because of poor facilities and uncooperative labor. Panamanian officials in turn blamed the United States for not maintaining the Canal's facilities before 1979 (a charge that Washington denied with many figures), and for making long-term planning impossible because Congress would only pass annual funding measures. Regardless of where the blame lay, the Canal was becoming dangerously less competitive.[9]

And, regardless of the 1978 treaties, Panama remained highly dependent on the United States. The U.S. Agency for International Development pumped in aid at one of the highest per capita levels in the world. The Pentagon poured in dollars as it carried out large military programs with the National Guard (or, as it was known after 1983, the Panama Defense Forces [PDF]). But congressional actions most dramatically revealed Panama's dependence. The Reagan administration and Congress set up a Caribbean Basin Initiative (CBI) in 1983 that aimed at stimulating development by opening U.S. markets to the region's products. CBI had little effect on Panama; some 90 percent of its commercial exports to the United States were already duty-free. Instead, the U.S. Congress, in order to protect uncompetitive domestic growers, cut Panama's rich sugar trade with North Americans by 67 percent between 1984 and 1987. Sugar mills closed, and Panamanians searched for work, even as North Americans paid well above the world price to their own country's protected sugar growers.[10]

Bananas were the single largest export commodity, but the crop was controlled by U.S.-owned United Brands, Inc., which sold over three-quarters of the export volume. (Panama's own growers actually produced nearly all the bananas.) Overall, however, foreign investment dropped like a stone. In 1987 U.S. direct investment amounted to $4.8 billion, the third largest in Latin America. Japan's had rocketed to $8

8. *Wall Street Journal,* July 10, 1987, p. 19; Andrew Zimbalist, "Panama," in Eva Paus, ed., *Struggle Against Dependence* (Boulder, Colo., 1988), pp. 87–97. Zimbalist's analysis is especially useful.

9. Zimbalist, "Panama," pp. 94–95; *Central America Report,* Oct. 3, 1986, p. 304; *ibid.,* Feb. 20, 1987, p. 51; *U.S. News and World Report,* Nov. 16, 1981, p. 47.

10. Economist Intelligence Unit, *Country Profile,* p. 50; Thomas John Bossert, "Panama," *Latin America and Caribbean Contemporary Record,* III (1983–1984), p. 633.

billion, but mostly in shipping and finance, not manufacturing. Between 1980 and 1985, new foreign investment nevertheless averaged only a paltry $30 million annually.[11] After 1985, the growing political and economic crises worsened the business climate. But it was crucial to note that those crises had deep roots in the pre-1985 years.

One root was especially deep historically. Since its independence in 1903, Panama's currency was not its own but based on the dollar. This meant that Panamanians could pay for new projects not by printing more money, but by increasing exports or by borrowing money on the international markets. As borrowing shot up, anxious lenders turned off the cash spigot. To obtain cash and keep its debt payments current, Panama received help from the International Monetary Fund (IMF) in 1983. But as its policies dictated, the IMF demanded tough terms. The Panamanian government had to reduce its budget radically, especially for public sector jobs, and consequently, unemployment headed upward. The IMF and the World Bank recognized that unemployment was "without doubt, the gravest economic and social problem" facing Panama, but they demanded continued crackdowns: less government spending, less job security and protection for laborers, an opening of the entire economy to world competition, and (of special note) increased production of goods for export—which meant an immediate decrease of goods for Panamanians.[12] It all sounded ominously like economic policies in Central America during the early 1970s, just as much of that region began to erupt in revolution.

One part of the economy, however, boomed. Some Panamanians close to the government found ready cash, and loads of it, by serving as a "drug and chemical transshipment point and money-laundering center for drug money," according to a 1985 report of the U.S. House of Representatives Foreign Affairs Committee. One Panama City businessman anticipated all this years before people in the United States noticed. "Trends here are horrendous," he declared in 1982. He was speaking of political as well as economic trends.[13]

11. Zimbalist, "Panama," p. 100; Economist Intelligence Unit, *Country Profile*, p. 50; Steve C. Ropp, *Panamanian Politics: From Guarded Nation to National Guard* (New York, 1982), p. 108; *Survey of Current Business, LXVIII* (Aug, 1988), 49.

12. World Bank, *Panama*, "Preface," pp. xvi–xx; United Nations, *Economic Survey*, p. 474; Ropp, "Panama's Struggle for Democracy," p. 422; John Weeks, "Panama: The Roots of Current Political Instability," *Third World Quarterly*, IX (July 1987), pp. 772–773—especially good on the currency problems.

13. *U.S. News and World Report*, Nov. 1, 1982, p. 31; *New York Times*, June 13, 1986, p. A15.

From Torrijos to Noriega

In 1980, Torrijos held unquestioned rule, but his power, resembling his nation's economy, was under attack from several directions. President Jimmy Carter pushed Panama to restore full civilian rule. The military was willing to give civilians the headache of governing Panama day to day. But this was to be done in a "semi-competitive system," as analyst Alain Rouquié termed it—a system in which elections of civilians would provide legitimacy for the exercise of power, but the real power would remain in military hands.[14] Torrijos spoke of "depoliticizing" the armed forces, but he actually further integrated them into the nation's development. More formally, he called for local elections in 1980, a national (including presidential) election in 1984, and a new Democratic Revolutionary Party (PRD) to secure the military's interests in those ballotings. The PRD included peasants, urban labor (whom Torrijos had earlier favored), and especially bourgeoisie who profited from the international banking services. On the left, the PRD identified with the Socialist International. But the only linchpin holding all of this together was Torrijos.[15]

In July 1981 the linchpin disappeared when Torrijos's private military plane crashed in Panama's mountains. He left behind no institutionalized means for transferring power.[16] It was certain the military would not allow the old white oligarchy (which the military had thrown out of power in 1968) to return. The fissures between the military and the oligarchy sharply separated Panama from such Central American nations as El Salvador and Guatemala, where the military and oligarchs embraced each other. Only revolution could break that embrace. In Panama, Torrijos had preempted any thoughts some Panamanians might have had about revolution by slashing oligarchical power and espousing the causes of peasants and especially urban labor.

The military had several special reasons for not sharing ultimate power with the *rabiblancos* (or "white tails"). The Guard, acting as state

---

14. Alain Rouquié, *The Military and the State in Latin America.* Translated by Paul E. Sigmund (Berkeley, 1988), p. 369.

15. Torrijos, *Imagen y Voz,* pp. 192–194; George Priestly, *Military Government and Popular Participation in Panama. The Torrijos Regime, 1968–1975* (Boulder, Colo., 1986), pp. 121–122.

16. *U.S. News and World Report,* March 28, 1988, p. 27.

authority, had by 1975 created thirty-five state agencies employing 30,000 people. These agencies included the Social Security Bank, the University of Panama, and a major sugar corporation. Some of these institutions (but not the University of Panama) formed the bases of the military's economic as well as political power, and it was not about to surrender them. Moreover, the cultural differences between the Guard and the *rabiblancos* were obvious. "When you look at the traditional [civilian] minister," a U.S. analyst noted in 1988, "he is white, from a rich family, speaks English fluently, was educated in the U.S. . . . " But "the typical Panamanian military guy comes from a rural area, is darker in color, does not speak English, was educated somewhere in Latin America and does not feel comfortable with Americans."[17] Those differences helped explain events in Panama in the early 1980s, as well as why a divided Reagan administration failed in its attempt to overthrow the Panamanian military regime in 1987–88.

The power lay in the Guard, and the fight for that power grew fierce. Three commanders-in-chief appeared between 1981 and 1983, until Manuel Antonio Noriega, who had controlled the feared G-2 intelligence wing of the Guard, used his knowledge of his colleagues' activities, and his own ruthlessness and links with the United States, to seize power in 1983. Born in poverty and illegitimacy in 1934, he won a scholarship to a Peruvian military school. Apparently at that early point he began working for the U.S. Central Intelligence Agency by informing on suspicious leftist fellow cadets. Returning to Panama as a Guard officer, he allegedly raped two women, one a thirteen-year-old, but Torrijos intervened to prevent punishment. The debt was handsomely repaid in 1969 when the *golpe* threatened to overthrow Torrijos's regime. Noriega's garrison at Chiriquí moved against the insurgents and maintained Torrijos's power. The young officer received a promotion to G-2. He rose despite reports that described him as "brutal"—he was "for rent but not for sale," as Noriega liked to describe himself later. A popular myth alleged that he had baskets on his desk marked "incoming mail," "outgoing mail," and—the fullest—"blackmail." One former employee called him frightening: "When you are near him, you feel you are near death."[18]

17. *Miami Herald*, Feb. 7, 1988, p. 1, reprinted in *Central America News Pak*, II (Feb. 1–Feb. 15, 1988), p. 9, has a superb summary; Ropp, *Panamanian Politics*, pp. 94–96; Priestly, *Military Government*, pp. 7–8, 118–119.
18. *Newsweek*, Feb. 15, 1988, p. 34; Richard Millett, "Looking Beyond Noriega," *Foreign Policy*, No. 71 (Summer 1988), p. 50.

Noriega had close links with the United States. He had passed on such useful information to intelligence officials during the 1950s and 1960s that the CIA made him one of its "assets." After he became boss of G-2 in 1970, his value rose, especially as he passed on CIA disinformation to stir up problems in Cuba. But by the mid-1970s, as George Bush headed the CIA, Noriega began to penetrate U.S. communications, paid U.S. soldiers to give him sensitive materials, and, most dangerously, apparently began acting as a double agent by passing information to Fidel Castro. Refusing to interfere after the soldiers were discovered helping Noriega, Bush said the U.S. Army should handle the case. The CIA chief met Noriega in 1976, and as Vice President under Ronald Reagan, held talks with him in 1983, just as Noriega consolidated his power and expanded a rich drug trade. Bush later denied he had any evidence then that Noriega was involved in that trade.[19]

Evidence abounded, however, that Noriega was seizing dictatorial control of Panama and using it to fill his own pockets. Neither Bush nor other Reagan officials publicly protested, despite their professed determination to spread "democracy" in the region. Within two months after taking control, Noriega integrated the military and police into a Panamanian Defense Force (PDF). The cycle was complete: starting with only a police force in the early 1940s, Panamanians and North Americans had built a separate professional military in the 1950s and 1960s, until now the creature swallowed up the police. Noriega took a force that had doubled from the 5,000 men in 1968, and increased it again to 15,000, including two new combat battalions. He expanded the officer corps to bring his own men into the ranks, then doubled his life insurance by creating a personal staff that dealt with economic, judicial, and international policies as well as military. The new officers enriched themselves by controlling businesses that monopolized communications, parts of the export-import trade, and even the duty-free shops at Omar Torrijos international airport—as well as the growing drug traffic. Meanwhile, the General strengthened his anti-riot squad, known as the "Dobermans." All this was known to Washington officials and, indeed, partially paid for by U.S. military aid.[20]

Nor was his drug-dealing a secret. As early as 1972, Nixon administra-

19. *New York Times,* Sept. 28, 1988, p. A24.

20. Bossert, "Panama," pp. 635–636; Ropp, *Panamanian Politics,* p. 46; Ropp, "General Noriega's Panama," p. 432; Larry Rohter, "America's Blind Eye," *New York Times Magazine,* May 29, 1988, p. 34.

tion officials considered stopping his deals by murder ("total and complete immobilization," in the words of the Nixon bureaucracy). Nothing was done; nor were the right questions asked when Reagan's intelligence analyses estimated Noriega's wealth in 1982 at $16 million. Noriega was proving too valuable to the CIA, especially as it tried to carry out Reagan's intention of overthrowing Nicaragua's Sandinista government. In 1984 the United States used economic pressure to force the Colombian government to ban the sale of chemicals used to make cocaine. But Washington did little when the needed acetone, ether, and hydrochloric acid required to transform the coca base began to move out of Panama instead.[21]

Nor did the Reagan administration protest when Noriega fixed the May 1984 Panamanian elections and then blatantly removed the man he had put in power. The election was held because the military understood its rule needed legitimacy. Changes in the Constitution were carefully crafted in 1983 to provide for elections but to keep real power in the PDF's officer corps. To reassure the United States, private banks that held over $3.5 billion of Panamanian securities, and the World Bank and IMF officers who had bailed him out in 1983, Noriega put Nicolas Ardito Barletta at the head of a five-party coalition ticket, UNADE. A University of Chicago–trained economist, Barletta had been a vice president of the World Bank. Opposing him was the inimitable and indomitable Arnulfo Arias, now eighty-one years old. As before, Arias and his political party (appealing especially to the lower-paid mulatto, mestizo, and black workers who felt the full force of the World Bank/IMF–ordered cutbacks), came out against military rule. For the first time, however, Arias did not run against the United States. The 1978 Canal treaties had removed anti-Yankeeism as a hot political topic.[22] (For Arias's colorful background, see pp. 73–77, 121–123.)

Publicly, the United States declared its neutrality and warned the PDF that it should support whoever won. Privately, the newly created National Endowment for Democracy, a semi-autonomous agency funded by the U.S. Congress, gave at least $20,000 to the American Institute for Free Labor Development to help Barletta win. On his own, Noriega allegedly moved $20 million to $25 million of his drug money through a Miami bank to improve Barletta's chances. Despite such encouragement, the CIA estimated that Barletta lost to Arias by 30,000 votes in

21. Ben Whitaker, *The Global Connection: The Crisis of Drug Addiction* (London, 1987), p. 340; *New York Times,* June 13, 1986, p. A1; *Miami Herald,* June 14, 1986, p. 17A.
22. Bossert, "Panama," p. 630; Priestly, *Military Government,* pp. 122–123.

a surprisingly open and fair election. The exact margin will never be known. Noriega ordered the counting stopped, and when it resumed and the result was announced, Barletta had somehow won by 1,713 votes out of some 650,000 cast. One reason for the victory was probably Noriega's "goon squad" that was sent to cow the electoral commission then counting the votes. When Arias supporters appeared to protest such tactics, gunmen recruited by the military opened fire, killing two and wounding forty. The CIA informed the Reagan administration about the fraudulent vote count, and the U.S. Embassy in Panama City sent detailed reports about the shootings. "Nothing happened," a U.S. diplomat recalled. "It was [like] throwing a ball into a pillow." At the moment the Embassy was sending home a long document on the vote fraud, Reagan received Barletta in the White House as camera shutters clicked. Both Vice President Bush and Secretary of State Shultz saw the reports on the fraud. Shultz nevertheless flew to Barletta's inauguration in October 1984 and praised the new regime for giving "Panamanians of all political persuasions a new opportunity for progress and national development."[23]

Noriega doubtless believed that his political corruption and drug trafficking would be ignored by Reagan, Bush, and Shultz as long as he and his PDF cooperated with the North Americans' crusade against the Sandinistas in Nicaragua. Shultz's visit thus seemed to be a stamp of approval not only for Barletta but for Noriega, who everyone involved understood held real power. Noriega's dramatic removal of Barletta in late 1985 must be understood in this context. The new President enforced the World Bank–IMF terms so forcefully that a large Panamanian labor group protested by calling a forty-eight-hour work stoppage in July 1985. Business groups complained that the new policies were opening them to deadly foreign competition.[24] Panama's economy had come apart in 1982–83, and now its social fabric threatened to tear. Barletta had outlived his usefulness months before the headless body of Noriega's enemy, Hugo Spadafora, was found in a mailbag on the Panama–Costa Rican border. As worldwide stories erupted, Barletta said he would ask for an investigation. In late September, the President instead, under intense PDF pressure, agreed to "separate himself" temporarily from the presidency.

23. *New York Times*, June 22, 1986, pp. 1, 2; Bossert, "Panama," p. 640; Raul Arías de Para, *Asi fue el fraude* (Panama, 1984), esp. pp. 17–18, 48–67, 71–114, is a detailed analysis of the 1984 election fraud: this account was widely circulated in Panama. The Miami bank funds are revealed in the *New York Times*, Oct. 13, 1988, p. D10.
24. Ropp, "General Noriega's Panama," p. 422.

The democratic cloak over Noriega's violent rule was being stripped away. Torrijos's old PRD, the party for whom Barletta had run in 1984, had, in historian Steve Ropp's words, "become something of an empty vessel housing the worst kind of opportunists."[25] Other political parties, never strong, were ground down by internal divisions, the lack of popular bases, poor leadership, and Noriega's pressure. With internal enemies defeated and others, including the Reagan administration, acquiescent, Noriega replaced Barletta with First Vice President Eric Arturo Delvalle. A wealthy sugar grower, Delvalle was as obedient to Noriega as he was rich. Washington showed its displeasure by cutting economic aid from $40 million to $6 million. Ambassador Everett Briggs apparently told Vice President Bush, among others, that it was the moment to force Noriega to behave. But the Reagan administration had created a monster that now forced it to face distasteful choices. If Washington got tough it would alienate the same military force that was helping the U.S. overthrow the Sandinistas, that was supposed to help protect the Canal, and that, if pressured, could protect itself by revving up the long-developed Panamanian dislike of Yankee intervention. If, however, Reagan did not get tough, he would continue to be linked to Noriega's corrupt, violent, drug-trafficking officer corps—"the closest thing to a government version of the Mafia anywhere in the world," as Representative Stephen Solarz (Dem.-N.Y.) described it.[26]

Why Reagan Got "into Bed with This SOB"

The Reagan administration's hatred of the Sandinistas proved to be stronger than its hatred of the international drug traffic. Noriega offered a superb base from which the United States could overthrow the Sandinistas and restore its control of the region, which had been slipping away during the Third Cold War. Indeed, Jimmy Carter's top intelligence agents had begun to treat Noriega as they did the closest U.S. allies in Europe, Israel, and Iran: in return for Noriega's passing information on Cuba and Central American affairs, no U.S. intelligence would operate within the National Guard. The National Security Agency (NSA), twice the size of the CIA, and the top-secret gatherer of information worldwide, increased its already impressive Panamanian base to listen in on all of Central America's and most of South America's communications. It

25. *Ibid.*, pp. 421, 432.
26. *U.S. News and World Report,* June 6, 1988, p. 30; ibid., Oct. 21, 1985, p. 46; Ropp, "General Noriega's Panama," pp. 423–424.

was "an intelligence feast," one official observed. But part of the food turned out to be plastic. One U.S. agent recalled being assured in Washington that Noriega was "our man." The official was therefore surprised when intercepts from Cuban intelligence messages said that Noriega was "their man." Reagan officials no doubt did believe that "Noriega may have been an s.o.b., but he was our s.o.b." They were only partly correct.[27]

But much more was expected of Noriega than merely supplying intelligence. A politician warned in 1982, "With Torrijos gone, Panama is a fragile place." Between 1982 and 1986 the country had five presidents. The United States nevertheless piled a good part of its Central American policy on Panamanian backs—until, indeed, Noriega became reluctant to carry it. Until that point in 1986, however, he allowed U.S. bases in Panama to be used for missions into Nicaragua and El Salvador, even though the 1978 treaties expressly stated that the bases could only be used to protect the Canal. The Canal region was also used for training and deploying advisers who helped anti-Sandinista forces. As the Canal's importance declined for U.S. commerce, Panama's importance rose dramatically as a base for military operations.

Assistant Secretary of State Elliott Abrams, who directed U.S. policy in Central America and Panama between 1985 and 1988, called "plain garbage" the stories that U.S.-formed, anti-Sandinista "contras" were training in Panama. But as early as August 3, 1982, the *Wall Street Journal* revealed that the U.S. Army's School of the Americas in Panama had become "a frontline" in fighting the Sandinistas. The country had become a base from which North American advisers were moving into "El Salvador and other hot spots," and a training facility for teaching "allied soldiers" about counterinsurgency. Panama's importance increased as the CIA stepped up its military effort against Nicaragua in 1983–84.[28]

"Rent-a-Colonel," as a U.S. official labelled Noriega, also performed other services at Washington's request. As the Central American blood-

27. *Newsweek*, June 6, 1988, p. 36; *Miami Herald*, June 13, 1986, p. 12A; *New York Times*, May 4, 1988, p. A27; *ibid.*, June 12, 1986, p. A14.

28. *U.S. News and World Report*, Nov. 1, 1982, p. 31 has the "fragile place" quote; John Weeks and Andrew Zimbalist, "The Failure of Intervention in Panama," *Third World Quarterly*, XI (January 1989), p. 5 is of particular importance and part of a larger study, *Panama's Political Economy: The Quest for Sovereignty* (Berkeley, Cal., 1990); Rohter, "America's Blind Eye," p. 34; *Wall Street Journal*, Aug. 3, 1982, pp. 1, 31; Royce Q. Shaw, "U.S. Policy Toward Central America During the Carter and Reagan Administrations," in Mary Ann Tetreault and Charles Frederick Abel, eds., *Dependency Theory and the Return of High Politics* (New York, 1986), p. 138.

shed threatened to spill over the entire region, four nations (Mexico, Panama, Venezuela, and Colombia) met on the Panamanian island of Contadora in January of 1983 to plan how the fighting might be stopped and peace negotiated. The United States opposed the Contadora nations because their plan threatened both to take initiative in the region out of Washington's hands and to leave the Sandinistas in power in Nicaragua. Noriega had no more entered the Contadora group than he began undercutting it by cooperating with U.S. military efforts—including an attempt to revive CONDECA, a U.S.-directed Central American military alliance. After Panama's Foreign Minister, Fernando Cardozo Fábrega, assured Shultz that they were "friends and partners" in late 1984, Washington sent $30 million to help cover Panama's budget deficit. In 1985, as the Contadora group tried to damp down military activities, Noriega's forces joined U.S. troops in a four-month-long military exercise in the region.[29] The CIA apparently had planned to train troops in Panama who would then move through Costa Rica (which was at peace with Nicaragua) and cut Nicaragua in half from the south while contras struck from the north.[30]

When the U.S. Congress discovered in 1984 that the CIA was directing the mining of harbors, and perhaps even encouraging assassinations, in Nicaragua, the lawmakers cut off aid to the contras. Noriega became even more important to Reagan's policy. No one around Reagan was more determined to make that policy work than CIA Director William Casey and his protégé on the White House National Security Council Staff, Lt. Col. Oliver North. In June 1985 North allegedly asked Noriega to train contras, in return for U.S. financial aid. Apparently Noriega was willing to help; at least, Panama received 200 million more dollars from U.S. and international agencies in 1986 that had been earlier promised. North, meanwhile, used Panama's relaxed banking rules to set up three dummy corporations to fund the contras. At the same time, however, stories spread that Noriega was helping infest the rich U.S. market with drugs. Senator Jesse Helms, who hated the 1978 treaties and the Panamanian regime that signed them, threatened to hold hearings on Noriega's ties to drug trafficking, Cuba, and Nicaragua. Helms also was ready to cut off U.S. aid to the Panamanian. Both Casey and a high State Department official told Helms to back off because Panama was going to help the contras. Noriega bragged that he could manipulate North

29. *Central America Report,* Jan. 11, 1985, pp. 1–2; Bossert, "Panama," p. 637; *Newsweek,* April 18, 1988, p. 39.
30. Bob Woodward, *Veil: The Secret Wars of the CIA, 1981–1987* (New York, 1987), pp. 232–233.

Americans as if they were "monkeys at the end of a chain." Later, when Reagan officials tried to disentangle themselves from Noriega, a Panamanian diplomat drew another image: "The U.S. has gotten so far into bed with this s.o.b. that it's now indebted to him."[31]

Trying to Get Out of Bed

In late December 1985, the United States began demanding better manners and more cooperation from its bed partner. Three months before, the headless body of Hugo Spadafora had been found. Tortured, sodomized, and with his testicles beaten until they were "monstrously swollen," as the autopsy report revealed, Spadafora had then been slowly beheaded with three separate incisions. Noriega was in France at the time, but Spadafora (who had been close to Torrijos and the Sandinistas before turning to support the contras—see p. 185), had accused Noriega of being a major drug trafficker. A U.S. National Security Council adviser, Norman Bailey, later charged that Noriega and top world drug dealers had met to plan Spadafora's murder.[32] Despite Barletta's unceremonious dismissal after he asked for an investigation of the murder, and despite U.S. Ambassador Everett Briggs' request that the United States get tough with Noriega, Washington officials did not immediately move. The Pentagon argued that Noriega was too valuable. State Department and NSC officials, however, began to wonder whether Noriega might not be forced to act more cooperatively, or face U.S. support for other PDF officers who would be willing to replace him.[33]

31. *Business Week*, Aug. 3, 1987, p. 42; *Newsweek*, Feb. 15, 1988, pp. 36, 38; *U.S. News and World Report*, May 2, 1988, p. 44. Especially important is the testimony of former U.S. State Department Intelligence officer and U.S. Ambassador to Costa Rica, Francis J. McNeil, in U.S. Congress, Subcommittees on International Economic Policy and Trade and on Western Hemisphere Affairs, 100th Cong., 2nd sess., *The Panama Democracy and Economic Recovery Act* (Washington, D.C., 1988), pp. 70–72. The North-Noriega talks, and conflicting evidence on the Noriega-Poindexter talk, as well as discussions Noriega had with Constantine Menges of the National Security Council, are in José Blandón's widely publicized testimony in U.S. Congress, Subcommittee on Terrorism, Narcotics and International Communications, 100th Cong., 1st sess., *Drugs, Law Enforcement, and Foreign Policy: Panama* (Washington, 1988), Part 2, pp. 158–164.
32. U.S. Congress, Committee on Foreign Relations, 100th Cong., 1st sess., *Resolution Pertaining to the Presidential Certification That Panama Has Fully Cooperated with the United States Anti-Drug Efforts* (Washington, D.C., 1987), p. 7; *Newsweek*, Feb. 15, 1988, p. 35.
33. Ropp, "General Noriega's Panama," p. 424; *Congressional Quarterly Weekly Report*, May 28, 1988, p. 1463.

In mid-December of 1985 NSC Director Admiral John Poindexter met secretly with Noriega in Panama. According to one report, Poindexter demanded more Panamanian help to undercut the Contadora plan and destroy the Sandinistas. Noriega indicated he could not do so. Poindexter then asked that Barletta be returned to the presidency and that Noriega resign as PDF commander. The General again refused. Other reports stated that Poindexter told Noriega to stop drug trafficking and selling high-tech goods to Communist countries.[34] Apparently little if anything was said about Spadafora's murder.

The frustrated Poindexter returned to Washington and apparently orchestrated a campaign to help the contras and depose Noriega. For the first objective he worked with Oliver North to divert funds from secret arms sales to Iran so military arms could be purchased for the contras. The two men pursued this scheme even though the U.S. Congress had prohibited the Executive from sending military aid to the contras. For the second objective, articles began appearing in leading U.S. newspapers that outlined Noriega's drug-running, human rights violations, and corruption. The *Wall Street Journal* emphasized these points on April 29, 1986, but pointedly added that opposition to pressuring Noriega was coming from the Pentagon and—of all places—the Drug Enforcement Agency (DEA), which had received Noriega's help in capturing drug traffickers and caches of drugs. The most dramatic story appeared on June 12 when the *New York Times* quoted "a White House official" on Noriega's role in both the international drug cartel and export companies that sold valuable U.S. technology to Communist countries. A "senior" Washington diplomat was quoted as saying, "It's precisely because we have long-term strategic interests in Panama, with the canal, that it's important to have reliable people we can deal with"—and, moreover, Panama had become of great importance for the U.S. monitoring of Central American revolutions.

From the available evidence, U.S. officials were apparently preparing for another intervention in Panama for a host of reasons—Noriega's involvement with the drug cartel and his refusal to give refuge to deposed Philippine dictator Ferdinand Marcos, among them. Reports circulated that Noriega was even allowing Soviet intelligence operations that covered Central America to be based in Panama. These problems seemed to form part of a larger pattern: Noriega was not sufficiently cooperating with U.S. policy in the entire region. He particularly was

34. *Central America Report*, June 12, 1987, pp. 169–170; *Miami Herald*, June 14, 1986, p. 1A.

reluctant to pick up the slack on the contra effort—an effort that by 1986 obsessed Reagan, Casey, Poindexter, and North, not least because it was so conspicuously collapsing.

Certainly it was not the single revelation of Noriega's drug-trafficking that caused the turn in U.S. policy. When the *Wall Street Journal* reported on November 3, 1983, that Panama's "banking system is swollen with excess dollars," and that the National Guard "may be helping launder money," Noriega's possible drug connections must have been well known to U.S. intelligence. As early as October 1984, an analysis in *Washington Report on the Hemisphere,* published by The Council on Hemispheric Affairs, was headlined: "U.S. Ignores Panamanian Drug Trade." By the mid-1980s Noriega had property in Paris, southern France, Israel, Spain, and Japan—an amount that would have been difficult to pay for with his $50,000 annual military salary.[35]

Even after U.S. officials, no doubt led by Poindexter, publicly raised the pressure on Noriega to step down, they continued to praise him for cooperating with the DEA. The Agency's chief, John C. Lawn, wrote six separate letters between 1982 and 1987 applauding Noriega's cooperation. The last, of May 2, 1987, "welcomed our close association." The DEA was pleased in part because Noriega willingly informed on lesser traffickers. Some of his information did lead to arrests in the United States. Noriega, meanwhile, continued to make a fortune working with the Colombian drug cartel and other big dealers. But it seems that another reason for Lawn's compliments was that so few people in the Reagan administration cared about Noriega's drug trafficking that no one—not even the White House and the NSC—told him about the evidence piling up against Noriega. When a U.S. Justice Department investigation began to put that evidence together, it was stopped on the order of Attorney General Edwin Meese.[36]

But as Noriega turned uncooperative on Central American and East-West policies, some of those officials who had not been disturbed by his drug dealing prepared to move against him. Their opportunity came on June 1, 1987, when his second in command, Roberto Diaz Herrera,

35. *Miami Herald,* June 13, 1986, p. 12A; *ibid.,* June 14, 1986, p. 17A—note the alleged Soviet link. Jim Southwick, "U.S. Ignores Panamanian Drug Trade," *Washington Report on the Hemisphere,* Oct. 2, 1984, pp. 1, 6; Jefferson Morley, "Dealing with Noriega: Bush's Drug Problem—and Ours," *The Nation,* Aug. 27–Sept. 3, 1988, pp. 149, 165–169. I am indebted to Bill Walker of Ohio Wesleyan University for these references.

36. U.S. Congress, *Drugs, Law Enforcement, and Foreign Policy,* Part 2, pp. 50–51; *Time,* Feb. 22, 1988, pp. 39–40; *Newsweek,* Feb. 15, 1988, p. 36; *Washington Post,* July 13, 1988, p. A12; Weeks and Zimbalist, "The Failure of Intervention in Panama," p. 13.

dramatically resigned under intense pressure from Noriega. Diaz Herrera's departure proved pivotal for three reasons. First, as he was a cousin of Torrijos and a champion of the late Maximum Chief's reforms of the 1970s, U.S. officials considered him leftist, anti–North American, and dangerous. They were reluctant to push Noriega out if Diaz Herrera were to replace him. Now that fear ended. Second, Diaz-Herrera's defection was the first split in Noriega's regime—the first time an insider was willing to talk. Third, Diaz Herrera publicly began to charge that Noriega had fixed the 1984 election, ordered Spadafora's murder, and was even responsible for the plane crash that killed Torrijos. None of this was news to U.S. officials, except, possibly, for the plane crash story. But that story, as well as Diaz Herrera's motives for spilling out his other allegations, was highly suspect. Herrera resigned, not because of any abhorrence of Noriega's crimes, but because Noriega and the PDF officer corps reneged on a 1983 deal that Diaz Herrera was to become Supreme Commander in 1987 after Noriega had served four years. The suspicions seemed warranted also when Diaz Herrera called in reporters, and, while eating McDonald hamburgers, told the press he had decided to talk publicly after receiving psychic instructions from an Indian mystic, Satya Sai Baba.[37]

Using Hammers to Put Out Fires: Abrams versus Noriega, 1987–1989

Diaz Herrera's revelations mixed with the economic disasters to produce an explosion of anti-Noriega protest. It was led by the new National Civic Crusade (NCC). Representing over one hundred civic groups, NCC members led huge street demonstrations while waving their symbol, a white handkerchief or flag. Especially surprising, the usually cautious Roman Catholic Church leaders publicly supported the protests. The United States, sensing a replay of the Philippine crisis in 1986 when street demonstrations and a cooperative army terminated the Ferdinand Marcos dictatorship, jumped in. The U.S. Senate re-

---

37. *U.S. News and World Report*, June 22, 1987, p. 18; Millett, "Looking Beyond Noriega," p. 51; Weeks and Zimbalist, "The Failure of Intervention in Panama," pp. 16–17. The 1983 deal is noted in Blandon's testimony in U.S. Congress, *Drugs, Law Enforcement, and Foreign Policy*, Part 2, pp. 84–85.

solved that Noriega follow Marcos's example, and that all aid, even Panama's sugar quota, be cut off until the NCC's demands were met. Assistant Secretary of State Elliott Abrams compared Panama with militarily controlled Chile and Haiti while he repeated the Reagan demands for "democracy."[38]

But the protests collapsed, and U.S. hopes suffered a severe blow. The NCC proved to be a weak reed with which to support an anti-Noriega movement. Indeed, between 1983 and 1987, its businessmen had accepted the IMF–World Bank demands to reinvigorate the economy by squeezing labor costs and reducing public expenditures. NCC leaders seemed highly ineffective in reaching out to worker and mass urban groups. They stood even less chance of weaning away from Noriega the PDF officers—men who differed racially and culturally from the NCC, and were being rewarded handsomely for their loyalty from Noriega's drug revenues. The General played on these divisions by proclaiming the NCC to be "bad Panamanians" who worked closely with Yankees. He organized his own groups of poor Panamanians, especially blacks and mestizos, who seldom identified with the white elite.[39]

Inside this political glove was an iron fist. Noriega organized a street march of 5,000 followers, who smashed windows and stoned vehicles at the U.S. Embassy, then overturned a statue of Theodore Roosevelt while the police disappeared. Two U.S. journalists were expelled, including Lucia Newman of Cable News Network, who was warned to leave or suffer "humiliation and physical abuse." As Abrams and Secretary of State Shultz expressed "outrage," Noriega arrested Diaz Herrera and forty-four others. The General imprisoned up to 600 opponents in July alone, while street clashes with his forces led to at least one death and over 1,000 injuries. Prisoners, according to Amnesty International reports, were "stripped, deprived of food and water and beaten with rifle butts, sticks and rubber hoses." These reports warned that for the first time in Panama's history, paramilitary squads—that is, vigilantes resembling the right-wing "death squads" in El Salvador—were becoming a major force. In August, secret police raided NCC headquarters. Many NCC leaders sped into exile. As violence increased, the powerful banking community's patience decreased. Over a billion dollars fled the coun-

38. Arias, "Panama," pp. 341–342; Ropp, "Panama's Struggle for Democracy," *Current History*, LXXXVI (Dec. 1987), 421.
39. Ropp, "Panama's Struggle for Democracy," pp. 422, 424, 434.

try, and twenty banks approached a severe cash shortage. Most bankers pulled away from the protest movement.[40]

Noriega searched for help. In late 1987 he gave landing rights to the Soviet's Aeroflot airlines and docking rights to the U.S.S.R.'s large fishing fleet. When he asked Libya's bitterly anti-U.S. strongman Muammar Qaddafi for money, that was too much even for those in the Pentagon who had stuck with Noriega. When, however, a top Pentagon official flew to Panama and asked the General to resign, he refused. On February 4, 1988, two Miami grand juries indicted Noriega on drug charges. U.S. Attorney Leon Kellner alleged that the Panamanian received more than $4.6 million in return for laundering drug cartel money and providing airstrips and safe havens for the traffickers. Noriega also was charged with helping smuggle one million pounds of marijuana into the United States.[41] The indictments might have been used as part of a larger, multilateral diplomacy to push Noriega out of power. Instead they led to one of the worst pages in the history of U.S.-Panamanian governmental relations.

The Miami grand juries wanted to name the entire Panamanian Defense Force a "racketeering enterprise." The U.S. Department of State, however, intervened to stop that move. Hoping to split the military and work with more pro-U.S. groups as it had in the Philippines, the State Department was clearly more concerned with getting rid of Noriega than with getting rid of all the military involved in Panama's corruption and drug trafficking.[42] Assistant Secretary of State Abrams now hoped to use the indictments to trigger a unilateral effort to topple Noriega and turn around stumbling Reagan policies in Latin America. His policy rested on two assumptions. The first was that the United States had the necessary power to go it alone. Apparently it was better not to bother with other Latin American leaders (some of whom had long been unwelcome in Washington anyway for opposing Reagan's policies in Nicaragua and El Salvador). The second assumption was that at the climactic moment, U.S. pressures would crack the PDF officer corps and turn it against Noriega.

Both assumptions proved to be tragically wrong. Just seven months before (July 1987), the U.S. Senate had resolved that Noriega should quit. The Organization of American States quickly responded by resolving that

40. Amnesty International USA, *Panama: Assault on Human Rights, March 1988* (New York, 1988), Introduction, pp. 2–3; U.S. Congress, Foreign Relations Committee, 100th Cong., 1st sess., *Restricting United States Assistance to Panama* (Washington, 1987), p. 2; *Central America Report*, Aug. 14, 1987, p. 245; *ibid.*, Oct. 2, 1987, p. 302; *U.S. News and World Report*, July 13, 1987, p. 17.
41. *Newsweek*, Feb. 15, 1988, p. 32; *Business Week*, Jan. 25, 1988, p. 53.
42. *New York Times*, March 27, 1988, p. 2E.

no outside interference should disturb Panama's internal affairs. By January of 1988, as Abrams was obviously preparing to move, a group of Latin American leaders quietly prepared their own approach to convince Noriega he should stand aside. At least one of those involved believed it was possible to have Noriega depart voluntarily. Whether that assessment is true or not will never be known. Abrams began a unilateral public campaign to depose the General. The Latin leaders backed away. In a March 1988 meeting, nations ranging ideologically from Cuba to Chile upheld nonintervention and condemned U.S. economic pressure on Panama. Venezuela's former (and soon to be reelected) President, Carlos Andres Perez, regretted that North Americans tried to be "the policeman of the continent," who wanted to decide "which countries are or are not democratic." He also feared that Abrams's policy "is turning Noriega into a sort of leader of anti-imperialism, of nationalism, of the defense of Latin American sovereignty." Washington's growing problems even went beyond the hemisphere. The Panamanian government later announced that France and Japan, as well as Mexico and Colombia, had given economic as well as moral support, while Taiwan had sent $10 million for housing. In June 1988, the West German Ambassador, while presenting his credentials to Noriega's regime, said the Bonn government would continue its present aid and even entertain new proposals.[43]

It was, again, ironic. The Reagan administration had constantly stressed the importance of studying history in high school and college curricula. In his farewell address of January 11, 1989, Reagan himself warned "of an eradication of the American memory," and declared: "If we forget what we did, we won't know who we are." But his own officials had forgotten the effects of eighty-five years of U.S. history in the Isthmian region and the historic opposition to U.S. interventionism when they cobbled together their policy toward Noriega.

Or else they relied on their second assumption—that they had the power to divide the Panamanian army quickly and neatly and then overthrow Noriega. This assumption also grew from an "American memory" rooted in 1903, the CIA's Guatemalan operation in 1954, the Dominican affair of 1965, and the overthrow of Salvador Allende's Chilean government in 1973. In each of those interventions the key to winning was ensuring that the native army was neutralized or on Washington's side. But Noriega also knew that history. Moreover, the conditions of 1988 did not resemble those of 1954 or 1973. Noriega not only controlled the army but

---

43. Author's interview, Nov. 5, 1988; Frank McNeil, *War and Peace in Central America* (New York, 1988), p. 258; *New York Times*, April 24, 1988, p. E3; *Central America Report*, June 17, 1988, p. 181;

also had eliminated other bases of power with which Abrams might work. That lack of alternatives became clear when President Delvalle, doubtless at Abrams's urging, publicly tried to fire Noriega. Instead, and in a legislative session in the middle of the night that lasted about five minutes, Noriega fired Delvalle, who fled into hiding (probably on a U.S. military base in Panama). Manuel Solís Palma became the puppet President.

Abrams worsened an already bad situation by treating Delvalle as the legal Panamanian government. The deposed President, however, had few important supporters. "Delvalle," a U.S. authority on the region wrote, "is perhaps the most hated man in Panama. Noriega could at least be admired for his machismo and cunning, but Delvalle became known as simply *la gallina* (the hen)." Nor did his popularity improve when, during the worst economic times in Panama, caused in large part by U.S. economic pressures, the wealthy Delvalle emerged long enough from hiding to travel to Miami to buy thoroughbred horses.[44] Of most importance, however, it had been Delvalle who willingly acted as Noriega's pawn when the General needed someone to replace the deposed Barletta in 1985. Delvalle had little political base and less reputation, but Abrams nevertheless hoped to use him to pressure Noriega out of power.

As Delvalle hid, the NCC called a general strike in late February. With strong support at first, it faded as the Chamber of Commerce became more interested in its annual trade fair than in protesting. Few NCC leaders appeared on the workers' barricades. A government employee complained, "They are all businessmen, and they run this like a business: Monday to Friday and then off to the beach for the weekend. You can't run a revolution that way."[45] Of course few NCC members wanted a revolution. They wanted Noriega to go somewhere else, and then have business as usual.

Delvalle, one anti-Noriega leader observed, "has no support except for the U.S. Embassy."[46] In earlier times that would have been sufficient. The United States had suspended economic aid during the July 1987 protests. In December the U.S. sugar quota was suspended. On March 2, 1988, Abrams turned the screw again by ordering U.S. banks to freeze Panama's $50 million of deposits in New York banks. Panama's banks closed the next day. A Reagan executive order told U.S. companies and personnel in Panama to make no more payments to Noriega.

44. John M. Zinder, "Opposition Outflanked," *NACLA Report on the Americas,* XXII (July/Aug. 1988), p. 38; *Wall Street Journal,* March 11, 1988, p. 1.
45. Carla Anne Robbins, "General Noriega's Freeze-Frame Fall," *U.S. News and World Report,* March 28, 1988, p. 27.
46. *Ibid.*

Reagan had condemned economic sanctions when Jimmy Carter used them against the Soviets after the invasion of Afghanistan in 1979, but Panama seemed much more vulnerable to direct U.S. pressure than did the Soviets. Of the country's $5 billion economy, the spending of the United States and its employees accounted for 11 percent. The entire currency system was tied to the dollar. As Noriega seemed about to fall, U.S. officials secretly told him that if he went abroad, they would not try to extradite him to face the Miami drug indictments. The General, however, demanded instead that all the indictments first be dropped. "He felt we were measuring him for the role of the 1988 winner of the Ferdinand Marcos award," one U.S. official declared, "and he was determined that it wasn't going to happen to him."[47] Noriega's demand was rejected. After all, time seemed to be on Washington's side.

But the man once called "Rent-a-Colonel" brought in forty-eight tons of weapons from Cuba and hired more Cuban advisers and Israeli-trained bodyguards. He then demanded that U.S. businesses pay according to contract, and noted that if North Americans did not pay for the use of the Canal as the 1978 treaties required, the treaties could also be ignored by Panamanians. When the U.S. Embassy obeyed Reagan's order not to pay its power bill, Noriega turned off its lights and air conditioning. The President then decided that North Americans could pay utility bills and also airport fees so they could leave Panama. Cornered U.S. corporations, including Texaco, United Brands, and Eastern Airlines, soon paid $3 million in taxes due rather than face difficulties. By late April 1988, U.S. officials had largely reversed Reagan's executive order. Noriega even made money personally when one of his many companies shipped thousands of pounds of melons daily to waiting North American customers. Melons are "obviously not as good as drugs," a U.S. official observed, "but it's a source of dollars."[48] In early 1989 the General even established his own bank so he would have more control over the laundering of drug profits. With these incomes and the creation of government scrip to replace the fast-disappearing dollar, Noriega kept the economy barely afloat and the army paid. As they had when applied to the Soviet Union, Iran, Libya, and Nicaragua, the economic sanctions threatened to claim U.S. businesses as their first victims. They were therefore soon quietly ignored.

47. *Washington Post*, May 16, 1988, p. A4.
48. *Ibid.*, June 2, 1988, p. A36; *Newsweek*, April 18, 1988, p. 39 reports the Cuban arms shipments; *U.S. News and World Report*, April 11, 1988, p. 13; *New York Times*, May 1, 1988, p. 22. The payments and the context are well analyzed in Weeks and Zimbalist, "The Failure of Intervention in Panama," pp. 1–27.

Amid the chaos of April 1988, the National Police Chief, Colonel Leonidas Macías, and a few other officers moved to overthrow Noriega. They had the indirect, if not the direct, encouragement of the State Department. But instead of following the script that overthrew Allende in Chile, the plotters seemed to follow Gilbert and Sullivan. Due to bad planning, they failed to arrest Noriega at the presidential palace because he did not appear there. Macías then apparently tried to take the main army garrison without a pistol. "He thought his personality and the stars on his shoulders would be enough," said one officer. Pro-Noriega troops simply arrested him. While Macías's fellow plotters awaited news, as one later put it, "Noriega walked in and they scattered like chickens before a rooster." Noriega shook up the officer corps, but most of it had remained loyal. One U.S. official explained why: "The top guys were passing it [money from drugs and other corruption] down more than we thought—down to captains and majors. . . . [Even captains] are getting more from corruption than from their salaries. Corruption is no longer just an aspect of [Panama's] society—it has become the whole point."[49]

Abrams had one fallback position: kidnap Noriega. Otherwise U.S. troops might have to go in. If a surgical strike could eliminate Noriega, Abrams reportedly said, the officer corps would fall "like a house of cards." The Pentagon, however, wanted no part of it. For one thing, U.S. military bases in other parts of the world could be under immediate pressure from host governments to close if bases in Panama were used to overthrow Noriega. For another, as a senior U.S. Army officer noted, "State always talks about a 'surgical' military operation. There is no such thing." Using adjectives such as "harebrained" and "idiotic," the Pentagon leaked Abrams's scheme to the press and thus killed it.[50] The Army did, however, send 1,300 more combat soldiers to Panama to raise the level of forces to 12,000.

On May 25, 1988, with the battle largely won for the time being, Noriega listened as U.S. officials asked him to give up his command and leave Panama until after the May 1989 elections. In return they were prepared to drop both the remaining economic sanctions and the drug indictments. Washington had virtually surrendered. Senator Al-

49. Carla Anne Robbins, "Waiting for the Next Coup to Topple Noriega," *U.S. News and World Report,* April 25, 1988, p. 36, is a well-told story of the coup attempt; *New York Times,* May 4, 1988, p. A27.

50. *Newsweek,* April 18, 1988, p. 39; *Wall Street Journal,* April 8, 1988, p. 1.

phonse D'Amato (Rep.-N.Y.), who was especially involved in fighting drug traffic, condemned the deal as plea-bargaining: "We're pleading and he's getting a pretty good bargain." Exiled Panamanian newspaper editor Roberto Eisenmann, who had long fought Noriega's rule, believed U.S. officials "were giving away the store. Unfortunately they were giving away *our* store."[51] Other Panamanians called it "Bay of Pigs II." But Noriega rejected the deal anyway. He would not give up his power over the PDF, even temporarily, and (some speculated) he feared leaving Panama on his own because drug dealers awaited to settle old scores. The international drug cartel was more feared than the Reagan administration.

That administration quietly tried to push Panama out of the spotlight while Vice President George Bush ran for the presidency. Bush had been the administration's "Drug Czar" in an anti-drug campaign that had tragically and conspicuously failed. He had also known Noriega since the mid-1970s. In mid-July of 1988, stories appeared that the CIA was planning a covert move to overthrow Noriega. Perhaps planted in the press to show voters that Bush and his colleagues in the administration had not forgotten the General, the story was disavowed by U.S. officials. When members of Congress asked for documents on Panama's drug trafficking, the White House quickly ordered all agencies to release no information. The issue clearly was political dynamite, and the administration was issuing no fuses.[52]

Meanwhile, the Panamanian economy spun into near chaos. One bank manager declared, "In many ways, we've gone back 400 years. It's almost a medieval economy."[53] Noriega, meanwhile, collected $40 million each month from U.S. military spending, $470 million annually from the Canal, and millions more from North American corporations. When Arnulfo Arias finally died in August 1988, Noriega's mass opposition had lost a key leader.

Senator D'Amato summarized eight years of the Reagan administration's close friendship with, and then sudden opposition to, Noriega: "The administration set its hair on fire and tried to put it out with a hammer."[54]

---

51. *Newsweek,* June 6, 1988, p. 39; *Washington Post,* June 16, 1988, p. A4; *ibid.,* May 26, 1988, p. A17.

52. *New York Times,* Aug. 18, 1988, p. A3; *ibid.,* Oct. 28, 1988, p. B6; *Washington Post,* July 28, 1988, p. A1, has the CIA story.

53. *New York Times,* Sept. 4, 1988, p. 14; *ibid.,* Jan. 9, 1989, p. A13.

54. *U.S. News and World Report,* May 23, 1988, p. 26.

Conclusion

Until 1985, few Reagan officials even knew the problem existed. The administration's Latin American policy focused on El Salvador and especially Nicaragua with an obsessiveness that largely blinded it to other dangers in the region. Noriega rode this obsession to ultimate power in Panama and also to immense wealth. In the end, the Reagan policies in Latin America saved neither Panama from Noriega nor Nicaragua from the Sandinistas. Both policies had virtually collapsed by the time Reagan and Abrams left office in January 1989. A former U.S. State Department official asked rhetorically, "Isn't narcotics a greater threat to national security than some little country in Central America?"[55]

The Reagan policy failed for many reasons. First, it placed too much hope in the National Civic Crusade, a group controlled by upper-middle-class business groups (but including intellectuals, students, and some labor leaders), that had the support of neither the masses nor possibly dissident elements in the military. The NCC consequently depended on the United States to save it—which actually damned it as another in a long line of tools used by Washington since 1903 to intervene in Panama's politics. Second, the policy depended too much on economic pressures when Noriega could both force sacrifices from Panamanians and find aid from Japan, Spain, Taiwan, West Germany, and Latin American nations who disagreed with—and were willing to take advantage of—crude U.S. interventionism. Third, when economic sanctions failed, U.S. officials had only the use of force remaining to them. A frustrated Abrams was apparently willing to use force. But cooler heads in the Pentagon and the White House realized that military pressure could be bloody and cause a firestorm of protest throughout the hemisphere. Around the globe, moreover, nations that sheltered U.S. bases could demand the removal or reduction of those outposts before they were used against home governments that might arouse the displeasure of Washington officials. Fourth, U.S. policy mistakenly bet that it could split Noriega's officer corps and turn good, uncorrupted officers against the bad and corrupted. But Noriega had fixed it so that few good officers existed. The high command, in the words of a U.S. military officer, was nothing more than "a band of thugs and thieves." Nevertheless, throughout the crisis Secretary of State Shultz praised the supposedly good members of the PDF, emphasized the need to "maintain its integrity

55. *Ibid.,* March 7, 1988, p. 21.

[*sic*]," and emphasized how the military had to play a "significant role" in Panama—especially in defending the Canal. One Panamanian, exiled in the United States, had a different view: "People say Noriega is a thug, but there is a group in the army that is far worse."[56] Fifth and finally, Panama was asked to do too much. Given the decline of its economy and politics between 1980 and 1985, it had no business trying to act, at the Reagan administration's request, as a regional point man for the massive effort against the Sandinistas and the Salvadoran revolutionaries.

A single thread ran through all these reasons for failure. They had deep roots in U.S.-Panamanian relations. It was as if the 1978 treaties were less a break, a turn for the better, than they were a footnote to a ruthlessly continuing narrative. Ancestors of the groups making up the NCC had fought among themselves and had looked more to the United States than to Panama's masses long before Torrijos's National Guard took matters out of those groups' hands in 1968. The economic distortions caused by the massive U.S. presence began in 1903, intensified in the interwar period, and reached one climax in the 1950s—and only sharpened, not lessened, Panama's anti-Washington nationalism. As for the use of force, it had been easily used in Panama before the 1930s, but after that time, and especially in the 1960s and 1970s, it had become a two-edged sword: angry Panamanians could use the Canal as a hostage against the threat of U.S. military intervention, and a deployment of troops by the Pentagon could trigger unacceptable reactions around the world. Perhaps the reaction of the PDF was most interesting historically, because the United States had played the major role in training and professionalizing the old *Guardia* in the 1950s and 1960s precisely to maintain order and to provide a stiff backbone that U.S. officials believed Panamanian civilians were incapable of providing. The PDF thus proved to be a Frankenstein that turned on its creator. This was not new. Other similar military forces that the United States had helped develop in Central America had failed miserably after the mid-1950s to protect U.S. interests and values. Finally, exploiting Panama as an instrument to carry out U.S. policies in the region had a long history. Washington had used Panamanian bases for the overthrow of an elected government in Guatemala in 1954, for the restoration of a friendly government in the Dominican Republic in 1965, and as a regional command post throughout the three Cold War eras. Panamanians had obligingly cooperated

---

56. *Time*, March 28, 1988, p. 33; Weeks and Zimbalist, "The Failure of Intervention in Panama," esp. pp. 10–27, has the Shultz quote and the context; *Washington Post*, May 16, 1988, p. A4, a superb postmortem on the failure; Millett, "Looking Beyond Noriega," p. 61; Rohter, "America's Blind Eye," p. 46.

until the mid-1980s, when Reagan officials encountered a different Panama, and, indeed, a different Latin America.

History's tide had turned in the post-1973 years, but Washington's Latin American policies had not made the turn. Shultz and Abrams emphasized that "democracy" was their goal in the region. To Latin Americans with long historical memories, the declaration rang hollow. Noriega nevertheless played the game. He held open elections in 1984, but of course fixed them and even had Bush and Shultz travel to Panama City to accept the results. In elections planned for 1989, Noriega again was determined to hold the balloting, but he used government agencies and influence to divide the political parties so his candidates would win. He could win, moreover, even though public opinion polls revealed that he was disliked and blamed for the nation's economic disasters by an overwhelming majority of Panamanians.[57]

The Canal, meanwhile, has remained a center of possible conflict. Under the treaties it is to be handed over to Panama at noon on the last day of 1999. But much earlier, in January 1990, the United States Senate must confirm a Panamanian nominated by Panama to become the administrator of the Panama Canal Commission. General Colin Powell, Reagan's National Security Adviser, warned that the United States would not give either more operating control in 1990 or full control in late 1999 to a government controlled by Noriega. A U.S. diplomat observed that in 1990: "I sincerely doubt you could get a Noriega nominee through the Senate. But if we don't, then we're not in compliance with the treaty."[58]

Meanwhile, the passageway itself has so badly suffered from a buildup of sediment and a growing lack of fresh water (caused in part by the multiplying Panamanian population's destroying the forests and basins around the Canal's water sources), that experts fear the waterway will be unusable by 2004. Studies have moved ahead for a sea--level canal that could cost $20 billion (with Japan providing much of the financing), or a widening of the present canal[59] that would require $400 million to $5 billion. Something has to be done soon, but nothing—neither widening the Canal nor turning it over to Panamanian administration—will be done until Noriega is somehow pushed out of power.

Even if the General disappeared, the political relationship between Panama and the United States must be rebuilt and rethought. The central problem is that, although Washington no longer has the leeway of 1903 (or the 1950s) to reshape Panama's government directly, the

57. *Washington Post,* Dec. 27, 1988, p. A11.
58. *New York Times,* Oct. 28, 1988, p. B6; *ibid.,* Jan. 27, 1989, p. A7.
59. *Central America Report,* June 27, 1986, pp. 190–191.

United States remains the most important fact of life for Panamanians. It exerts such "overwhelming influence . . . over the day-to-day political life of Panamanians," economist John Weeks wrote, "that it is possible that the term 'domestic politics' is a misuse of words" in Panama.[60] In 1984, as Central American affairs heated up, the Pentagon moved the Southern Command back to Panama. Once a lazy rest-and-rehabilitation base for U.S. officers, it became one of the most active military centers on the globe. It not only housed 12,000 troops and acted as the region's intelligence nerve center, but became the base for U.S. forces charged with conducting low-intensity conflicts (as in El Salvador and against Nicaragua).[61]

U.S. power was indeed immeasurably greater in the 1980s than it had been in 1903, the 1920s, or even the 1950s. But history has transformed the arena in which that power operated. North Americans of course have had to deal with Noriega, but above all they have had to deal with the history that had brought him to power—a history they had played a large role in shaping. The 1977 treaties were a long stride in the right direction because they took both the United States' and Panama's interests into account. The Reagan policies of the 1980s were steps backward because they tried to use Panama with little sense of history, with little thought of the effect on Panama, and with little understanding of the effect of these policies on U.S. interests in the region. The question for the critical decade of the 1990s, the decade when a healthy Canal is supposed to come under full control of a friendly Panama, is whether that history can be learned.

60. Weeks, "Panama," p. 764.
61. *Central America Report*, Dec. 19, 1986, p. 388; *ibid.*, March 4, 1988, p. 66; *Washington Post*, June 2, 1988, p. A36.

Conclusion: Five Questions

1. Was Ronald Reagan correct in claiming that the Canal Zone was sovereign United States territory just the same as Alaska?

Articles II and III of the 1903 treaty (analyzed in Chapter II) triggered the never-ending debate on this question. During the first twenty years of the agreement, the United States acted, to use the treaty's words, "as if it were sovereign" in the Zone. A 1907 Supreme Court decision stated that the area was United States territory. A neutrality act of World War I considered the Canal and its environs as part of the United States. In 1920 a congressional act defined Zone ports as "domestic." Other legislation, especially affecting shipping and defense, considered the area as "territory under the jurisdiction of the United States." In 1922–23 conversations with Panamanian officials, Secretary of State Charles Evans Hughes went as far as any North American statesman has gone in claiming full sovereign rights in the Zones (see Chapter III).

Even during these early years, however, the claim was ambiguous. Theodore Roosevelt, John Hay, and William Howard Taft, the three most important figures in establishing the fundamental United States position, agreed that Panama retained—to use Taft's famous phrase—

"titular sovereignty," although all three downplayed its importance. More significant was the testimony from Philippe Bunau-Varilla: "The United States, without becoming sovereign, received the exclusive use of the rights of sovereignty, while respecting the sovereignty itself of the Panama Republic." That judgment remained definitive not only because the Frenchman wrote the 1903 treaty, but tried to give the United States every possible advantage in the pact.

For a half-century the United States admitted in a variety of acts that it did not own the Zone as it "owned" Texas or Alaska. Taft's 1904 agreement (noted in Chapter II), recognized that Zonal boundary authorities were not fully sovereign, for the United States surrendered the right to apply its tariff to goods entering from Panama. Congress enacted a separate Canal Zone Code which expressly excluded United States general law (such as the criminal code), from having force in the area. The United States Constitution never automatically applied; the Zone's governor, for example, could single-handedly deport undesirables. Notably, children born of Panamanians in the Zone remained Panamanian. Born in Louisiana or Alaska, they would be United States citizens. A 1930 Supreme Court decision defined the Zone's ports as "foreign," and a Circuit Court of Appeals explicitly said the area was not "a part of the United States." Finally, a 1948 Supreme Court decision flatly declared that while Congress controlled the Zone, the United States did not possess "sovereignty."[1]

This historical checkerboard led a distinguished legal scholar to conclude that the debate over sovereignty held "greater interest for the legal metaphysician than for the lawyer. The legal status of the waterway is not to be determined by reference to these abstract concepts," R. R. Baxter wrote, "but by a consideration of the relations established among Panama, the United States, and user nations by treaty and the customary law."[2]

Baxter's point provided the key to answering the question. During the 1970s crisis the 1903 treaty language had to be interpreted in the light of nearly 75 years of United States-Panamanian relations. Examined from this historical perspective, the answer was clear: the United States did

1. These points, pro and con, are discussed in R. R. Baxter, *The Laws of International Waterways* (Cambridge, Mass., 1964), pp. 84–87; Lawrence O. Ealy, *Yanqui Politics and the Isthmian Canal* (University Park, Pa., 1971), pp. 106, 172; Charles J. Maechling, "The Panama Canal: A Fresh Start," *Orbis*, XX(Winter 1977), 1007–1023; Helen C. Low, "Panama Canal Treaty in Perspective," Overseas Development Council Monograph Series #29 (1976).

2. Baxter, *Laws of International Waterways*, p. 87.

not own the Zone or enjoy all sovereign rights in it. The turning point perhaps occurred in the 1936 treaty (examined in Chapter III), which termed the Zone the "territory of the Republic of Panama under the jurisdiction of the United States of America." The U.S. Senate constitutionally ratified that pact. After World War II, Washington officials repeatedly recognized Panama's sovereign powers in the Zone. Every President, starting with Dwight D. Eisenhower, allowed the Panamanian flag to fly with Old Glory in the area, an act not allowed in Alaska or Texas. By 1967 Johnson administration officials searched the record then privately concluded that the United States could not claim full sovereignty in the Zone (see Chapter V). In 1976, Ellsworth Bunker, heading the North American negotiating team, summarized the official consensus of the previous four decades by declaring that Washington did not purchase the Zone in 1903, but paid Panama for certain rights: "We bought Louisiana; we bought Alaska. In Panama, we bought not territory, but rights. . . . It is clear that under law we do not have sovereignty in Panama."

Senator Strom Thurmond was mistaken in his belief that "We own it, title in fee simple."[3] If the United States "owned" it, no argument over sovereignty could have arisen, just as no major argument over North American sovereign control of, say, Florida, has occurred since it was purchased in 1819. Of equal importance, the title was not in "fee simple." The United States at no time claimed that it purchased the Zone outright. After 1903 it paid annual annuities to Panama, a payment which implicitly recognized less than full ownership of the waterway area. In no territorial transaction involving the mainland or such overseas acquisitions as Hawaii or the Philippines did the United States recognize the continuing rights of the sellers by paying annuities.

The Zone cannot be thought of as comparable to either a state or a territory, but more aptly, as Baxter declared, to a "great government reservation."[4] After the reorganization acts of 1948 and 1950, the Panama Canal Company became a corporation controlled by its sole stockholder, the Secretary of the Army, who acted as agent for the President of the United States. No territory, and certainly no state, was ever so controlled. The Secretary of the Army appointed a nine- to thirteen-member board of directors to manage the corporation. Private property in the Zone was virtually non-existent. The governmental corporation owned and operated everything from homes to stores to bowling alleys,

3. *Congressional Record*, 93d Cong., 2nd Sess., March 29, 1974, p. S4730.
4. Baxter, *Laws of International Waterways*, p. 86.

partly because of the belief that the land could one day revert to Panama. The same cannot be said about Texas.

2. Since the Canal has not yet been paid for, should not Panama pay the United States for the original cost and later improvements?

The original cost of building the Canal was about $400 million when wages of the workers and prices of materials were roughly one-tenth to one-twentieth of current levels. Whether the investment has been amortized is an unanswerable question. The variables created by time and changed circumstances, as well as the different criteria used by experts who have studied the problem, make it comparable to a thousand-piece jigsaw puzzle which has important pieces missing.

It is unarguable, however, that from the beginning Congressmen cared little about amortizing the investment. They were primarily concerned about subsidizing United States shipping that used the canal. Tolls were set not to recoup expenses, but to help shippers. "Basically," two experts on the question concluded, "the policy of the Panama Canal system is that charges to shippers be set to recover only the actual cost of providing the service." Tolls were never set to pay for the original construction cost.[5] It is too late to ask Panama to do immediately what, for understandable reasons, the United States refused to do over a period of sixty years, even if a figure could be agreed upon.

3. Does the Canal remain a vital interest of the United States?

The importance of the Canal decreased notably after 1974, when military traffic to Vietnam declined and the Suez Canal reopened. The Panama Canal Company made good profits until the early 1970s, but after 1973 losses required the raising of tolls three times in four years. The raises occurred after 59 years in which the tolls were not raised at all.

Two other special reasons might be noted for its declining importance. First, the Canal machinery operates efficiently, but it is a superb antique whose parts date back to 1914. The Canal will require expensive modification in the not distant future simply to continue moving its present rate of traffic. Large tankers, which form the arteries of the international oil

5. Norman J. Padelford and Stephen R. Gibbs, *Maritime Commerce and the Future of the Panama Canal* (Cambridge, Md., 1975); Georgetown University Center for Strategic Studies, *Panama; Canal Issues and Treaty Talks* (Washington, D.C., 1967), p. 12; and see ECLA report in *Latin America*, May 3, 1974, pp. 133–134. A Latin American view of the difficulty in measuring the economic (and social) costs of the Canal is Gorostiaga, *Panama y la Zona del Canal*, pp. 11–15.

system, cannot squeeze through the waterway. The need to modernize was one reason the Panamanians demanded billions of dollars from the United States when the 1977 treaty was negotiated.

A second reason why it is slipping in importance is an ongoing revolution in international trade. The Canal accommodates ships carrying no more than 65,000 long tons of cargo. In 1964 no bulk carriers went above 80,000 tons; ten years later more than 100 ships carried more than 125,000 tons, and some approached 300,000 tons. In early 1977 as many as 1000 vessels were too large, either in width or tonnage, to travel the passageway.

Of equal importance, ships that formerly journeyed from Asia through the Canal and on to eastern United States ports now anchor instead at West Coast ports and lift their huge, transferable containers directly on eastbound railway cars. A week of transit time and as much as 10 percent in costs can thereby be saved. One container vessel carries the cargo formerly carried by three to five of the merchant ships using the Canal. The container phenomenon has grown so rapidly that hard-hit eastern port authorities recently joined with International Longshoremen to ask the government that the practice be restricted.[6] Containerization, larger ships, air freight, truck trailer rigs with cargo roll-on, roll-off techniques, and the increased processing of raw materials near their sources—all are reducing the Canal's value. (See p. 190.)

A Library of Congress study concluded that while the waterway remained important for United States and world commerce, "it is not of overwhelming or critical economic importance." Ten to 17 percent of United States oceangoing commerce, representing less than one percent of the gross national product, uses the Canal. It is more important to several Latin American nations (who, under the new treaty, can help guarantee the waterway's security), and to Japan, South Korea, New Zealand, and Taiwan than to the United States. As one economic consultant on the Canal remarked in late 1976, "Now that people are fighting not to give it up, the thing isn't worth fighting about."[7]

Militarily, supporting warships and merchantmen carrying supplies continue to use the Canal. But its strategic value has also rapidly declined. Aircraft carriers cannot use it, and nuclear submarines must surface while going through. In 1903 the waterway was vital for Mahan's

---

6. *Wall Street Journal,* Nov. 15, 1976, p. 6:1; an excellent summary by Zone officials is in U.S. Congress, House, Subcommittee of the Committee on Appropriations, 94th Cong., 1st Sess., *Department of Transportation and Related Agencies Appropriations for 1976* (Washington, D.C., 1975), especially pp. 4–5.

7. *Business Week,* Dec. 6, 1976, pp. 84–86.

famous strategy of keeping the one-ocean U.S. Navy together in force while shifting it from sea to sea. But three-quarters of a century later, the nation has long possessed a two-ocean navy. A former senior officer responsible for overseeing transportation expenditures believed that using routes other than the Canal would not have adversely affected the Vietnam war effort; added costs would have been negligible.[8] In a war the Canal would be defenseless against sabotage or missiles. Perhaps Panamanian diplomat Carlos Lopez Guevara put it best: "If the Canal really were vital to the United States, we would not have a chance" of obtaining a treaty.

4. If Congress had refused to accept a new treaty, or the United States later decided not to carry out its provisions, what could Panama do about it?

The government and most Panamanians are determined to obtain the Canal at a fixed future date, but they are not foolish enough to believe they can wage a war, even a Vietnam type of conflict, against the United States. (Graham Greene made the interesting observation that "The Panamanians are not romantic."[9] That characterization at least seems to fit the National Guard leaders who rule the country.) Realism could dictate guerrilla attacks or small acts of sabotage which raise tensions in the area without closing down the Canal. Sabotage would be easy. Torrijos once accurately described the Canal "as vulnerable as a newborn baby." The area cannot be defended unless an army in excess of 100,000 men was stationed in the Zone, preferably along a Berlin-type wall. Even that defense would be neither impregnable, nor, needless to add, acceptable to many North Americans and most Latin Americans. General George Brown, chairman of the U.S. Joint Chiefs of Staff, believed the Canal's safety was impossible to guarantee without a new treaty: "It is more efficiently and effectively defended in partnership with Panama."[10]

After conferring on the problem, CIA, Defense Department, and State Department officials agreed with General Brown that the waterway was nearly impossible to protect against sabotage, and if the United States was required to defend it against an internal Panamanian threat under the 1903 treaty, it "could not expect much sympathy from Latin

8.   Cox, "Choices" in Silvert, ed., *Americas in Changing World*, p. 140.
9.   Greene, "Country with Five Frontiers," p. 13.
10.   *Latin American Report*, IV (July 1976), p. 6.

American countries."[11] A United States military officer worried about fighting alone: "For those of us who really care about the Army, [the atrocities committed against Vietnamese civilians at] My Lai was an awful blow. We know what that's done to our reputation. The last thing in the world we want now is to be ordered to start shooting into a crowd of Panamanians."[12]

5. Since the United States operated the Canal so efficiently and Panama made hundreds of millions of dollars annually from the traffic and the annuities, why did the Panamanians insist on assuming total control?

Panamanians wanted the Canal for two principal reasons. Of possibly lesser significance is a nationalism that developed long before 1903; as Chapters I and II emphasized, Panamanian separatism long preceded Theodore Roosevelt's taking of the Canal. That nationalism finally accepted the Bunau-Varilla treaty only because Panama both needed United States protection and feared Washington's power. The nationalism ripened particularly with the appearance of student political organizations and a small but active middle class in the 1930s (Chapters III and IV). North Americans never understood this nationalism, partly because they were ignorant of nineteenth-century Panamanian history, partly because they became enchanted with Theodore Roosevelt's self-propagated myth that he created the country on the third day of November 1903.

Panamanians increasingly resented the division of their country by a Zone which for many years they could cross only with difficulty, and they feared a colonial control to which, rightly or wrongly, they attributed many of their nation's problems. The control was not a figment of their imagination. In 1944, John F. Muccio, the acute chargé of the U.S. Embassy in Panama City, detailed the extent of the domination. United States influence, even if

> we should be able to keep our mouths tightly shut and take no overt action, is inescapable. . . . For instance, any cantina or restaurant can be closed by the Public Health authorities. The Army can completely and thoroughly sabotage Panamanian commercial life through simply declaring either all Panama or specific business enterprises "off limits" to soldiers. . . . Our control over water works and other utilities can completely

11. Enclosure in Robert J. McCloskey to Senator Dick Clark, June 30, 1976, manuscript copy.
12. Franck and Weisband, "Panama," pp. 186–187.

estop the development of whole sections of the cities of Panama and
Colon. . . .

Every realistic Panamanian, just as every realistic American, is fully
aware that this influence over the daily life of Panama exists, and there is
always a question in the minds of the Panamanians as to how this power
will be used.[13]

Muccio wrote during wartime, but most of his statements applied to
pre-1941 Panama and many to the post-1945 years. In 1950 a confidential State Department analysis concluded that "the virtual dependence
of Panamanian economic life on US activities in the Canal Zone and the
inferiority complex inherently felt by a small, undeveloped country having close relations with a large and powerful state" caused Panamanians
to feel "a highly nationalistic sensitivity and resentment toward the
United States." Despite such "resentment," however, the State Department urged greater private investment in Panama, particularly since "by
the Constitution of 1946 American businessmen are in a position of
economic equality with Panamanians."[14] The 1972 Constitution changed
that equal relationship, but the Constitution and the 1977 pacts affected
only the degree, not the fact, of Panamanian dependence. The United
States possessed $1.8 billion of investments in the country, and North
American banks, multinational corporations, mineral-processing companies, and agribusinesses continued to dominate the nation's economy.
The National Guard depended on Washington for its matériel and much
of its officer training. The small oligarchy had long since been integrated
into a North American marketing system.

Finally, Panama needs the Canal for economic reasons. As this account has repeatedly shown, Panamanian governments tried to solve
fundamental economic problems with a variety of programs, but always
returned to the area's greatest resource, the Canal. For good reason,
Panamanians never believed the United States paid them enough for the
use of the Zone. While they received between $1.9 million and $2.3
million in annual rental, the United States paid Spain $20 million to $30
million each year for the use of airbases in Spanish territory.

A United Nations report believed the Canal could produce $2 billion
annually in revenue for Panama. In addition, the country could develop
such new industries as shipbuilding, repair, and drydocks, while expanding existing warehousing and transshipment operations.[15] The 1977

13. Muccio to Phillip W. Bonsal, Department of State, June 6, 1944, 819.00/6–644, Box
3729, NA, RG 59.
14. *FRUS, 1950*, II, 974, 977.
15. *Washington Post*, June 3, 1977, p. A24:4.

treaty was by no means a cure-all for either the Panamanian or North American problems on the Isthmus, but it was a long step forward in making relationships between the two nations more equitable. In a sense the agreement was most important because it demonstrated a mutual understanding that was impossible to achieve in the previous relationship between the colonial power and the colony. Such a colonial relationship had begun to be historically outdated in Asia and Africa even in 1903 when it was established between the United States and Panama. Certainly it was a dangerous anachronism by the mid-1970s.

Appendix

THE 1903 TREATY. THE "HAY-BUNAU-VARILLA" CONVENTION

Between the United States and Panama, Signed at Washington, November 18, 1903.

The Treaty was ratified by the President of the United States, February 25, 1904.

Article 1

The United States guarantees and will maintain the independence of the Republic of Panama.

Article 2

The Republic of Panama grants to the United States in perpetuity the use, occupation and control of a zone of land and land under water for the construction, maintenance, operation, sanitation and protection of said Canal of the width of ten miles extending to the distance of five miles on each side of the center line of the route of the Canal to be constructed; the said zone beginning in the Caribbean Sea three marine miles from mean low water mark and extending to and across the Isthmus of Panama into the Pacific ocean to a distance of three marine miles from mean low water mark with the proviso that the cities of Panama and Colon and the harbors adjacent to said cities, which are included within the boundaries of the zone above described, shall not be included within this grant. The Republic of Panama further grants to the United States in perpetuity the use, occupation and control of any other lands and waters outside of the zone above described which may be necessary and convenient for the construction, maintenance, operation, sanitation and protection of the said Canal or of any auxiliary canals or other works necessary and convenient for the construction, maintenance, operation, sanitation and protection of the said enterprise.

The Republic of Panama further grants in like manner to the United States in perpetuity all islands within the limits of the zone above described and in addition thereto the group of small islands in the Bay of Panama, named Perico, Naos, Culebra and Flamenco.

Article 3

The Republic of Panama grants to the United States all the rights, power and authority within the zone mentioned and described in Article 2 of this agreement and within the limits of all auxiliary lands and waters mentioned and described in said Article 2 which the United States would possess and exercise if it were the sovereign of the territory within which said lands and waters are located to the entire exclusion of the exercise by the Republic of Panama of any such sovereign rights, power or authority.

Article 4

As rights subsidiary to the above grants the Republic of Panama grants in perpetuity to the United States the right to use the rivers, streams, lakes and other bodies of water within its limits for navigation, the supply of water or water-power or other purposes, so far as the use of said rivers, streams, lakes and bodies of water and the waters thereof may be necessary and convenient for the construction, maintenance, operation, sanitation and protection of the said Canal.

Article 5

The Republic of Panama grants to the United States in perpetuity a monopoly for the construction, maintenance and operation of any system of communication by means of canal or railroad across its territory between the Caribbean Sea and the Pacific ocean.

Article 6

The grants herein contained shall in no manner invalidate the titles or rights of private land holders or owners of private property in the said zone or in or to any of the lands or waters granted to the United States by the provisions of any Article of this treaty, nor shall they interfere with the rights of way over the public roads passing through the said zone or over any of the said lands or waters unless said rights of way or private rights shall conflict with rights herein granted to the United States in which case the rights of the United States shall be superior. All damages caused to the owners of private lands or private property of any kind by reason of the grants contained in this treaty or by reason of the operations of the United States, its agents or employees, or by reason of the construction, maintenance, operation, sanitation and protection of the said Canal or of the works of sanitation and protection herein provided for, shall be appraised and settled by a joint Commission appointed by the Governments of the United States and the Republic of Panama, whose decisions as to such damages shall be final and whose awards as to such damages shall be paid solely by the United States. No part of the work on said Canal or the Panama railroad or on any auxiliary works relating thereto and authorized by the terms of this treaty shall be prevented, delayed or impeded by or pending such proceedings to ascertain such damages. . . .

Article 7

The Republic of Panama grants to the United States within the limits of the cities of Panama and Colon and their adjacent harbors and within the territory adjacent thereto the right to acquire by purchase or by the exercise of the right of eminent domain, any lands, buildings, water rights or other properties necessary and convenient for the construction, maintenance, operation and protection of the Canal and of any works of sanitation, such as the collection and disposition of sewage and the distribution of water in the said cities of Panama and Colon, which, in the discretion of the United States may be necessary and convenient for the construction, maintenance, operation, sanitation and protection of the said Canal and railroad. . . .

The Republic of Panama agrees that the cities of Panama and Colon shall comply in perpetuity with the sanitary ordinances whether of a preventive or curative character prescribed by the United States and in case the Government of Panama is unable or fails in its duty to enforce this compliance by the cities of Panama and Colon with the sanitary ordinances of the United States the Republic of Panama grants to the United States the right and authority to enforce the same.

The same right and authority are granted to the United States for the maintenance of public order in the cities of Panama and Colon and the territories and harbors adjacent thereto in case the Republic of Panama should not be, in the judgment of the United States, able to maintain such order.

Article 8

The Republic of Panama grants to the United States all rights which it now has or hereafter may acquire to the property of the New Panama Canal Company and the Panama Railroad Company as a result of the transfer of sovereignty from the Republic of Colombia to the Republic of Panama over the Isthmus of Panama and authorizes the New Panama Canal Company to sell and transfer to the United States its rights, privileges, properties and concessions as well as the Panama Railroad and all the shares or part of the shares of that company; but the public lands situated outside of the zone described in Article 2 of this treaty now included in the concessions to both said enterprises and not required in the construction or operation of the Canal shall revert to the Republic of Panama except any property now owned by or in the possession of said companies within Panama or Colon or the ports or terminals thereof.

Article 9

The United States agrees that the ports at either entrance of the Canal and the waters thereof, and the Republic of Panama agrees that the towns of Panama and Colon shall be free for all time so that there shall not be imposed or collected custom house tolls, tonnage, anchorage, lighthouse, wharf, pilot, or quarantine dues or any other charges or taxes of any kind upon any vessel using or passing through the Canal or belonging to or employed by the United States, directly or indirectly, in connection with the construction, maintenance, operation, sanitation and protection of the main Canal, or auxiliary works, or upon the cargo, officers, crew, or passengers of any such vessels, except such tolls and charges as may be imposed by the United States for the use of the Canal and other works, and except tolls and charges imposed by the Republic of Panama upon merchandise destined to be introduced for the consumption of the rest of the Republic of Panama, and upon vessels touching at the ports of Colon and Panama and which do not cross the Canal.

The Government of the Republic of Panama shall have the right to establish in such ports and in the towns of Panama and Colon such houses and guards as it may deem necessary to collect duties on importations destined to other portions of Panama and to prevent contraband trade. The United States shall have the right to make use of the towns and harbors of Panama and Colon as places of anchorage, and for making repairs, for loading, unloading, depositing, or trans-shipping cargoes either in transit or destined for the service of the Canal and for other works pertaining to the Canal.

Article 10

The Republic of Panama agrees that there shall not be imposed any taxes, national, municipal, departmental, or of any other class, upon the Canal, the railways and auxiliary works, tugs and other vessels employed in the service of the Canal, store houses, work shops, offices, quarters for laborers, factories of all kinds, warehouses, wharves, machinery and other works, property, and effects appertaining to the Canal or railroad and auxiliary works, or their officers or employees, situated within the cities of Panama and Colon, and that there shall not be imposed contributions or charges of a personal character of any kind upon officers, employees, laborers, and other individuals in the service of the Canal and railroad and auxiliary works.

Article 11

The United States agrees that the official dispatches of the Government of the Republic of Panama shall be transmitted over any telegraph and telephone lines established for canal purposes and used for public and private business at rates not higher than those required from officials in the service of the United States.

Article 12

The Government of the Republic of Panama shall permit the immigration and free access to the lands and workshops of the Canal and its auxiliary works of all employees and workmen of whatever nationality under contract to work upon or seeking employment upon or in any wise connected with the said Canal and its auxiliary works, with their respective families, and all such persons shall be free and exempt from the military service of the Republic of Panama.

Article 13

The United States may import at any time into the said zone and auxiliary lands, free of custom duties, imposts, taxes, or other charges, and without any restrictions, any and all vessels, dredges, engines, cars, machinery, tools, explosives, materials, supplies, and other articles necessary and convenient in the construction, maintenance, operation, sanitation and protection of the Canal and auxiliary works, and all provisions, medicines, clothing, supplies and other things necessary and convenient for the officers, employees, workmen and laborers in the service and employ of the United States and for their families. If any such articles are disposed of for use outside of the zone and auxiliary lands granted to the United States and within the territory of the Republic, they shall be subject to the same import or other duties as like articles imported under the laws of the Republic of Panama.

Article 14

As the price or compensation for the rights, powers and privileges granted in this convention by the Republic of Panama to the United States, the Government of the United States agrees to pay to the Republic of Panama the sum of ten million dollars ($10,000,000) in gold coin of the United States on the exchange of the ratification of this convention and also an annual payment during the life of this convention of two hundred and fifty thousand dollars ($250,000) in like gold coin, beginning nine years after the date aforesaid.

The provisions of this Article shall be in addition to all other benefits assured to the Republic of Panama under this convention.

But no delay or difference of opinion under this Article or any other provisions of this treaty shall affect or interrupt the full operation and effect of this convention in all other respects. . . .

Article 18

The Canal, when constructed, and the entrances thereto shall be neutral in perpetuity, and shall be opened upon the terms provided for by Section I of Article three of and in conformity with all the stipulations of the treaty entered into by the Governments of the United States and Great Britain on November 18, 1901.

Article 19

The Government of the Republic of Panama shall have the right to transport over the Canal its vessels and its troops and munitions of war in such vessels at all times without paying charges of any kind. The exemption is to be extended to the auxiliary railway for the transportation of persons in the service of the Republic of Panama, or of the police force charged with the preservation of public order outside of said zone, as well as to their baggage, munitions of war and supplies. . . .

Article 23

If it should become necessary at any time to employ armed forces for the safety or protection of the Canal, or of the ships that make use of the same, or the railways and auxiliary works, the United States shall have the right, at all times and in its discretion, to use its police and its land and naval forces or to establish fortifications for these purposes.

Article 24

No change either in the Government or in the laws and treaties of the Republic of Panama shall, without the consent of the United States, affect any right of the United States under the present convention, or under any treaty stipulation between the two countries that now exists or may hereafter exist touching the subject matter of this convention.

If the Republic of Panama shall hereafter enter as a constituent into any other Government or into any union or confederation of states, so as to merge her sovereignty or independence in such Government, union or confederation, the rights of the United States under this convention shall not be in any respect lessened or impaired.

Article 25

For the better performance of the engagements of this convention and to the end of the efficient protection of the Canal and the preservation of its neutrality, the Government of the Republic of Panama will sell or lease to the United States lands adequate and necessary for naval or coaling stations on the Pacific coast and on the western Caribbean coast of the Republic at certain points to be agreed upon with the President of the United States. . . .

PANAMA CANAL TREATY: 1977–1978

The United States of America and the Republic of Panama,

Acting in the spirit of the Joint Declaration of April 3, 1964, by the Representatives of the Governments of the United States of America and the Republic of Panama, and of the Joint Statement of Principles of February 7, 1974, initialed by the Secretary of State of the United States of America and the Foreign Minister of the Republic of Panama, and

Acknowledging the Republic of Panama's sovereignty over its territory,

Have decided to terminate the prior Treaties pertaining to the Panama Canal and to conclude a new Treaty to serve as the basis for a new relationship between them and, accordingly, have agreed upon the following:

Article I
Abrogation of Prior Treaties and Establishment of a New Relationship

1. Upon its entry into force, this Treaty terminates and supersedes:

(a) The Isthmian Canal Convention between the United States of America and the Republic of Panama, signed at Washington, November 18, 1903;

(b) The Treaty of Friendship and Cooperation signed at Washington, March 2, 1936, and the Treaty of Mutual Understanding and Cooperation and the related Memorandum of Understandings Reached, signed at Panama, January 25, 1955, between the United States of America and the Republic of Panama;

(c) All other treaties, conventions, agreements and exchanges of notes between the United States of America and the Republic of Panama concerning the Panama Canal which were in force prior to the entry into force of this Treaty. . . .

2. In accordance with the terms of this Treaty and related agreements, the Republic of Panama, as territorial sovereign, grants to the United States of America, for the duration of this Treaty, the rights necessary to regulate the transit of ships through the Panama Canal, and to manage, operate, maintain, improve, protect and defend the Canal. The Republic of Panama guarantees to the United States of America the peaceful use of the land and water areas which it has been granted the rights to use for such purposes pursuant to this Treaty and related agreements.

3. The Republic of Panama shall participate increasingly in the management and protection and defense of the Canal, as provided in this Treaty.

4. In view of the special relationship established by this Treaty, the United States of America and the Republic of Panama shall cooperate to assure the uninterrupted and efficient operation of the Panama Canal.

Article II
Ratification, Entry Into Force, and Termination

1. This Treaty shall be subject to ratification in accordance with the constitutional procedures of the two Parties. . . .

2. This Treaty shall terminate at noon, Panama Time, December 31, 1999.

Article III
Canal Operation and Management

1. The Republic of Panama, as territorial sovereign, grants to the United States of America the rights to manage, operate, and maintain the Panama Canal, its complementary works, installations and equipment and to provide for the orderly transit of vessels through the Panama Canal. The United States of

America accepts the grant of such rights and undertakes to exercise them in accordance with this Treaty and related agreements.

2. In carrying out the foregoing responsibilities, the United States of America may:

(a) Use for the aforementioned purposes, without cost except as provided in this Treaty, the various installations and areas (including the Panama Canal) and waters, described in the Agreement in Implementation of this Article, signed this date, as well as such other areas and installations as are made available to the United States of America under this Treaty and related agreements, and take the measures necessary to ensure sanitation of such areas;

(b) Make such improvements and alterations to the aforesaid installations and areas as it deems appropriate, consistent with the terms of this Treaty;

(c) Make and enforce all rules pertaining to the passage of vessels through the Canal and other rules with respect to navigation and maritime matters, in accordance with this Treaty and related agreements. The Republic of Panama will lend its cooperation, when necessary, in the enforcement of such rules;

(d) Establish, modify, collect and retain tolls for the use of the Panama Canal, and other charges, and establish and modify methods of their assessment;

(e) Regulate relations with employees of the United States Government;

(f) Provide supporting services to facilitate the performance of its responsibilities under this Article;

(g) Issue and enforce regulations for the effective exercise of the rights and responsibilities of the United States of America under this Treaty and related agreements. The Republic of Panama will lend its cooperation, when necessary, in the enforcement of such rules; and

(h) Exercise any other right granted under this Treaty, or otherwise agreed upon between the two Parties.

3. Pursuant to the foregoing grant of rights, the United States of America shall, in accordance with the terms of this Treaty and the provisions of United States law, carry out its responsibility by means of a United States Government agency called the Panama Canal Commission, which shall be constituted by and in conformity with the laws of the United States of America.

(a) The Panama Canal Commission shall be supervised by a Board composed of nine members, five of whom shall be nationals of the United States of America, and four of whom shall be Panamanian nationals proposed by the Republic of Panama for appointment to such positions by the United States of America in a timely manner.

(b) Should the Republic of Panama request the United States of America to remove a Panamanian national from membership on the Board, the United States of America shall agree to such request. In that event, the Republic of Panama shall propose another Panamanian national for appointment by the United States of America to such position in a timely manner. In case of removal of a Panamanian member of the Board at the initiative of the United States of America, both Parties will consult in advance in order to reach agreement concerning such removal, and the Republic of Panama shall propose another Panamanian national for appointment by the United States of America in his stead.

(c) The United States of America shall employ a national of the United States of America as Administrator of the Panama Canal Commission, and a Panamanian national as Deputy Administrator, through December 31, 1989. Beginning January 1, 1990, a Panamanian national shall be employed as the Administrator and a national of the United States of America shall occupy the position of Deputy Administrator. Such Panamanian nationals shall be proposed to the United States of America by the Republic of Panama for appointment to such positions by the United States of America.

(d) Should the United States of America remove the Panamanian national from his position as Deputy Administrator, or Administrator, the Republic of Panama shall propose another Panamanian national for appointment to such position by the United States of America. . . .

5. The Panama Canal Commission shall reimburse the Republic of Panama for the costs incurred by the Republic of Panama in providing the following public services in the Canal operating areas and in housing areas set forth in the Agreement in Implementation of Article III of this Treaty and occupied by both United States and Panamanian citizen employees of the Panama Canal Commission: police, fire protection, street maintenance, street lighting, street cleaning, traffic management and garbage collection. The Panama Canal Commission shall pay the Republic of Panama the sum of ten million United States dollars ($10,000,000) per annum for the foregoing services. It is agreed that every three years from the date that this Treaty enters into force, the costs involved in furnishing said services shall be reexamined to determine whether adjustment of the annual payment should be made because of inflation and other relevant factors affecting the cost of such services.

6. The Republic of Panama shall be responsible for providing, in all areas comprising the former Canal Zone, services of a general jurisdictional nature such as customs and immigration, postal services, courts and licensing, in accordance with this Treaty and related agreements.

7. The United States of America and the Republic of Panama shall establish a Panama Canal Consultative Committee, composed of an equal number of high-level representatives of the United States of America and the Republic of Panama, and which may appoint such subcommittees as it may deem appropriate. This Committee shall advise the United States of America and the Republic of Panama on matters of policy affecting the Canal's operation. In view of both Parties' special interest in the continuity and efficiency of the Canal operation in the future, the Committee shall advise on matters such as general tolls policy, employment and training policies to increase the participation of Panamanian nationals in the operation of the Canal, and international policies on matters concerning the Canal. The Committee's recommendations shall be transmitted to the two Governments, which shall give such recommendations full consideration in the formulation of such policy decisions.

8. In addition to the participation of Panamanian nationals at high management levels of the Panama Canal Commission, as provided for in paragraph 3 of this Article, there shall be growing participation of Panamanian nationals at all other levels and areas of employment in the aforesaid commission, with the objective of preparing, in an orderly and efficient fashion, for the assumption by the Republic of Panama of full responsibility for the management, operation and maintenance of the Canal upon the termination of this Treaty. . . .

10. Upon entry into force of this Treaty, the United States Government agencies known as the Panama Canal Company and the Canal Zone Government shall cease to operate within the territory of the Republic of Panama that formerly constituted the Canal Zone.

Article IV
Protection and Defense

1. The United States of America and the Republic of Panama commit themselves to protect and defend the Panama Canal. Each Party shall act, in accordance with its constitutional processes, to meet the danger resulting from an armed attack or other actions which threaten the security of the Panama Canal or of ships transiting it.

2. For the duration of this Treaty, the United States of America shall have primary responsibility to protect and defend the Canal. The rights of the United States of America to station, train, and move military forces within the Republic of Panama are described in the Agreement in Implementation of this Article, signed this date. The use of areas and installations and the legal status of the armed forces of the United States of America in the Republic of Panama shall be governed by the aforesaid Agreement.

3. In order to facilitate the participation and cooperation of the armed forces of both Parties in the protection and defense of the Canal, the United States of America and the Republic of Panama shall establish a Combined Board comprised of an equal number of senior military representatives of each Party. These representatives shall be charged by their respective governments with consulting and cooperating on all matters pertaining to the protection and defense of the Canal, and with planning for actions to be taken in concert for that purpose. Such combined protection and defense arrangements shall not inhibit the identity or lines of authority of the armed forces of the United States of America or the Republic of Panama. The Combined Board shall provide for coordination and cooperation concerning such matters as:

(a) The preparation of contingency plans for the protection and defense of the Canal based upon the cooperative efforts of the armed forces of both Parties;

(b) The planning and conduct of combined military exercises; and

(c) The conduct of United States and Panamanian military operations with respect to the protection and defense of the Canal.

4. The Combined Board shall, at five-year intervals throughout the duration of this Treaty, review the resources being made available by the two Parties for

the protection and defense of the Canal. Also, the Combined Board shall make appropriate recommendations to the two Governments respecting projected requirements, the efficient utilization of available resources of the two Parties, and other matters of mutual interest with respect to the protection and defense of the Canal.

5. To the extent possible consistent with its primary responsibility for the protection and defense of the Panama Canal, the United States of America will endeavor to maintain its armed forces in the Republic of Panama in normal times at a level not in excess of that of the armed forces of the United States of America in the territory of the former Canal Zone immediately prior to the entry into force of this Treaty.

Article V
Principle of Non-Intervention

Employees of the Panama Canal Commission, their dependents and designated contractors of the Panama Canal Commission, who are nationals of the United States of America, shall respect the laws of the Republic of Panama and shall abstain from any activity incompatible with the spirit of this Treaty. Accordingly, they shall abstain from any political activity in the Republic of Panama as well as from any intervention in the internal affairs of the Republic of Panama. The United States of America shall take all measures within its authority to ensure that the provisions of this Article are fulfilled.

Article VI
Protection of the Environment

1. The United States of America and the Republic of Panama commit themselves to implement this Treaty in a manner consistent with the protection of the natural environment of the Republic of Panama. To this end, they shall consult and cooperate with each other in all appropriate ways to ensure that they shall give due regard to the protection and conservation of the environment. . . .

Article VII
Flags

1. The entire territory of the Republic of Panama, including the areas the use of which the Republic of Panama makes available to the United States of America pursuant to this Treaty and related agreements, shall be under the flag of the Republic of Panama, and consequently such flag always shall occupy the position of honor. . . .

Article IX
Applicable Laws and Law Enforcement

1. In accordance with the provisions of this Treaty and related agreements, the law of the Republic of Panama shall apply in the areas made available for the use of the United States of America pursuant to this Treaty. The law of the Republic

of Panama shall be applied to matters or events which occurred in the former Canal Zone prior to the entry into force of this Treaty only to the extent specifically provided in prior treaties and agreements.

2. Natural or juridical persons who, on the date of entry into force of this Treaty, are engaged in business or non-profit activities at locations in the former Canal Zone may continue such business or activities at those locations under the same terms and conditions prevailing prior to the entry into force of this Treaty for a thirty-month transition period from its entry into force. The Republic of Panama shall maintain the same operating conditions as those applicable to the aforementioned enterprises prior to the entry into force of this Treaty in order that they may receive licenses to do business in the Republic of Panama subject to their compliance with the requirements of its law. Thereafter, such persons shall receive the same treatment under the law of the Republic of Panama as similar enterprises already established in the rest of the territory of the Republic of Panama without discrimination.

3. The rights of ownership, as recognized by the United States of America, enjoyed by natural or juridical private persons in buildings and other improvements to real property located in the former Canal Zone shall be recognized by the Republic of Panama in conformity with its laws. . . .

11. The Parties shall conclude an agreement whereby nationals of either State, who are sentenced by the courts of the other State, and who are not domiciled therein, may elect to serve their sentences in their State of nationality.

Article X
Employment with the Panama Canal Commission

1. In exercising its rights and fulfilling its responsibilities as the employer, the United States of America shall establish employment and labor regulations which shall contain the terms, conditions and prerequisites for all categories of employees of the Panama Canal Commission. These regulations shall be provided to the Republic of Panama prior to their entry into force.

2. (a) The regulations shall establish a system of preference when hiring employees, for Panamanian applicants possessing the skills and qualifications required for employment by the Panama Canal Commission. The United States of America shall endeavor to ensure that the number of Panamanian nationals employed by the Panama Canal Commission in relation to the total number of its employees will conform to the proportion established for foreign enterprises under the law of the Republic of Panama.

(b) The terms and conditions of employment to be established will in general be no less favorable to persons already employed by the Panama Canal Company or Canal Zone Government prior to the entry into force of this Treaty, than those in effect immediately prior to that date.

3. (a) The United States of America shall establish an employment policy for the Panama Canal Commission that shall generally limit the recruitment of

personnel outside the Republic of Panama to persons possessing requisite skills and qualifications which are not available in the Republic of Panama.

(b) The United States of America will establish training programs for Panamanian employees and apprentices in order to increase the number of Panamanian nationals qualified to assume positions with the Panama Canal Commission, as positions become available.

(c) Within five years from the entry into force of this Treaty, the number of United States nationals employed by the Panama Canal Commission who were previously employed by the Panama Canal Company shall be at least twenty percent less than the total number of United States nationals working for the Panama Canal Company immediately prior to the entry into force of this Treaty. . . .

6. With regard to wages and fringe benefits, there shall be no discrimination on the basis of nationality, sex, or race. Payments by the Panama Canal Commission of additional remuneration, or the provision of other benefits, such as home leave benefits, to United States nationals employed prior to entry into force of this Treaty, or to persons of any nationality, including Panamanian nationals who are thereafter recruited outside of the Republic of Panama and who change their place of residence, shall not be considered to be discrimination for the purpose of this paragraph.

7. Persons employed by the Panama Canal Company or Canal Zone Government prior to the entry into force of this Treaty, who are displaced from their employment as a result of the discontinuance by the United States of America of certain activities pursuant to this Treaty, will be placed by the United States of America, to the maximum extent feasible, in other appropriate jobs with the Government of the United States in accordance with United States Civil Service regulations. For such persons who are not United States nationals, placement efforts will be confined to United States Government activities located within the Republic of Panama. Likewise, persons previously employed in activities for which the Republic of Panama assumes responsibility as a result of this Treaty will be continued in their employment to the maximum extent feasible by the Republic of Panama. The Republic of Panama shall, to the maximum extent feasible, ensure that the terms and conditions of employment applicable to personnel employed in the activities for which it assumes responsibility are no less favorable than those in effect immediately prior to the entry into force of this Treaty. . . .

Article XI
Provisions for the Transition Period

1. The Republic of Panama shall reassume plenary jurisdiction over the former Canal Zone upon entry into force of this Treaty and in accordance with its terms. In order to provide for an orderly transition to the full application of the jurisdictional arrangements established by this Treaty and related agree-

ments, the provisions of this Article shall become applicable upon the date this Treaty enters into force, and shall remain in effect for thirty calendar months. The authority granted in this Article to the United States of America for this transition period shall supplement, and is not intended to limit, the full application and effect of the rights and authority granted to the United States of America elsewhere in this Treaty and in related agreements.

2. During this transition period, the criminal and civil laws of the United States of America shall apply concurrently with those of the Republic of Panama in certain of the areas and installations made available for the use of the United States of America pursuant to this Treaty, in accordance with the following provisions:

(a) The Republic of Panama permits the authorities of the United States of America to have the primary right to exercise criminal jurisdiction over United States citizen employees of the Panama Canal Commission and their dependents, and members of the United States Forces and civilian component and their dependents, in the following cases:

(i) for any offense committed during the transition period within such areas and installations, and

(ii) for any offense committed prior to that period in the former Canal Zone.

The Republic of Panama shall have the primary right to exercise jurisdiction over all other offenses committed by such persons, except as otherwise provided in this Treaty and related agreements or as may be otherwise agreed.

(b) Either Party may waive its primary right to exercise jurisdiction in a specific case or category of cases.

3. The United States of America shall retain the right to exercise jurisdiction in criminal cases relating to offenses committed prior to the entry into force of this Treaty in violation of the laws applicable in the former Canal Zone.

4. For the transition period, the United States of America shall retain police authority and maintain a police force in the aforementioned areas and installations. . . .

5. The courts of the United States of America and related personnel, functioning in the former Canal Zone immediately prior to the entry into force of this Treaty, may continue to function during the transition period for the judicial enforcement of the jurisdiction to be exercised by the United States of America in accordance with this Article. . . .

Article XII
A Sea-Level Canal or a Third Lane of Locks

1. The United States of America and the Republic of Panama recognize that a sea-level canal may be important for international navigation in the future. Consequently, during the duration of this Treaty, both Parties commit themselves to study jointly the feasibility of a sea-level canal in the Republic of Panama, and in the event they determine that such a waterway is necessary, they shall negotiate terms, agreeable to both Parties, for its construction.

2. The United States of America and the Republic of Panama agree on the following:

(a) No new interoceanic canal shall be constructed in the territory of the Republic of Panama during the duration of this Treaty, except in accordance with the provisions of this Treaty, or as the two Parties may otherwise agree; and

(b) During the duration of this Treaty, the United States of America shall not negotiate with third States for the right to construct an interoceanic canal on any other route in the Western Hemisphere, except as the two Parties may otherwise agree.

3. The Republic of Panama grants to the United States of America the right to add a third lane of locks to the existing Panama Canal. This right may be exercised at any time during the duration of this Treaty, provided that the United States of America has delivered to the Republic of Panama copies of the plans for such construction.

4. In the event the United States of America exercises the right granted in paragraph 3 above, it may use for that purpose, in addition to the areas otherwise made available to the United States of America pursuant to this Treaty, such other areas as the two Parties may agree upon. The terms and conditions applicable to Canal operating areas made available by the Republic of Panama for the use of the United States of America pursuant to Article III of this Treaty shall apply in a similar manner to such additional areas.

5. In the construction of the aforesaid works, the United States of America shall not use nuclear excavation techniques without the previous consent of the Republic of Panama.

Article XIII
Property Transfer and Economic Participation by the Republic of Panama

1. Upon termination of this Treaty, the Republic of Panama shall assume total responsibility for the management, operation, and maintenance of the Panama Canal, which shall be turned over in operating condition and free of liens and debts, except as the two Parties may otherwise agree. . . .

4. The Republic of Panama shall receive, in addition, from the Panama Canal Commission a just and equitable return on the national resources which it has dedicated to the efficient management, operation, maintenance, protection and defense of the Panama Canal, in accordance with the following:

(a) An annual amount to be paid out of Canal operating revenues computed at a rate of thirty hundredths of a United States dollar ($0.30) per Panama Canal net ton, or its equivalency, for each vessel transiting the Canal after the entry into force of this Treaty, for which tolls are charged. The rate of thirty hundredths of a United States dollar ($0.30) per Panama Canal net ton, or its equivalency, will be adjusted to reflect changes in the United States wholesale price index for total manufactured goods during biennial periods. The first adjustment shall take place five years after entry into force of this Treaty, taking into account the changes that occurred in such price index during the preceding two years. Thereafter, successive adjustments shall take place at the end of each biennial period. If the United States of America should decide that another indexing method is preferable, such method shall be proposed to the Republic of Panama and applied if mutually agreed.

(b) A fixed annuity of ten million United States dollars ($10,000,000) to be paid out of Canal operating revenues. This amount shall constitute a fixed expense of the Panama Canal Commission.

(c) An annual amount of up to ten million United States dollars ($10,000,000) per year, to be paid out of Canal operating revenues to the extent that such revenues exceed expenditures of the Panama Canal Commission including amounts paid pursuant to this Treaty. In the event Canal operating revenues in any year do not produce a surplus sufficient to cover this payment, the unpaid balance shall be paid from operating surpluses in future years in a manner to be mutually agreed.

Article XIV
Settlement of Disputes

In the event that any question should arise between the Parties concerning the interpretation of this Treaty or related agreements, they shall make every effort to resolve the matter through consultation in the appropriate committees established pursuant to this Treaty and related agreements, or, if appropriate, through diplomatic channels. In the event the Parties are unable to resolve a particular matter through such means, they may, in appropriate cases, agree to submit the matter to conciliation, mediation, arbitration, or such other procedure for the peaceful settlement of the dispute as they may mutually deem appropriate.

DONE at Washington, this 7th day of September, 1977, in duplicate, in the English and Spanish languages, both texts being equally authentic.

TREATY CONCERNING THE PERMANENT NEUTRALITY AND OPERATION OF THE PANAMA CANAL: 1977–1978

The United States of America and the Republic of Panama have agreed upon the following:

Article I

The Republic of Panama declares that the Canal, as an international transit waterway, shall be permanently neutral in accordance with the regime established in this Treaty. The same regime of neutrality shall apply to any other international waterway that may be built either partially or wholly in the territory of the Republic of Panama.

Article II

The Republic of Panama declares the neutrality of the Canal in order that both in time of peace and in time of war it shall remain secure and open to peaceful transit by the vessels of all nations on terms of entire equality, so that there will be no discrimination against any nation, or its citizens or subjects, concerning the conditions or charges of transit, or for any other reason, and so that the Canal, and therefore the Isthmus of Panama, shall not be the target of reprisals in any armed conflict between other nations of the world. The foregoing shall be subject to the following requirements:

(a) Payment of tolls and other charges for transit and ancillary services, provided they have been fixed in conformity with the provisions of Article III(c);

(b) Compliance with applicable rules and regulations, provided such rules and regulations are applied in conformity with the provisions of Article III;

(c) The requirement that transiting vessels commit no acts of hostility while in the Canal; and

(d) Such other conditions and restrictions as are established by this Treaty.

Article III

1. For purposes of the security, efficiency and proper maintenance of the Canal the following rules shall apply:

(a) The Canal shall be operated efficiently in accordance with conditions of transit through the Canal, and rules and regulations that shall be just, equitable and reasonable, and limited to those necessary for safe navigation and efficient, sanitary operation of the Canal;

(b) Ancillary services necessary for transit through the Canal shall be provided;

(c) Tolls and other charges for transit and ancillary services shall be just, reasonable, equitable and consistent with the principles of international law;

(d) As a pre-condition of transit, vessels may be required to establish clearly the financial responsibility and guarantees for payment of reasonable and adequate indemnification, consistent with international practice and standards, for damages resulting from acts or omissions of such vessels when passing through the Canal. In the case of vessels owned or operated by a State or for which it has acknowledged responsibility, a certification by that State that it shall observe its obligations under international law to pay for damages resulting from the act or omission of such vessels when passing through the Canal shall be deemed sufficient to establish such financial responsibility;

(e) Vessels of war and auxiliary vessels of all nations shall at all times be entitled to transit the Canal, irrespective of their internal operation, means of propulsion, origin, destination or armament, without being subjected, as a condition of transit, to inspection, search or surveillance. However, such vessels may be required to certify that they have complied with all applicable health, sanitation and quarantine regulations. In addition, such vessels shall be entitled to refuse to disclose their internal operation, origin, armament, cargo or destination. However, auxiliary vessels may be required to present written assurances, certified by an official at a high level of the government of the State requesting the exemption, that they are owned or operated by that government and in this case are being used only on government noncommercial service.

2. For the purposes of this Treaty, the terms "Canal," "vessel of war," "auxiliary vessel," "internal operation," "armament" and "inspection" shall have the meanings assigned them in Annex A to this Treaty.

Article IV

The United States of America and the Republic of Panama agree to maintain the regime of neutrality established in this Treaty, which shall be maintained in order that the Canal shall remain permanently neutral, notwithstanding the termination of any other treaties entered into by the two Contracting Parties.

Article V

After the termination of the Panama Canal Treaty, only the Republic of Panama shall operate the Canal and maintain military forces, defense sites and military installations within its national territory.

Article VI

1. In recognition of the important contributions of the United States of America and of the Republic of Panama to the construction, operation, maintenance, and protection and defense of the Canal, vessels of war and auxiliary vessels of those nations shall, notwithstanding any other provisions of this Treaty, be entitled to transit the Canal irrespective of their internal operation, means of propulsion, origin, destination, armament or cargo carried. Such vessels of war and auxiliary vessels will be entitled to transit the Canal expeditiously.

2. The United States of America, so long as it has responsibility for the operation of the Canal, may continue to provide the Republic of Colombia toll-free transit through the Canal for its troops, vessels and materials of war. Thereafter, the Republic of Panama may provide the Republic of Colombia and the Republic of Costa Rica with the right of toll-free transit.

Article VII

1. The United States of America and the Republic of Panama shall jointly sponsor a resolution in the Organization of American States opening to accession by all nations of the world the Protocol to this Treaty whereby all the signatories will adhere to the objectives of this Treaty, agreeing to respect the regime of neutrality set forth herein.

2. The Organization of American States shall act as the depositary for this Treaty and related instruments.

Article VIII

This Treaty shall be subject to ratification in accordance with the constitutional procedures of the two Parties. The instruments of ratification of this

Treaty shall be exchanged at Panama at the same time as the instruments of ratification of the Panama Canal Treaty, signed this date, are exchanged. This Treaty shall enter into force, simultaneously with the Panama Canal Treaty, six calendar months from the date of the exchange of the instruments of ratification.

DONE at Washington, this 7th day of September, 1977, in the English and Spanish languages, both texts being equally authentic.

Protocol to the Treaty Concerning the Permanent Neutrality and Operation of the Panama Canal

Whereas the maintenance of the neutrality of the Panama Canal is important not only to the commerce and security of the United States of America and the Republic of Panama, but to the peace and security of the Western Hemisphere and to the interests of world commerce as well;

Whereas the regime of neutrality which the United States of America and the Republic of Panama have agreed to maintain will ensure permanent access to the Canal by vessels of all nations on the basis of entire equality; and

Whereas the said regime of effective neutrality shall constitute the best protection for the Canal and shall ensure the absence of any hostile act against it;

The Contracting Parties to this Protocol have agreed upon the following:

Article I

The Contracting Parties hereby acknowledge the regime of permanent neutrality for the Canal established in the Treaty Concerning the Permanent Neutrality and Operation of the Panama Canal and associate themselves with its objectives.

Article II

The Contracting Parties agree to observe and respect the regime of permanent neutrality of the Canal in time of war as in time of peace, and to ensure that vessels of their registry strictly observe the applicable rules.

Article III

This Protocol shall be open to accession by all States of the world, and shall enter into force for each State at the time of deposit of its instrument of accession with the Secretary General of the Organization of American States.

Senate additions to Neutrality Treaty March 16, 1978

Resolved (two-thirds of the Senators present concurring therein), That the Senate advise and consent to the ratification of the Treaty Concerning the Permanent Neutrality and Operation of the Panama Canal, together with Annexes A and B thereto and the Protocol relating thereto, done at Washington on September 7, 1977 (Executive N, Ninety-fifth Congress, first session), subject to the following—

(a) Amendments:

(1) At the end of Article IV, insert the following:

"A correct and authoritative statement of certain rights and duties of the Parties under the foregoing is contained in the Statement of Understanding issued by the Government of the United States of America on October 14, 1977, and by the Government of the Republic of Panama on October 18, 1977, which is hereby incorporated as an integral part of this Treaty, as follows:

" 'Under the Treaty Concerning the Permanent Neutrality and Operation of the Panama Canal (the Neutrality Treaty), Panama and the United States have the responsibility to assure that the Panama Canal will remain open and secure to ships of all nations. The correct interpretation of this principle is that each of the two countries shall, in accordance with their respective constitutional processes, defend the Canal against any threat to the regime of neutrality, and consequently shall have the right to act against any aggression or threat directed against the Canal or against the peaceful transit of vessels through the Canal.

" 'This does not mean, nor shall it be interpreted as, a right of intervention of the United States in the internal affairs of Panama. Any United States action will be directed at insuring that the Canal will remain open, secure, and accessible, and it shall never be directed against the territorial integrity or political independence of Panama.'."

(2A) At the end of the first paragraph of Article VI, insert the following:

"In accordance with the Statement of Understanding mentioned in Article IV above: 'The Neutrality Treaty provides that the vessels of war and auxiliary vessels of the United States and Panama will be entitled to transit the Canal expeditiously. This is intended, and it shall so be interpreted, to assure the transit of such vessels through the Canal as quickly as possible, without any impediment, with expedited treatment, and in case of need or emergency, to go to the head of the line of vessels in order to transit the Canal rapidly.' "

(b) Conditions:

(1) Notwithstanding the provisions of Article V or any other provision of the Treaty, if the Canal is closed, or its operations are interfered with, the United States of America and the Republic of Panama shall each independently have the right to take such steps as each deems necessary, in accordance with its constitutional processes, including the use of military force in the Republic of Panama, to reopen the Canal or restore the operations of the Canal, as the case may be.

(2) The instruments of ratification of the Treaty shall be exchanged only upon the conclusion of a Protocol of Exchange, to be signed by authorized representatives of both Governments, which shall constitute an integral part of the Treaty documents and which shall include the following:

"Nothing in the Treaty shall preclude the Republic of Panama and the United States of America from making, in accordance with their respective constitutional processes, any agreement or arrangement between the two countries to facilitate performance at any time after December 31, 1999, of their responsibilities to maintain the regime of neutrality established in the Treaty, including agreements or arrangements for the stationing of any United States military forces or the maintenance of defense sites after that date in the Republic of Panama that the Republic of Panama and the United States of America may deem necessary or appropriate.".

(c) Reservations:. . . .

(4) To carry out the purposes of Article III of the Treaty of assuring the security, efficiency, and proper maintenance of the Panama Canal, the United States of America and the Republic of Panama, during their respective periods of responsibility for Canal operation and maintenance, shall, unless the amount of the operating revenues of the Canal exceeds the amount needed to carry out the purposes of such Article, use such revenues of the Canal only for purposes consistent with the purposes of Article III.

(d) Understandings:

(1) Paragraph 1(c) of Article III of the Treaty shall be construed as requiring, before any adjustment in tolls for use of the Canal, that the effects of any such toll adjustment on the trade patterns of the two Parties shall be given full consideration, including consideration of the following factors in a manner consistent with the regime of neutrality:

(A) the costs of operating and maintaining the Panama Canal;

(B) the competitive position of the use of the Canal in relation to other means of transportation;

(C) the interests of both Parties in maintaining their domestic fleets;

(D) the impact of such an adjustment on the various geographical areas of each of the two Parties; and

(E) the interests of both Parties in maximizing their international commerce.

The United States of America and the Republic of Panama shall cooperate in exchanging information necessary for the consideration of such factors.

(2) The agreement "to maintain the regime of neutrality established in this Treaty" in Article IV of the Treaty means that either of the two Parties to the Treaty may, in accordance with its constitutional processes, take unilateral action to defend the Panama Canal against any threat, as determined by the Party taking such action.

(3) The determination of "need or emergency" for the purpose of any vessel of war or auxiliary vessel of the United States of America or the Republic of Panama going to the head of the line of vessels in order to transit the Panama Canal rapidly shall be made by the nation operating such vessel.

(4) Nothing in the Treaty, in Annex A or B thereto, in the Protocol relating to the Treaty, or in any other agreement relating to the Treaty, obligates the United States of America to provide any economic assistance, military grant assistance,

security supporting assistance, foreign military sales credits, or international military education and training to the Republic of Panama.

(5) The President shall include all amendments, conditions, reservations, and understandings incorporated by the Senate in this resolution of ratification in the instrument of ratification to be exchanged with the Government of the Republic of Panama.

U.S. Senate additions to Canal Treaty April 18, 1978

Resolved (two-thirds of the Senators present concurring therein), That the Senate advise and consent to the ratification of the Panama Canal Treaty, together with the Annex and Agreed Minute relating thereto, done at Washington on September 7, 1977 (Executive N, Ninety-fifth Congress, first session), subject to the following—

(a) Reservations:

(1) Pursuant to its adherence to the principle of nonintervention, any action taken by the United States of America in the exercise of its rights to assure that the Panama Canal shall remain open, neutral, secure, and accessible, pursuant to the provisions of the Panama Canal Treaty, the Treaty Concerning the Permanent Neutrality and Operation of the Panama Canal, and the resolutions of ratification thereto, shall be only for the purpose of assuring that the Canal shall remain open, neutral, secure, and accessible, and shall not have as its purpose or be interpreted as a right of intervention in the internal affairs of the Republic of Panama or interference with its political independence or sovereign integrity.

(2) The instruments of ratification of the Panama Canal Treaty to be exchanged by the United States of America and the Republic of Panama shall each include provisions whereby each Party agrees to waive its rights and release the other Party from its obligations under paragraph 2 of Article XII of the Treaty.

(3) Notwithstanding any provision of the Treaty, no funds may be drawn from the Treasury of the United States of America for payments under paragraph 4 of Article XIII wthout statutory authorization.

(4) Any accumulated unpaid balance under paragraph 4(c) of Article XIII of the Treaty at the date of termination of the Treaty shall be payable only to the extent of any operating surplus in the last year of the duration of the Treaty, and nothing in such paragraph may be construed as obligating the United States of America to pay, after the date of the termination of the Treaty, any such unpaid balance which shall have accrued before such date.

(5) Exchange of the instruments of ratification of the Panama Canal Treaty and of the Treaty Concerning the Permanent Neutrality and Operation of the Panama Canal shall not be effective earlier than March 31, 1979, and such Treaties shall not enter into force prior to October 1, 1979, unless legislation necessary to implement the provisions of the Panama Canal Treaty shall have been enacted by the Congress of the United States of America before March 31, 1979.

(6) After the date of entry into force of the Treaty, the Panama Canal Commission shall, unless otherwise provided by legislation enacted by the Congress of the United States of America, be obligated to reimburse the Treasury of the United States of America, as nearly as possible, for the interest cost of the funds or other assets directly invested in the Commission by the Government of the United States of America and for the interest cost of the funds or other assets directly invested in the predecessor Panama Canal Company by the Government of the United States of America and not reimbursed before the date of entry into force of the Treaty. Such reimbursement for such interest costs shall be made at a rate determined by the Secretary of the Treasury of the United States of America and at annual intervals to the extent earned, and if not earned, shall be made from subsequent earnings. For purposes of this reservation, the phrase "funds or other assets directly invested" shall have the same meaning as the phrase "net direct investment" has under section 62 of title 2 of the Canal Zone Code.

(b) Understandings:

(1) Before the first day of the three-year period beginning on the date of entry into force of the Treaty and before each three-year period following thereafter, the two Parties shall agree upon the specific levels and quality of services, as are referred to in paragraph 5 of Article III of the Treaty, to be provided during the following three-year period and, except for the first three-year period, on the reimbursement to be made for the costs of such services, such services to be limited to such as are essential to the effective functioning of the Canal operating areas and the housing areas referred to in paragraph 5 of Article III. If payments made under paragraph 5 of Article III for the preceding three-year period, including the initial three-year period, exceed or are less than the actual costs to the Republic of Panama for supplying, during such period, the specific levels and quality of services agreed upon, then the Panama Canal Commission shall deduct from or add to the payment required to be made to the Republic of Panama for each of the following three years one-third of such excess or deficit, as the case may be. There shall be an independent and binding audit, conducted by an auditor mutually selected by both Parties, or any costs of services disputed by the two Parties pursuant to the reexamination of such costs provided for in this understanding.

(2) Nothing in paragraph 3, 4, or 5 or Article IV of the Treaty may be construed to limit either the provisions of the first paragraph of Article IV providing that each Party shall act, in accordance with its constitutional processes, to meet danger threatening the security of the Panama Canal, or the provisions of paragraph 2 of Article IV providing that the United States of America shall have primary responsibility to protect and defend the Canal for the duration of the Treaty.

(3) Nothing in paragraph 4(c) of Article XIII of the Treaty shall be construed to limit the authority of the United States of America, through the United States

Government agency called the Panama Canal Commission, to make such financial decisions and incur such expenses as are reasonable and necessary for the management, operation, and maintenance of the Panama Canal. In addition, toll rates established pursuant to paragraph 2(d) of Article III need not be set at levels designed to produce revenues to cover the payment to the Republic of Panama described in paragraph 4(c) of Article XIII.

(4) Any agreement concluded pursuant to paragraph 11 of Article IX of the Treaty with respect to the transfer of prisoners shall be concluded in accordance with the constitutional processes of both Parties.

(5) Nothing in the Treaty, in the Annex or Agreed Minute relating to the Treaty, or in any other agreement relating to the Treaty obligates the United States of America to provide any economic assistance, military grant assistance, security supporting assistance, foreign military sales credits, or international military education and training to the Republic of Panama.

(6) The President shall include all reservations and understandings incorporated by the Senate in this resolution of ratification in the instrument of ratification to be exchanged with the Government of the Republic of Panama.

Bibliographical Essay

General Works

Foreign Relations of the United States, published by the U.S. Department of State, is the indispensable primary source; it is cited in the book as *FRUS,* followed by year and, when necessary, volume number. It was begun in 1861, and its publication date was changed in the early twentieth century so a volume was published twenty years after the events it documented. The gap has grown to nearly thirty years, and the volumes on Latin America are only down into the mid-1950s. Because the State Department's Declassification Office is so slow, and so unnecessarily secretive about events of more than thirty years before, an increasingly important source for information on U.S. policy—and a less-censored source—will be the Foreign Office documents in the British Public Record Office in Kew, England: these documents are automatically opened thirty years after the event. Documents are also available at the National Archives in Washington, D.C., mostly in Record Group #59. These are cited in the book as NA, RG 59. Most of the documents through 1929 are available on microfilm.

Important periodicals are *Department of State Bulletin,* containing speeches of State Department officials and also some documents; *Latin America* (London), probably the best weekly newsletter on the 1960s and 1970s; *Latin America Report* (Guatemala City); and—of special importance—*Central America News-*

Pak, published biweekly by the Central America Resource Center, Austin, Texas, and containing key articles from North American and Latin American newspapers. The United Nations' Economic Commission for Latin America, *Economic Survey of Latin America,* is thorough and authoritative. Other periodical material is listed in the *Reader's Guide to Periodical Literature* and *Social Science Index.*

Published documentary material on presidential pronouncements can be found in James D. Richardson, *Messages and Papers of the Presidents* (New York, 1897–1914), and *Public Papers of the Presidents,* a well-indexed annual source published by the Government Printing Office and covering every Chief Executive since Truman. The best sources for congressional work on Panama, other than the *Congressional Record,* are the publications of the Senate Foreign Relations Committee, the House Foreign Affairs Committee, and the House Merchant Marine and Fisheries Committee (especially its Panama Canal Subcommittee).

An indispensable secondary source is Thomas E. Weil *et al., Area Handbook for Panama* (Washington, D.C., 1972). Good surveys are Sheldon B. Liss, *The Canal: Aspects of United States–Panamanian Relations* (Notre Dame, Ind., 1967); William D. McCain, *The United States and the Republic of Panama* (Durham, N.C., 1937), a superb treatment of the 1903–1936 years; and especially Steve Ropp, *Panamanian Politics: From Guarded Nation to National Guard* (New York, 1982), the best recent overview. David N. Farnsworth and James W. McKinney, *U.S.-Panama Relations, 1903–1978* (Boulder, Colo., 1983) is especially strong on the politics. Herbert and Mary Knapp, *Red, White, and Blue Paradise: The American Canal Zone in Panama* (San Diego, 1984), is an outspoken and colorful Zonian view. Michael L. Conniff, *Black Labor on a White Canal: Panama, 1904–1981* (Pittsburgh, 1985) is definitive. Panamanian perspectives are available in Ernesto J. Castillero Reyes, *Historia de Panamá* (Panama, 1955); and Ernesto Castillero Pimental, *Politica Exterior de Panamá* (Panama, 1961), a small handbook on the objectives and bases of Panamanian foreign policy. Castillero Reyes' *El Canal de Panama* (n. p., n. d., but approximately mid-1960s) emphasizes the pre-1904 era. Lawrence O. Ealy has written two important accounts: *The Republic of Panama in World Affairs, 1903–1950* (Philadelphia, 1951), the best work in English on Panamanian foreign policy in those years; and *Yanqui Politics and the Isthmian Canal* (University Park, Pa., 1971), good on the North American debates.

Some of the best analyses of Panama and its relations with the United States can be found in articles: Jules B. Billard, "Panama, Link Between Oceans and Continents," *National Geographic,* CXXXVII (March 1970), pp. 402–440, a splendid, well-illustrated introduction; Daniel Goldrich, "Panama," in Martin C.Needler, ed., *Political Systems of Latin America* (Princeton, 1964), an excellent survey by one of the best scholars of Panamanian affairs; Louis Harris, "Panama," in Ben G. Burnett and Kenneth F. Johnson, eds., *Political Forces in Latin America* (Belmont, Calif., 1968); two articles by a dean of Latin American studies in the United States, E. Bradford Burns, "Panama's Struggle for Independence," *Current History*, LXVI (January 1974), and "Panama: The Search for Independence," *Current History*, LXXII (February 1977); and Lester D. Langley, "The United States and Panama: The Burden of Power," *Current History*, LVI (January 1969). Langley's work on U.S.-Panamanian relations is crucial; several of his essays, listed below, are standard on the years they cover. Note especially his "U.S.-Panamanian Relations Since 1941," *Journal of Inter-American Studies*, XII (July 1970). A useful overview, stressing the post-1960 era, is Robert E. Looney, *The Economic Development of Panama* (New York, 1976); and an insider's account of United Fruit is Thomas P. McCann, *An American Company: The Tragedy of United Fruit* (New York, 1976). McCann notes the extensive earlier work on United Fruit in Latin America. Standard on legal questions is R. R. Baxter, *The Laws of International Waterways, with Particular Regard to Interoceanic Canals* (Cambridge, Mass., 1964). In a class by itself is Alain Rouquié, *The Military and the State in Latin America*, translated by Paul E. Sigmund (Berkeley, Calif., 1988), especially good for post-1968 Panamanian development.

Documents from the early nineteenth century through the 1955 treaty, including some private reports as well as the treaties and other agreements, are usefully compiled in Diogenes A. Arosemena G., *Documentary Diplomatic History of the Panama Canal* (Panama, 1961).

The Early Years (to 1904)

A well-written introduction for the Panamanian side is David Howarth, *Four Hundred Years of Dreams and Cruelty* (New York, 1966). The most important scholarly work on Panamanian nationalism is Ricaurte Soler's writings, especially *Pensamiento Panameño y Concepión de la Nacionalidad durante el Siglo XIX* (Panama, 1954); and *Formas Ideológicas de la Nación Panameña* (San Jose, Costa Rica, 1972). The Burns essays, noted above, are of special significance.

The nineteenth-century North American movement into Panamanian affairs is analyzed in Charles S. Campbell's excellent *The Transformation of American Foreign Relations, 1865–1900* (New York, 1976); Richard D. Challener's *Admirals, Generals, and American Foreign Policy, 1898–1914* (Princeton, 1973), a pioneering account of military strategy with a valuable chapter on isthmian intervention; and Kenneth J. Hagan's fine monograph, *American Gunboat Diplomacy and the Old Navy, 1877–1889* (Westport, Conn., 1973). The broad background through the 1903 revolution has been covered many times in superb accounts: Dwight C. Miner, *The Fight for the Panama Canal Route* (New York, 1940); Miles P. DuVal, *Cadiz to Cathay* (Stanford, 1940), especially useful for the Colombian side; Gerstle Mack, *The Land Divided* (New York, 1944), exhaustive on the pre-1921 years; Lester D. Langley, *Struggle for the American Mediterranean: United States-European Rivalry in the Gulf-Caribbean, 1776–1904* (Athens, Ga., 1976), an excellent survey placed within the larger international framework; and two definitive articles by Charles D. Ameringer, "The Panama Canal Lobby of Philippe Bunau-Varilla and William Nelson Cromwell," *American Historical Review*, LXVII (January 1963); and "Philippe Bunau-Varilla: New Light on the Panama Canal Treaty," *Hispanic American Historical Review*, XLVI (February 1966). Much of this has now been synthesized in David McCullough's readable *The Path Between the Seas: The Creation of the Panama Canal, 1870–1914* (New York, 1977). A new and fresh account is Richard L. Lael, *Arrogant Diplomacy: U.S. Policy Toward Colombia, 1903–1922* (Wilmington, Del., 1987). Theodore Roosevelt's letters are available in Elting E. Morison, ed., *The Letters of Theodore Roosevelt*, 6 vols. (Cambridge, Mass., 1951). Central figures are analyzed in Richard W. Leopold, *Elihu Root and the Conservative Tradition* (Boston, 1954); Stanford University Libraries, *Francis Butler Loomis and the Panama Crisis* (Stanford, Calif., 1965), although much remains to be done on Loomis. Bunau-Varilla tells his story with all the considerable egomania, overstatement, and drama at his command in *Panama: The Creation, Destruction, and Resurrection* (London, 1913). An important account of the opposition to T. Roosevelt's work is Terence Graham, *The "Interests of Civilization"? Reaction in the United States Against the Seizure of the Panama Canal Zone, 1903–1904* (Lund Studies in International History, 19, Lund, Sweden, 1983). The public sentiments on both sides are given at length in *Public Opinion*, especially volumes 35 and 36, which cover 1903–1904; and are noted in David S. Patterson's fine study, *Toward a Warless World: The Travail of the American Peace Movement, 1887–1914* (Bloomington, Ind., 1976). A leading Panamanian historian provides little-known vignettes in Ernesto J. Castillero Reyes, *Episodios de la Independencia de Panama* (Panama, 1957); a Colombian historian gives his perspective in Germán Arciniegas, *Caribbean: Sea of the New World* (New York, 1954); and Latin American reaction to the U.S. involvement is analyzed in J. Patterson, "Latin-American Reaction to the Panama Revolution of 1903," *Hispanic American Historical Review*, XXIV (May 1944).

The 1904 policies are analyzed in Dana G. Munro's *Intervention and Dollar Diplomacy in the Caribbean, 1900–1921* (Princeton, 1964); G. A. Mellander, *The United States in Panamanian Politics* (Danville, Ill., 1971), a useful synthesis; two important works by Ralph E. Minger, "Panama, the Canal Zone, and Titular Sovereignty," *Western Political Quarterly*, XIV (June 1961); *idem, William Howard Taft and United States Foreign Policy: The Apprenticeship Years, 1900–1908* (Urbana, Ill., 1975); and William D. McCain's classic, *The United States and the Republic of Panama* (Durham, N.C., 1937).

See also the footnotes to Chapters I and II: some of those references are not repeated here. And see especially Richard Dean Burns, *Guide to American Foreign Relations Since 1700* (Santa Barbara, Calif., 1983).

The Middle Years (1904–1960)

The best account is McCain, *U.S. and Republic of Panama*, cited above, which concludes in the mid-1930s. Wilsonian policy is well described in G. W. Baker, Jr., "The Wilson Administration and Panama, 1913–1921," *Journal of Inter-American Studies*, VIII (April 1966); Joseph Tulchin, *The Aftermath of War:*

World War I and U.S. Policy Towards Latin America (New York, 1971), which has a short account of Hughes' dealings with Panama; George Westerman, "Gold vs. Silver Workers in the Canal Zone," *Common Ground,* VIII (No. 2, 1948), by an eminent black Panamanian who traces racial discrimination in the Zone; Willis J. Abbot, *The Panama Canal: An Illustrated Historical Narrative* (New York, 1922), which stands apart as a traveler's account and seems to catch perfectly the growing tensions on the Isthmus; Frank Otto Gattell, "Canal in Retrospect—Some Panamanian and Colombian Views," *Americas,* XV (July 1958), a good essay on intellectual currents. Harmodio Arias, *The Panama Canal: A Study in Institutional Law and Diplomacy* (London, 1911) is a crucial analysis by one of the leading Panamanian political figures.

An excellent introduction to the 1920s and 1930s is R. L. Buell, "Panama and the United States," *Foreign Policy Reports,* VII (January 20, 1932). The pivotal work has been done by Lester Langley in two articles: "Negotiating New Treaties with Panama: 1936," *Hispanic American Historical Review,* XLVIII (May 1968); and "World Crisis and the Good Neighbor Policy in Panama, 1936–1941," *Americas,* XXIV (October 1967). Roosevelt's views are best discovered in two primary sources: Edgar B. Nixon, ed., *Franklin D. Roosevelt and Foreign Affairs,* 3 vols. (Cambridge, Mass., 1969); and Samuel I. Rosenman, ed., *The Public Papers and Addresses of Franklin D. Roosevelt,* (New York, 1938–50). The standard one-volume work is now Robert Dallek, *Franklin D. Roosevelt and American Foreign Policy, 1932–1945* (New York, 1979); while crucial insights, especially into Latin American policy, are to be found in Lloyd C. Gardner, *Economic Aspects of New Deal Diplomacy* (Madison, Wisc., 1964).

The best introduction to the 1940s is David Green, *The Containment of Latin America* (Chicago, 1971). Important articles are Norman J. Padelford, "American Rights in the Panama Canal," *American Journal of International Law,* XXIV (July 1940); Arthur P. Whitaker's superb article in *Inter-American Affairs, 1941* (New York, 1942), which Whitaker edited; A. R. Wright, "Defense Sites Negotiations Between the United States and Panama, 1936–1948," *Department of State Bulletin,* XXVII (Aug. 11, 1952); and material in *Records of Meetings,* especially volume VI, at the Council on Foreign Relations in New York City.

For the 1950s one book stands alone: Larry LaRae Pippin, *The Remón Era: An Analysis of a Decade of Events in Panama, 1947–1957* (Stanford, 1964). The growing economic crisis is traced in Pedro C. M. Teichert, *Economic Policy, Revolution and Industrialization in Latin America* (Oxford, Miss., 1959). C. G. Fenwick, "Treaty of 1955 Between the United States and Panama," *American Journal of International Law,* IL (October 1955), provides the starting place, along with Pippin, for the treaty. The background of the 1959 riots can be found in Milton S. Eisenhower, *The Wine is Bitter. The United States and Latin America* (New York, 1963); and Ricardo J. Alfaro, *Medio Siglo de Relaciones entre Panama y los Estados Unidos* (Panama, 1959), for a key Panamanian view.

The critical development of the middle class in Panama is traced in several works: the essays by Carolina de Campbell and Ofelia Hopper, and another by

John Biesanz, in Theo R. Crevenna, ed., *Materiales para el estudio de la clase media en la América Latina*, vol. IV (Washington, D.C., 1950); John and Mavis Biesanz, *The People of Panama* (New York, 1955), a broad, important work; and Richard N. Adams, *Cultural Surveys of Panama, Nicaragua. . . .* (Washington, D.C., 1957), important for its study of the *campesino* in the interior; and for the economic aspects, E. A. Cleugh, *Panama: Economic and Commercial Conditions. . . .* (London, 1955).

See also the footnotes in Chapters III and IV. Some of those references are not repeated here. Of special importance, check with Richard Dean Burns, ed., *Guide to American Foreign Relations Since 1700* (Santa Barbara, Calif., 1983), unsurpassed as a reference to work on United States diplomacy to the early 1980s.

The Recent Years (post-1960)

The framework can be found in Geoffrey Barraclough, *Introduction to Contemporary History* (New York, 1965), a crucial interpretive work; John Gerassi, *The Great Fear; The Reconquest of Latin America by Latin Americans* (New York, 1963). The two standard studies on U.S.-Panamanian relations are Kent Jay Minor, "United States-Panamanian Relations: 1958–1973," unpublished doctoral dissertation, Case Western Reserve University, 1974; and Lester D. Langley, "U.S.-Panamanian Relations Since 1941," *Journal of Inter-American Studies*, XII (July 1970). Ernest A. Duff *et al.*, *Violence and Repression in Latin America* (New York, 1976) emphasizes the cohesiveness in Panamanian society. Panama is not considered an integral part of Central America, as is made evident in C. F. Denton, "Interest Groups in Panama and the Central American Common Market," *Inter-American Economic Affairs*, XXI (Summer 1967). Some of the most important work on the 1960s has been done by Daniel Goldrich: *Sons of the Establishment: Elite Youth in Panama. . . .* (Chicago, 1966); *idem*, "Requisites for Political Legitimacy in Panama," *Public Opinion Quarterly*, XXVI (Winter 1962); *idem*, "Developing Political Orientations of Panamanian Students," *Journal of Politics*, XXIII (February 1961).

The 1964 tragedy is anticipated in Mercer D. Tate, "The Panama Canal and Political Partnership," *Journal of Politics*, XXV (February 1963), an excellent overview. Lyndon Johnson's view is given in his *The Vantage Point* (New York, 1971); to be tempered with Philip Geyelin, *Lyndon B. Johnson and the World* (New York, 1966); and several essays in Robert A. Divine, ed., *Exploring the Johnson Years* (Austin, Tex., 1981) that exploit newly opened Johnson materials. The 1964 rioting is analyzed in detail in International Commission of Jurists, *Report on the Events in Panama, January 9–12, 1964* (Geneva, Switzerland, 1964); and Lyman M. Tondel, Jr., ed., *The Panama Canal* (Dobbs Ferry, N.Y., 1965); Jules Dubois, *Danger Over Panama* (Indianapolis, 1964), highly critical of Panama; J. Fred Rippy, "United States and Panama, The High Cost of Appeasement," *Inter-American Economic Affairs*, XVII (Spring 1964), is required reading, as are all of Rippy's works on Latin America. The aftermath, especially the inexorable economic problems, can be studied in Georgetown University Center for Strategic Studies, *Panama; Canal Issues and Treaty Talks* (Washington, D.C., 1967); Carl R. Jacobsen, "Basic Data on the Economy of the Republic of Panama," *Overseas Business Reports* (June 1968), published by the U.S. Department of Commerce; and especially Larry L. Pippin, "Challenge in Panama," *Current History,* L (January 1966).

For the 1970s and 1980s, two books are crucial for understanding the context: Lars Schoultz, *National Security and United States Policy toward Latin America* (Princeton, 1987); and Abraham F. Lowenthal, *Partners in Conflict: The United States and Latin America* (Baltimore, 1987). A number of good articles introduce the 1970s: Helen C. Low, "Panama Canal Treaty in Perspective," Overseas Development Council Monograph Series #29 (1976); Thomas M. Franck and Edward Weisband, "Panama Paralysis," *Foreign Policy,* No. 29 (Winter 1975–1976); Jan Morris, "A Terminal Case of American Perpetuity," *Rolling Stone,* No. 203 (Jan. 1, 1976), which has brilliant reporting; E. J. Kahn, Jr., "Letter from Panama," *The New Yorker,* Aug. 16, 1976; and Ben S. Stephansky, " 'New Dialogue' on Latin America: The Cost of Policy Neglect," in Ronald G. Hellman and H. Jon Rosenbaum, eds., *Latin America: The Search for a New International Role* (New York, 1975).

Good introductions to the Torrijos era and the conditions that produced his rule are George Priestly, *Military Government and Popular Participation in Panama. The Torrijos Regime, 1968–1975* (Boulder, Colo., 1986); the Rouquié and Ropp volumes, both superb, noted in the "General Works" section above; Omar Torrijos's own words in *Imagen y Voz* (Panama, 1985); and the distinguished British novelist's account, *Getting to Know the General,* by Graham Greene (New York, 1984). Martin C. Needler, "Omar Torrijos, The Panamanian Enigma," *Intellect,* CV (February 1977) is critical and important. Steve C. Ropp's brilliant analysis can be found in "Military Reformism in Panama: New Directions or Old Indications," *Caribbean Studies,* XII (October 1972). Organization of American States, *Constitution of Panama, 1972* (Washington, D.C., 1974) is a key primary document.

Panama's growth as an international banking center is examined in Harry Johnson, "Panama as a Regional Financial Center: A Preliminary Analysis of Development Contribution," *Economic Development and Cultural Change,* XXIV (January 1976); and Robin Pringle, "Panama—A Survey," *The Banker,* CXXV (October 1975); while T. V. Greer provides a fascinating survey in "Mercantile Potpourri Called Panama," *Journal of Inter-American Studies,* XIV (August 1972). The overall picture is given in Looney, *Economic Development of Panama,* cited above; and William C. Merrill *et al., Panama's Economic Development; The Role of Agriculture* (Ames, Iowa, 1975).

The introduction to the treaty negotiations and debate can best be found in detail in William J. Jorden, *Panama Odyssey* (Austin, Tex., 1984), written by the U.S. Ambassador to Panama and a former journalist; a contemporary view of the framework is in Commission on United States–Latin American Relations,

The United States and Latin America: Next Steps (n.p., 1976), written by the Commission headed by Sol Linowitz; also Xavier Gorostiaga, *Panama y la Zona del Canal* (Buenos Aires, 1975), a fact-filled Latin American analysis. A fine overview of the Carter administration's policies is Gaddis Smith, *Morality, Reason, and Power: American Diplomacy in the Carter Years* (New York, 1986). The insider, pro-treaty works are Jimmy Carter, *Keeping Faith: Memoirs of a President* (New York, 1982); Cyrus R. Vance's thoughtful *Hard Choices* (New York, 1983); and Zbigniew Brzezinski's blunt *Power and Principle: Memoirs of the National Security Adviser, 1977–1981* (New York, 1983). They are joined on the pro-treaty side by Robert G. Cox, "Choices for Partnership or Bloodshed in Panama," in Kalman H. Silvert, ed., *The Americas in a Changing World* (New York, 1975), an important analysis. The anti-treaty argument can be found in Philip M. Crane, *Surrender in Panama,* with an introduction by Ronald Reagan (Ottawa, Ill., 1978); and Charles Maechling, Jr., "The Panama Canal: A Fresh Start," *Orbis,* XX (Winter 1977), a thoughtful criticism of the State Department position. Daniel Flood's views can be found in "Projected Surrender of the U.S. Canal Zone," *Vital Speeches,* Aug. 1, 1975. Balanced, scholarly contributions are George D. Moffett III, *The Limits of Victory. The Ratification of the Panama Canal Treaties* (Ithaca, N.Y., 1985), especialy good on the international context and the effect of declining U.S. power; J. Michael Hogan, *The Panama Canal in American Politics* (Carbondale, Ill., 1986), a fine overview and especially useful on public opinion; William L. Furlong and Margaret E. Scranton, *The Dynamics of Foreign Policymaking: The President, The Congress and the Panama Canal Treaties* (Boulder, Colo., 1984), based on Scranton's dissertation and important for the 1958 to 1976 background; G. Harvey Summ and Tom Kelly, eds., *The Good Neighbors: America, Panama, and the 1977 Canal Treaties* (Athens, Ohio, 1988), important analytical essays on post-1958 negotiations and a useful annotated bibliography; General Accounting Office, Comptroller General, *Implementing the Panama Canal Treaty of 1977—Good Planning But Many Issues Remain* (Washington, 1980), a good rundown on future problems. Important for the Canal's future working is U.S. Congress, House Subcommittee of the Committee on Appropriations, 94th Cong., 1st sess., *Department of Transportation and Related Agencies Appropriations for 1976,* especially Part 4 (Washington, D.C., 1975): the Leon M. Cole study deserves notice.

On the 1980s, especially useful are the Schoultz and Lowenthal volumes noted above; *Panama en Cifras. Años 1980–1984* (Panama, 1985), a comprehensive source for the figures on everything from migration, to debt, to politics; U.S. Congress, House Subcommittee on Western Hemisphere Affairs, 100th Cong., 2nd sess., *The Political Situation in Panama and Options for U.S. Policy* (Washington, D.C., 1988), important for the Pritchard, Moss, Ropp, and Kozak testimony; Andrew Zimbalist, "Panama," in Eva Paus, ed., *Struggle Against Dependence: Nontraditional Export Growth in Central America and the Caribbean* (Boulder, Colo., 1988), especially instructive for its analysis of the Canal's economy; José Antonio Perez Gomez and William Hughes Ortega, *Desarrollo, Cri-*

sis, Deuda y Política Económica en Panamá (Panama, 1985), which places the crisis within the larger Latin American "dependency" framework; John Weeks and Andrew Zimbalist, "The Failure of Intervention in Panama," *Third World Quarterly*, XI (January 1989), which greatly influenced the interpretation in the final chapter of this book; and the reporting of Carla Anne Robbins in *U.S. News and World Report* weekly magazine.

Check also the footnotes to Chapters V, VI, VII, and VIII: many of the sources listed in those footnotes are not repeated here. Most important, consult Richard Dean Burns, ed., *Guide to American Foreign Relations Since 1700* (Santa Barbara, Calif., 1983) for the most thorough list of monographs and articles for the pre-1981 years.

Index